Working with the Masters

Sacred Adventure Series

Book 1: THE SPIRITUAL QUEST

Book 2: MEETING THE MASTERS

Book 3: WORKING WITH THE MASTERS

SACRED ADVENTURE SERIES ◆ 3

Working with the Masters

TEACHINGS OF THE ASCENDED MASTERS®

MARK L. PROPHET ◆ ELIZABETH CLARE PROPHET

Staff of Summit University®

SUMMIT UNIVERSITY PRESS®

WORKING WITH THE MASTERS

For information, contact Summit University, 63 Summit Way,
Gardiner, MT 59030 USA. Tel: 1-800-245-5445 or 406-848-9500.
www.SummitUniversity.org
www.SacredAdventureSeries.org

Library of Congress Control Number: 2003101394
ISBN: 978-1-60988-296-9
ISBN: 978-1-60988-297-6 (eBook)

This book is based on the teachings of the ascended masters delivered by Mark L. Prophet and Elizabeth Clare Prophet.

SUMMIT UNIVERSITY PRESS®

21 20 19 18 1 2 3 4

To those who see their whole life as a sacred adventure,
to those who push ever onward, daring to conquer,
daring to challenge the vast seas and to
scale the highest mountains of consciousness,
to those who remember always that
the trek upward is worth the inconvenience,
we dedicate this book as the next step on the spiritual path.

We offer this book with the greatest love to the Ascended Masters Jesus Christ, Kuthumi, El Morya, and Djwal Kul and to the messengers Mark L. Prophet and Elizabeth Clare Prophet, without whom it would never have come into existence.

SUMMIT UNIVERSITY®

A College of Religion, Science, and Culture

In 1971, Mark L. Prophet founded Summit University in Santa Barbara, California, to provide in-depth courses of study on health, spirituality and consciousness. SU is a modern mystery school based on the teachings of the world's spiritual traditions and the great lights of East and West who have come out of these paths, the ascended masters. Summit University served as a platform for the release of the original teachings of the ascended masters for nearly three decades. Its staff is currently organizing this abundance of teachings into well-defined seminars and courses available to spiritual seekers worldwide. A Sacred Adventure is Summit University's first independent study program for those interested in exploring and assimilating the teachings of the ascended masters in the privacy of their own homes.

Recent SU seminars have included programs like "Experience the Light Within," "The Way of the Christian Mystic," and "The Path of the Eastern Adept." The programs draw on the mystical essence of the major world religions and sacred traditions. Online courses include topics such as "Understanding Yourself," "Cosmic Law," "Discipleship," and "Buddhism—Loving-Kindness in Action." Summit University students find ample opportunity for experiential work through introspective and interactive exercises, meditations and prayer work.

Summit University programs include online study courses as well as national and international weekend seminars and retreats that provide in-depth topical studies. SU events are a truly mystical experience for many, since each seminar or retreat is sponsored by one or more of the ascended masters. The masters work with students to give them profound insights into their psychology and provide them with inner guidance for their spiritual development. Summit University offers a powerful transformational experience for newer students as well as longtime students on the spiritual path.

For more information about Summit University:
www.SummitUniversity.org
Learn more about our online courses here:
www.SummitUniversity.org/courses
Email us at: info@SummitUniversity.org

CONTENTS

ONLINE EXERCISES

This book contains a number of inspiring and transformative spiritual exercises such as meditations and spoken prayers. To do the exercises online with recorded audio tracks, look for this symbol to locate the links!

INTRODUCTION

Welcome to *Working with the Masters*, the third volume in the Sacred Adventure series. This book is the continuation of a detailed discussion, begun in Book 2, of the seven rays of the divine consciousness and the path of self-mastery as taught to us by the ascended masters. It picks up where Book 2 left off: with the fourth, the white ray of purity, and its fierce master, Serapis Bey.

After the white ray comes the fifth, or green ray, an oasis of wholeness and whole-eye vision under the rulership of its presiding chohan, the Ascended Master Hilarion, who was once embodied as the apostle Paul. Governing the sixth ray—purple and gold flecked with ruby—we find an ascended lady master. Her name is Nada. Her embodiments take us back as far as Atlantis where she served as an advocate of the people, which preeminently qualifies her to teach us the way of service to life. Chapter 7 introduces the illustrious Ascended Master Saint Germain, Lord of the Seventh Ray. This violet-colored ray brings us the buoyant energy of alchemy, freedom, liberation and self-transcendence.

In between the chapters on the seven rays you'll find wonderful treatises on related subjects. For the white ray, we're focusing on the light of the Divine Mother. The green ray is augmented by a discussion of the power of music and sound. Following the chapter on the sixth ray there's a unique description of elemental life—the invisible beings of fire, air, water and earth who sustain the physical platform for mankind's evolution.

The last chapter in this book is where the rubber meets the road. You'll find out how the seven rays are the framework for your own spiritual path and how one ray in particular—your major ray—serves as the stepping-stone to your own development of higher consciousness. Book 3 culminates in a detailed overview of what it means to enter into a working relationship with one of the great ascended masters and let that master guide you all the way back to the realm of Spirit from whence you came.

Each of the first seven chapters contains several sections. "Wisdom Teachings of the Masters" is based on instructions and insights from the ascended masters. "Introducing..." offers a brief profile of the embodiments as well as the divine personality of an ascended master related to the topic of that chapter.

The "Liberating Power of the Word" section in these chapters explains various aspects of the science of the spoken Word, a unique system of spiritual techniques that includes the use of dynamic spoken prayers called "decrees," visualization and meditation. These techniques are given to help you invoke divine light into your life to produce constructive change. These empowering tools and the many exercises in this book can greatly enhance your spiritual path. If you are unfamiliar with this spiritual science, we recommend that you refer to the first book in the Sacred Adventure series, *The Spiritual Quest,* for a good foundational understanding.

Happy traveling as you embark on the third leg of the Sacred Adventure journey!

Synopsis of the first two books in the Sacred Adventure Series

Book 1, The Spiritual Quest

Ideally, preparation for the second leg of your spiritual journey includes reading the first book in the series. In case you haven't had that opportunity, here is a brief summary of its chapter topics, since these concepts are foundational to understanding much of the material in the present book.

1. **Your Divine Origin** explains how we were created as spiritual beings and how we fit into the great cosmic scheme. It describes how our souls descended from realms of Spirit into matter and clarifies our connection to the I AM Presence, our individual manifestation of the Divine. It also gives an overview of the ultimate goal of our soul, our reunion with the I AM Presence, known as the ascension.

2. **Your Higher Self** explores the relationship between the basic components of our spiritual makeup, including the soul and the Higher Self—the I AM Presence and Holy Christ Self. It also demonstrates how we can attune to our innate divinity through the divine spark, the threefold flame in our heart.

3. **Living a Spiritual Life in a Material World** explains how knowing that you are a spiritual being does not always mean that you feel spiritual. This highly practical teaching takes the material previously presented and shows how you can be a spiritual being even as you live in a material world. It gives specifics about how the aspects of your spiritual nature interrelate, function and are affected positively and negatively by the encounters of everyday life.

4. **Expanding the Flow of Light Within** covers how the light of Spirit flows within the human organism and how you can invoke more of this light into your world at will. It explains your spiritual centers, the chakras, and how the presence or absence of light in the chakras can affect your consciousness and daily life. Ways to protect and expand your aura, the forcefield of light

around your body, are also discussed. Perhaps most importantly, it details how your uses of divine light relate to the ascension, the ultimate goal of your soul.

5. **Karma: Good, Bad and Balanced** probes the circumstances and history that have led us to where we are today as souls. It explains how our freewill choices—both good and bad—have affected and will affect our experience in the physical world. It shows how the Eastern concept of karma, the result of these freewill choices, relates to Western theology. And it offers ways to help minimize some of the difficult effects of returning negative karma.

6. **Reincarnation: Beyond the Veil of This Life** explores the concept of reincarnation as a key component in the mystery of life. It covers the history of the belief in reincarnation worldwide. And, just as it was previously shown how the Eastern concept of karma fits into Christianity, this section shows how reincarnation fits into Western theology. It presents a thorough explanation of the argument for reincarnation and its ramifications, including why we must reincarnate and how we can ultimately break this cycle of returning again and again to physical embodiment.

7. **Your Ultimate Destiny** describes the ideal final episode of your many lifetimes. It defines the process of the ascension: the glorious reunion with God that marks the pinnacle of your soul's experiences in the physical world. It clarifies the process of the ascension, what it requires, and how others before us have achieved this victory of immortality.

Book 2, Meeting the Masters

This volume began a detailed study of the seven major aspects or "rays" of the divine consciousness. These rays are represented in the seven chakras in our own bodies. They are also represented by a group of seven spiritual teachers called the seven lords, or chohans, of the rays.

1. **Exploring Our Teeming Cosmos** sets the framework for the teachings on the seven rays in this book. It describes the spiritual hierarchy of the Great White Brotherhood, reviews what is known as the three kingdoms—angelic beings, human beings and elemental life—and introduces the seven rays and their spiritual governors, the seven chohans of the rays. It also discusses how we contact this spiritual hierarchy by means of the science of the spoken Word.

2. **The Strength of Divine Will** covers the first ray and its powerful chohan, El Morya, who lived as Thomas Becket, Sir Thomas More and the Mogul emperor Akbar the Great. Specific aspects of this ray are discussed in detail:

- Qualities: Power, will, faith, protection
- Color: Electric blue
- Chakra: Throat chakra
- Etheric retreat: The Temple of Good Will over Darjeeling, India

3. **Soul Travel** explains the process of how the soul leaves the physical body while we sleep and is able to travel to the etheric retreats of the ascended masters for spiritual instruction and out-of-the-body work. How to safely do this and where to go are topics included in this chapter.

4. **The Brilliance of Divine Wisdom** focuses on the second ray. Its chohan is Lord Lanto, a wise teacher whose roots go back to ancient China. Some of the details of this ray are:
   - Qualities: Understanding, wisdom, illumination
   - Color: Golden yellow
   - Chakra: Crown chakra
   - Etheric retreat: The Royal Teton Retreat, congruent with the Grand Teton in Wyoming, USA

5. **The Angelic Kingdom** is a delightful chapter about the reality of angels in our lives. It covers historic instances of angelic intercession, the nature and purpose of angels, and the curious fact of embodied angels living among us. Sections on the seven archangels and how to work with angels complete this overview.

6. **The Comfort of Divine Love** is the last ray discussed in this book. It covers the beauty of the third ray and the path of love of its chohan, Paul the Venetian, whose last embodiment was that of the Italian Renaissance painter by that name. Included are:
   - Qualities: Love, devotion, creativity, beauty
   - Color: Rose pink
   - Chakra: Heart chakra
   - Etheric retreats: The Château the Liberté (Castle of Freedom), located over the Rhone River in southern France; and the Temple of the Sun over Manhattan in New York City

7. **The Threefold Flame** discusses the divine spark in your heart—the potential of your divinity. This tiny etheric flame consists of a brilliant white sphere from which spring three fiery plumes of the divine consciousness: blue (power), golden yellow (wisdom) and pink (love). After immersing themselves in the first three rays as introduced in this book, readers gain a profound understanding of how the primary divine qualities of power, wisdom and love shape their lives and enfire their spiritual quest.

GETTING THE MOST OUT OF SACRED ADVENTURE

The Sacred Adventure series is an independent course of self-study that progressively leads you through the practical steps of spiritual development and helps you assimilate the teachings of the ascended masters. The following recommendations and study tips can assist you to maximize your enjoyment of a Sacred Adventure while reaping the greatest possible benefits from the material.

Recommendations

1. **Keep a journal.** This course is designed for use with a journal or notebook to record your personal insights and reflections. Journal pages are included for your use at the end of the book, or you may want to purchase your own notebook. You might want to reserve one section in your journal for your experiences with the exercises and meditations, and keep another section for taking notes.

2. **Begin at the beginning.** The chapters and books in the Sacred Adventure course are progressive, building upon the information previously given. You stand to gain the most by starting with chapter 1 in Book 1, *The Spiritual Quest,* and going through the book in sequence, and by regularly using the interactive components. If you are currently reading *Meeting the Masters* and have not yet read *The Spiritual Quest,* be sure to also read Book 1 to gain the proper foundation necessary for a complete understanding of the concepts presented in Book 2.

3. **Take a dynamic role.** Active participation will improve your ability to assimilate the wisdom teachings of the ascended masters. By practicing the exercises and meditations, you will also make the material more applicable to your daily life. It is recommended that you take advantage of the interactive applications (and the online audio tracks that guide you through several of them) by setting aside ample time and a hallowed space to practice them.

Study Tips

1. **Pick a regular time to study and try to stick to it.** Establishing a regular study rhythm and allowing time in between study periods can maximize your gains.

2. **Keep study periods short.** Research has proven that shorter study periods produce the most beneficial learning experiences.

3. **Frequently review the material.** If more than a few days go by between your studies, it is helpful to do a quick review of the information you last read. The review process reinforces key concepts and prepares you to grasp new ideas. If you have taken notes on the material, you may wish to study them before proceeding. Likewise, revisiting how you personally interpreted your experiences through the various exercises and meditations can help refresh your learning and bring new insights.

4. **Refer to the glossary.** The glossary included at the end of the book contains definitions and explanations for many terms that may be new or unfamiliar. Feel free to refer to it whenever a new term or concept seems unclear.

CHAPTER 1

The Joy of Divine Purity

The Pure Fount of Divinity

The fourth ray, composed of fiery white-light essence, carries a unique vibration that is markedly different from that of the other color rays. At first glance, there's a strange contradiction hidden in its nature: its intense energy coalesces as structure and order, and yet, the white light is also a buoyant, joyous flame that brings us an abiding sense of joy. Looking more closely, we can see that this joyous feeling is an expression of the satisfaction that bubbles up in our hearts and souls when we know with certainty that all is in divine order; all is well.

Situated at the midpoint between the seven rays, the fourth (or white) ray holds unique keys for our spiritual path. It encompasses all the other rays just as the color white contains all the hues of the physical spectrum. This pivotal ray is crucial not only for each individual but also for the victory of our planet and its many evolutions.

The Ascended Master Kuthumi said the following about the intense energy of this ray, which is often referred to as the Mother light or Mother flame:

> The white of purity (the fourth ray) is a stellar radiance. While composed of all of the colors of the rainbow, it has its own gigantic sheath that, as a sea of liquid flame, holds before the children of men the longing to be a part of that which can never be contaminated by reason or by deceitful act. Purity—the mind of God, the nature of God, the character of God, freedom from stain, freedom from blame, the triumphant merging of the many colors into the purity of the One.[1]

The fourth ray is the ray of architects and builders. Its devotees love order and symmetry and take delight in the grand design and intricate architecture of the Matter cosmos. Enthusiasts of this ray truly enjoy mathematics, geometry, astronomy, astrophysics and nuclear physics, biochemistry and the beauty of divine design mirrored in the physical sciences. They also are attracted to the music of the spheres, the science of sound and the precipitation of the Word, though these areas are shared with the fifth and seventh rays as well. The fourth ray therefore influences many careers and areas of life.

The pure white light of the fourth ray is focused in the base-of-the-spine chakra. It springs up like a fountain from the base chakra to nourish the other chakras with its life-giving, creative energy. It releases the love, comfort and care of the Mother flame—

1 *Pearls of Wisdom,* vol. 11, no. 17.

the feminine presence of God—into our souls and four lower bodies.

The fourth ray is unique because making our ascension ultimately depends on it. We must master its light and raise it within our body temple and chakras before we can reunite with our I AM Presence.

Serapis Bey is the fierce master and chohan of this ray—an "altogether different chohan" as one of his fellow chohans once described him. Serapis has little tolerance for human foibles, spurred on by a deep love for the victory of our souls over all unreality. He guides us with a firm hand in building a reliable spiritual foundation for our path to the ascension, all the way home to the heart of our Father-Mother God.

The White Ray—Key to Self-Mastery

Let's take a look now at how the fourth ray nourishes our entire spiritual being with its intense white energy, which is the light of the Divine Mother. In addition to being its own ray anchored in the base-of-the-spine chakra, the white light is also found in the center of each of the other six rays. Here it acts as the fiery spiritual core that nourishes and sustains the divine consciousness and expression of the qualities of these rays in the outer world.

Threefold Flame

It is located as well in our threefold flame, the individualized spark of divinity placed in our own hearts. This threefold flame, with its fiery plumes of blue (power), yellow (wisdom) and pink (love), springs from a base of sacred fire, our white-fire core of being. We can visualize this as a small ball of brilliant white light at the base of the three plumes.

The fourth ray is critical to our spiritual achievement since the victory of the ascension hinges on mastering its energy. There must be a sufficiency of light in our chakras to ascend. Raising the light from the base-of-the-spine up through the other chakras creates an upward sweep that eventually results in bonding to our Holy Christ Self and achieving our ultimate victory, the ascension in the light, when it is time to take our leave of earth for the last time. So, the light of the Divine Mother in the fourth ray actually fuels the fire of the ascension flame.

The Ascended Master Lord Ling, an Eastern master also known as the God of Happiness, compares our progress on the spiritual path to building a "pyramid of life," under the direction of our Holy Christ Self. Mastering the energy of the Mother is fundamental to raising up the Mother light through the chakras to build this pyramid, whose four sides represent the four lower bodies. He noted, "Your own Christ Self will not allow you to erect the sides of the pyramid until you have built a firm foundation in this white light."[2]

Among other prerequisites, it takes mastery of the white ray in combination with balancing at least 51 percent of our karma to permanently bond with our Holy Christ Self and become a living Christ. When the light of the Mother rises from the base-of-the-spine chakra to the secret chamber of the heart, it magnetizes the light of the

2 *Pearls of Wisdom*, vol. 24, no. 4.

Father from the crown chakra. When the light of Mother and Father meet in the heart, we give birth to Christ consciousness. As the Mother light rises through the throat, third eye and ultimately to the crown, we will experience the bliss of enlightenment. Therefore, our individual mastery of the Mother light is critical to our ultimate spiritual attainment.

Qualities of the Fourth Ray

Steeping our consciousness in white-ray qualities until they become part of us helps us make steady progress on the spiritual path. While reading about the qualities listed below, consider which traits you already embody and which ones you would like to develop more fully.

Harmony

Divine harmony is the smooth and steady vibration of being in tune with God's consciousness. It is similar to harmony in music—pleasing and uplifting to the soul. Staying harmonious in the face of whatever comes our way is a large part of mastering the white ray. It can be helpful to remember that our existence depends on the stream of light that our I AM Presence releases daily and hourly into our chakras and four lower bodies, and that we can keep this light-energy pure by keeping our harmony. When we hold light in harmony it also assists those around us to come into a similar vibration, thereby producing a unified feeling of comfort and oneness.

The Ascended Master God Harmony—a true master of this quality—explained the importance of harmony and balance in accelerating spiritually:

> Harmony, then, is the balance of light, of sun centers, electronic forcefields. When there is balance, then there is harmony. When there is balance and harmony, then and only then can there be acceleration.
>
> You may have wondrous gifts of virtue, but often in a lifetime or many lifetimes an individual lifestream does not exceed a certain level of attainment professionally or a certain level of virtue because the individual reaches the line where there is no longer balance, where he cannot carry into an accelerated momentum that virtue which may function at a lesser vibration.
>
> Take, for example, a top that spins. In order to spin, it must have a certain acceleration and a certain balance. Thus when the law of harmony functioning within you goes below the level of a certain acceleration, it can no longer be maintained. And this is when discord enters in with disintegration and ultimately self-destruction. Thus in order to have the key of harmony, you must have the key of the acceleration of love.[3]

3 *Pearls of Wisdom*, vol. 23, no. 24.

Purity

Purity is the brilliant light of Spirit attained by souls who crave a high level of intensity within their being and aura. A strong desire not to taint the pristine consciousness of God impels us to lead lives based in honor and integrity. People with a deep affinity to the white ray have a unique quality of awareness, a crystalline clarity like the unpolluted, sparkling waters of a mountain stream. They have purity beyond the ordinary sense of the word and a consciousness that is a clear vessel for the mind of God, which allows them to cut to the quick of any situation.

The author Surya Das illustrates this quality in the following story of Geshé Ben, an erudite eleventh-century monk who was known for his rigorous attention to the pure mind.

> Wandering in search of alms one day, the young monk Ben was invited into the home of a devout couple. While the faithful householders went out of the room to prepare some food for the poor young mendicant, youthful Ben suddenly awoke—as if from a reverie—to find himself with his hand in the cookie jar, as it were, pinching some delectable tea for himself from a sack in one corner. There he was, caught red-handed—if only by his own meticulous conscience.
>
> Shouting, "Thief, thief!" Ben created such an uproar that the entire family came running, makeshift weapons in hand. To their amazement and relief, they beheld the novice accusing himself of pilfering and threatening to cut off his offending hand at once if it ever acted so disgracefully again. Thus the novice met his inner guru, the innate integrity of wisdom itself, from whom he was never thereafter parted.[4]

Purity of heart is a chalice ever filled by the crystal clear waters of Life.[5]

—SAINT GERMAIN

All the fourth-ray angels as well as the legions of purity stand ready and willing to teach us and help us make right choices that lead to the ascension through purity's flame. But by cosmic law, they cannot enter our world until they are invited by calls given in the flame of love. The Goddess of Purity, who earned her ascension by embodying the quality of purity, said that purity cannot exist without love. Purity of the heart, which is the seat of love, is therefore an essential quality on the spiritual path.

The crystal is the lens of the Mother's mind. Therefore, with crystal clarity let us go forth to find purity. And where we find it not, let us raise it up! Let us raise it up in a mighty fountain of light![6]

—ARCHANGEL RAPHAEL

---

4 Surya Das, *The Snow Lion's Turquoise Mane: Wisdom Tales from Tibet* (New York: HarperCollins Publishers, 1992), p. 25.

5 *Pearls of Wisdom*, vol. 30, no. 29.

6 *Pearls of Wisdom*, vol. 24, no. 14.

Discipline

We need inner discipline to simultaneously hold increasing amounts of light and maintain our harmony. True discipline goes well beyond following rules. It springs from the soul's commitment to follow the straightest path to her inner goal of reunion with the Divine. It therefore involves making daily decisions that raise our consciousness bit by bit toward the Higher Self. These may range from small things such as not watching television programs that have a negative impact on the emotions to larger things such as not choosing friends whose spiritual values are disturbingly different from our own.

Serapis Bey, Chohan of the Fourth Ray, encourages the development of discipline as an invaluable boost on the path. He said: "Do not think of the white fire as simply a stern discipline. It is the correctness of the way. It contains the geometry of being, the foundation stone from which you will rise . . . like a space shuttle into the arms of the everlasting God."[7]

In society, the white ray's design and goal are reflected in law and order. Branches of the military also have much fourth-ray training in individual and group discipline, as well as in upholding standards of law and order.

> *May you develop a new zest by the zeal of the fourth ray, the joy of the white light and the means whereby this light does facilitate your service!*
>
> *There is nothing sterile about the white light, for it is, after all, the acceleration of all paths and color bands.*[8] —AMEN BEY

Joy

The quality of joy is invaluable for anyone pursuing spiritual wholeness. The ascended masters have referred to it as the "motor of life." Joy makes our lives *move* in an upward trajectory. As a soul walks the spiritual path in earnest and gains mastery on the white ray, an inner joy begins to grow within. It is a bliss that radiates from people who know they are going in the right direction. It is the happiness of one who has charted his course and set his sails to reach his destination. It's also a by-product from a no-nonsense sense of determination to do what needs to be done as quickly and as well as possible. Joy can indeed be an exuberance that turns all difficulties into challenges that are met with enthusiasm and gusto.

At the same time, pure joy is deep and abiding, not superficial. It is reflected in the calm, contented vibration and smile of someone who knows he is doing his best. It is seen in devout souls or saints such as Gandhi or Mother Teresa, who smiled with their whole being in the midst of what others deemed terrible hardships. Joy also comes from recognizing and honoring the light of the Divine Mother infilling the four lower bodies and chakras.

7 *Pearls of Wisdom*, vol. 46, no. 50.

8 *Pearls of Wisdom*, vol. 34, no. 29.

Hope

Hope is the quality of looking forward to and expecting the best possible outcome in a given situation. It holds fast to the vision of the desired end, knowing that there may be obstacles but that there is a divine way that leads to the goal. Hopeful people see light at the end of any tunnel. The ability to hold on to a sense of promise in the face of challenging events is valuable for everyone in these changeable times. The Archeia Hope spoke eloquently of this quality, in the context of the ascension:

> *Hope springs eternal in the human breast.*[10]
> —ALEXANDER POPE

> And what is hope but the ascension flame itself? What is hope but life itself? Life without hope is not life at all. Every newborn child comes with hope—hope of surmounting the past incarnation, hope for the clean white page that is given and the new opportunity. . . .
>
> And remember, dearest hearts, that the goal of the ascension is not merely a goal of reunion with God, but the goal of the ascension is to intensify ascending currents in the aura, in the garment, in the sacred fire that rises upon the spinal altar. This blazing, accelerating flame that swirls around one's presence becomes that very garment, first of the transfiguration, then the resurrection, then the ascension. . . .
>
> The ascension flame as the flame of the hope of the Divine Mother . . . is pure light! light! light! light! light![9]

> *For we are saved by hope.*
> —ROMANS 8:24

> *True hope is swift, and flies with swallow's wings;*
> *Kings it makes gods, and meaner creatures kings.*[11]
> —SHAKESPEARE

Excellence

Excellence is another impressive characteristic of the fourth ray. In fact, it is through excellence that the white ray can most easily be seen as affecting all the other rays. While the pursuit of excellence is an integral part of the personality of fourth-ray people, those in all professions and walks of life who strive for perfection in their calling are actually developing their mastery of this ray.

> *It is a wretched taste to be gratified with mediocrity when the excellent lies before us.*[13]
> —ISAAC D'ISRAELI

The Great Divine Director, a powerful cosmic being, emphasized its importance when he said, "Excellence in all one does denotes a candidate for the ascension."[12] Elizabeth Clare Prophet commented that a person who is constantly excelling is constantly accelerating toward the ascension. When excellence is accompanied by pure motive and working unselfishly to the glory of God and as a gift to humanity, it becomes a part of the path of the ascension. However, if striving for excellence is just the pride

9 *Pearls of Wisdom,* vol. 30, no. 4.

10 *McGraw-Hill Dictionary of American Idioms and Phrasal Verbs,* s.v. "Hope springs eternal."

11 William Shakespeare, *King Richard III,* act 5, sc. 2, lines 24–25.

12 *Pearls of Wisdom,* vol. 3, no. 20.

13 Isaac D'Israeli, *Curiosities of Literature* (1834), quoted in John Bartlett, *Familiar Quotations,* 16th ed., (Boston: Little, Brown and Company, 1992), p. 368.

of a person glorying in the ego and looking for human rewards, it does not earn us any grace on the path.

Everyday experiences with mediocrity make us appreciate and value excellence when we come across it. Mediocrity versus excellence is the difference between going to a car repair shop that does haphazard work and charges a lot versus going to a shop where the mechanics do a great job for a fair price. It's the distinction between watching a ball game with so-so teams or a game with superb players that keeps you on the edge of your seat. It's the contrast between a straight-A student versus one who simply puts in a basic level of effort to get a passing grade. If we prefer to be treated with excellence in our dealings with others, it is wise to strive for it ourselves and express it as much as we can in how we live our lives.

> *Badness you can get easily, in quantity: the road is smooth, and it lies close by. But in front of excellence the immortal gods have put sweat, and long and steep is the way to it, and rough at first. But when you come to the top, then it is easy, even though it is hard.*[14]
>
> —HESIOD

Negative White-Ray Qualities: Detours on the Way Home

Understanding how the light of the Divine Mother is qualified as it flows through our chakras can help us to avoid many pitfalls on the path. The positive white-ray qualities are clear enough—but as with all of the seven rays, there are ways this crystalline energy can be misused. Elizabeth Clare Prophet explained that the misuse of the base-of-the-spine chakra can have negative physical outcomes like breaking down the immune system, weakening and depleting the physical body, and making the person more vulnerable to disintegration, disease, old age, and death. So it is good to know about the possible misqualifications of purity's ray. Here are some of the more common ones:

- Discord in its many manifestations is contrary to the innate harmony of the white ray.
- Distorted, ugly or unwholesome images are the antithesis of the divine design and symmetry of the fourth ray.
- Amorality, impurity, sensuality and lustful energies misuse the sacred fire in the base-of-the-spine chakra and keep it from being able to rise up through the chakras.
- Discouragement and despair indicate a deficiency of hope.
- Lack of self-control, lawlessness, anarchy and chaos are contrary to the discipline of the white ray.
- Settling for mediocrity undermines the striving for perfection and excellence.

14 *The Theogony,* l. 287, quoted in *Familiar Quotations,* p. 54.

If you recognize any of these qualities in yourself, you can determine to replace them with positive characteristics. While working on this it is vital to invoke the violet flame to clear away any negative karma and to firmly establish positive qualities that can help you move forward spiritually. The following exercise illustrates one way to accomplish this.

EXERCISE: SEPARATING THE REAL FROM THE UNREAL

Serapis Bey gave us some concrete, practical instructions on how to separate the Real Self from the unreal in ourselves in the following exercise. It is a great tool for reinforcing our divine identity as well as for helping us see what negative energies we can cast into the sacred fire of the violet flame.

1. Reserve several pages in your journal or a separate notebook for this exercise, since it is intended to be an ongoing practice.
    - Label this section of your journal *My Christhood.*
    - Make two columns on the page.
    - Label the first column—*Myself, What Is Real.*
    - Label the second column—*Myself, What Is Unreal.*
    - Then head the first column with the words *God, the I AM THAT I AM; Christ, the only begotten Son.* This is what is real within you.
    - Head the second column with: *the human ego, the human will, the human intellect, the human pride.* This is what is unreal in you.
2. In the first column, list the virtues of light, the virtues of the Christ and of God which you know to be real and manifest within you.
3. In the second column, list those faults that are not real but that you observe in yourself.
4. Then return to the first column and list those attributes that you desire to have as real, that you know exist, that you honor and adore but which you have not yet mastered.
5. Claim these attributes as yourself, as reality, by giving the following call:

    In the name of my mighty I AM Presence and beloved Serapis Bey, I claim as my personal reality the qualities of [name the virtues you listed in the first column]**. According to God's will, let it be done.**

6. Whenever you give your violet-flame decrees, name the faults or sins you listed in the second column and ask God to transmute them. This exercise is ongoing because you can continually add and subtract from your two lists to gain scientific self-mastery on the path of the ascension. Serapis said:

    > This is the starting place of the ascension. That which is in the first column must rise; that which is in the second must be transmuted before the energy thereof can rise.

Then, step by step, each day with rejoicing in your heart you take the power, the dominion of the God qualities you have listed in the first column and all energies that you have listed there and you use them as your authority, your substance, your collateral to invoke the grace of God, his will, and his healing to remove the stain of sin and all unreality which you have listed as the misqualified energies and momentums in the second column. This, then, becomes an objective and practical exercise in the demonstration of the science of the laws of God.[15]

Simple Ways to Amplify the White Ray

Gemstones or crystals can magnify the energy of the seven rays since they are molecular chalices with a crystalline structure that can hold a great quantity of light. Specific stones amplify particular qualities that correspond to each of the rays. Diamond, pearl, zircon and quartz crystal can increase the energy of the fourth ray.

As the highest vibrating crystal, diamond is a symbol of Spirit. It is used by all the chohans of the rays as a powerful focus often associated with kingship, priesthood or authority. In Sanskrit this stone is called *vajra,* meaning "thunderbolt." It has also been called "adamant," which stems from the Greek word *adamas,* signifying "unconquerable." In ancient times, the diamond was said to endow the wearer with superior strength, fortitude and courage, strengthen body and mind, induce purity and fearlessness, and defend against enemies. Edgar Cayce said in his readings that diamonds are good for attunement with infinity.

Zircon is a man-made stone that comes in many colors. Crystals forged in nature or artificially in a laboratory carry the same vibration as long as they have the same molecular structure and mineral content. So while it is wonderful to have real stones, man-made gemstones make the beneficial vibrations available to a larger number of people. Among other things, zircon is said to allay jealousy and to protect one from fever, edema and jaundice. Clear zircons, which are commonly used, look like and carry the same vibration as diamonds. So these two stones can be used interchangeably to enhance the energy of the white ray.

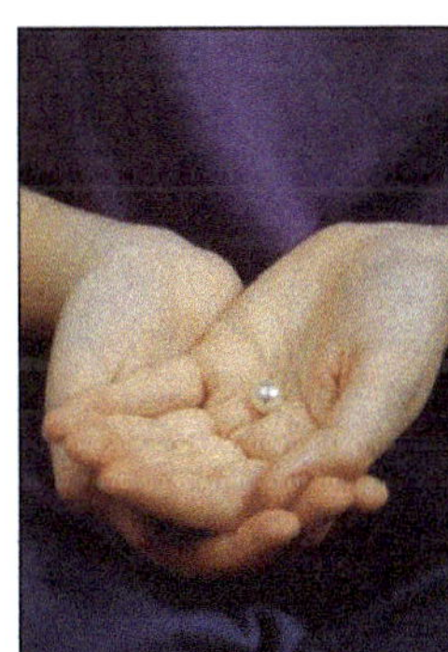

The pearl is a symbol of the soul. The ancient text *The Book of the Glory of Kings* says that Archangel Gabriel was directed to protect all who carry a pearl. In Chinese tradition, the initiate wears a coarse garment but hides a pearl on his breast representing the mystic center and transformation of the not-self. Also in China, powdered pearls were taken for stomach ailments. They were also mixed with distilled water and given to lunatics to restore reason. Edgar Cayce said that pearls strengthen the body and should be worn close to the skin. The primary effect of pearl is on the emotions; it facilitates developing harmony and an even temperament.

Quartz crystal is known for its healing properties. Some clear single quartz

15 Mark L. Prophet and Elizabeth Clare Prophet, *Lords of the Seven Rays* (Gardiner, Mont.: Summit Publications, Inc., 1986), p. 152.

crystals are called "generator" crystals, which are believed to conduct and ground pure healing energy. They are six-sided and may be of any size. Crystal is a great repository of energy and it has the property of holding devotion and light. If we keep even a tiny piece of quartz crystal where we do our mantras or meditations, the energy of our devotions will begin to concentrate in that crystal. The addition of crystals to an altar adds to the aura of devotion and sanctity in the room, and it may even be possible to feel the presence of angels who have been drawn there by prayers and who can also use crystals as a physical focus.

Aside from using gemstones, the light of the fourth ray is amplified on earth on Fridays. We may increase its light in our aura by wearing white, especially on that day.

The Base-of-the-Spine Chakra

The base-of-the-spine chakra is the fourth-ray chakra where the white light of the Divine Mother resides. This light is also called the Kundalini, which literally means "coiled-up serpent." This points to the fact that the Kundalini energy is coiled up in a latent state in the base chakra before it begins to rise through the chakras as we develop spiritually.

The Sanskrit name of this chakra is *Muladhara,* meaning "root," "base," or "foundation." It has four petals, which set the pattern for the flowing of the Mother light through the physical form. The base chakra is the place of the release of the sacred fire for procreation and for harmonizing the four lower bodies. The guarding of the sacred fire within it and the raising of the Kundalini energy nourishes and increases the light in all the chakras above it.

Full mastery of this chakra can lead to attaining omnipresent consciousness. Mastery of the energies of the fourth ray and raising the Kundalini light can also give an adept mysterious powers called *siddhis* in Hinduism. Examples are bilocation, clairvoyance, clairaudience, the power to materialize objects and the ability to make oneself invisible, fly through the air or walk through fire unharmed.... Although such feats may seem implausible, extremely pure saints have demonstrated these abilities. For example, the twentieth-century mystic Padre Pio was renowned for knowing a person's innermost thoughts and for his ability to bilocate while maintaining full awareness in both places.

Spiritual progress only occurs if the Mother light is raised naturally as we progress along the spiritual path. Some people desire the siddhis excessively, and they therefore resort to haphazard use of various forms of yoga or breathing exercises to force the Kundalini to rise and awaken their higher chakras. However, there can be grave danger in forcing the raising of the Kundalini when one is not yet ready for its powerful energies.

The ascended masters and their messengers, as well as other enlightened teachers, strongly caution against attempting to awaken the serpent fire prematurely. They speak about the tremendous creative power locked in this sacred energy that may not be easy to control once fully aroused. When this fire rises up through chakras that are not yet purified, it contacts the impure energy and magnifies it—sometimes to such an extent that the individual is unable to deal with the consequences. An uncontrolled rising of the Kundalini may cause physical pain as well as psychological problems. In extreme cases, it may even lead to insanity.

With this in mind, the Goddess of Purity explained that purity is a prerequisite to raising the Mother light: "I counsel you, then, in pure *seeing,* pure *knowing,* pure *feeling,* pure *loving,* pure *desiring,* pure *speaking,* pure *entering in* to the secret chamber of the heart. In purity of service and ministration, all these things, then, shall give to you the power, ultimately, of the raising of the sacred fire of the Kundalini."[16]

Serapis Bey explains that the ascension and the abilities that result from raising the Mother light must be desired ordinately, i.e., in moderation and with the right motivation. The ascended masters teach that divine powers are best achieved naturally by simply following the spiritual path and using the violet flame.

Serapis is therefore a strong proponent of using the violet flame, the energy of the seventh ray, even though he is our teacher on the fourth ray. The more deeply we study the rays, the more we see how they intertwine and work together to lead us to the ascension. In fact, though our souls are in embodiment to master a major and a minor ray, we must attain a certain level of mastery in each of the seven rays to achieve our victory in the light.

> *Let the Mother flame, then, increase within you and let your protection be commensurate with your need. For the Mother flame is great power. I place it under the control of Brahma, Vishnu, and Shiva within you, that it may not cause insanity or derangement or quicken anger or emotions, but be kept in the very heart of fire for the release and control of the planetary home and changes that are to come.*[17]
>
> —ASCENDED LADY MASTER VESTA

Assessing Your Mastery of the Base-of-the-Spine Chakra

As you strive to attain mastery in the base-of-the-spine chakra, it's beneficial to have a snapshot of just where you stand in regard to the fourth ray. The following exercise is intended to help you evaluate your white-ray qualities and take steps toward strengthening those in which you may be less accomplished. It is based on four areas of action that build and sustain positive qualities of this ray.

1. Valuing the material world and your physical body as chalices for Spirit
2. Honoring the sacred in nature and applying its lessons to your life
3. Honoring, respecting and nurturing the feminine in yourself and others
4. Conserving the energy of the sacred fire

16 *Pearls of Wisdom,* vol. 31, no. 79.
17 *Pearls of Wisdom,* vol. 28, no. 7.

SELF-ASSESSMENT: YOUR BASE-OF-THE-SPINE CHAKRA

1. On a scale of 1 to 5, where 1 is "never true of me" and 5 is "always true of me," please rate the following statements based on your current perceptions.

1 Never true of me
2 Rarely true of me
3 Sometimes true of me
4 Often true of me
5 Always true of me

a) **I value the material world and my body as chalices for Spirit.**	1	2	3	4	5
1. When my body shows signs that it is out of balance or needs something, I tend to those needs.					
2. I treat my body with reverence—as if it were the temple of God's Spirit.					
3. I give my body the care it needs—good food, rest and exercise.					
4. I maintain positive images/thoughts about the health of my body.					
5. I care for my physical surroundings and my home.					
6. I am practical and perform effectively in my physical environment.					
7. My home and work space encourage and inspire my creativity.					

b) **I honor the sacred in nature and apply its lessons to my life.**	1	2	3	4	5
1. I spend time in activities where I commune with nature, such as planting a garden, growing houseplants or hiking.					
2. I am conscious of how my actions impact the environment; I treat the environment with respect.					
3. I look beyond physical expressions to recognize God in nature.					
4. I take time to express my gratitude for the blessings of nature.					

c) **I honor, respect and nurture the feminine in others and myself.**	1	2	3	4	5
1. I treat women as respectfully as I treat men.					
2. I consider women's contributions to be of equal value to men's.					
3. I make a point of expressing my gratitude for the role of mother in family and society.					
4. I take adequate time to nurture my feminine side by doing things that make me feel emotionally balanced and spiritually fulfilled.					
5. I rely on my intuition as well as my reasoning mind.					

d) I conserve the energy of the sacred fire.	1	2	3	4	5
1. I work gently and safely on raising the sacred fire upward from my base-of-the-spine chakra into my other chakras for their awakening and expansion.					
2. I honor the sacred fire as the source of my creativity and do not waste it by engaging in sensual pleasures.					
3. I use the energy of the sacred fire to cultivate relationships that preserve my innate dignity and divinity.					

2. After completing the assessment, add up your score in each one of the four sections and divide it by the number of statements in that section to get an average.

3. Use the following action plan to formulate a personal strategy that will enhance your performance in every area where your average score was "3" or below.

Base-of-the-Spine Chakra Action Plan

a) I value the material world and my body as chalices for Spirit.

I resolve to improve in this area by doing the following: ____________________

____

____

____

b) I honor the sacred in nature and apply its lessons to my life.

I resolve to improve in this area by doing the following: ____________________

____

____

____

c) I honor, respect and nurture the feminine in others and myself.

I resolve to improve in this area by doing the following: ____________________

____

____

____

d) I conserve the energy of the sacred fire.

I resolve to improve in this area by doing the following: ____________________

____

____

____

4. Put your action plan into practice for three months. Then take the assessment again and note the positive changes in your journal.

MEDITATION: RAISING THE LIGHT OF THE DIVINE MOTHER

The ascended masters released the following exercise as the best meditation for safely raising the light of the Divine Mother. It focuses our consciousness on the chakras above the heart, which in most people are less polluted than the chakras below the heart. Since the chakras above and below the heart are connected in a figure-eight pattern, drawing light into the chakras above the heart will automatically also have a purifying effect on the chakras below the heart without a need to focus our attention there and risking the amplification of negative energy that may be lodged there.

www.SummitLighthouse.org/SA3-1

The white-fire ball in the meditation represents what the ascended masters call the "seed atom," another term for the Kundalini.

Chart of Your Divine Self

1. Be seated in a meditation posture that is comfortable and hold your spine erect.
2. Draw all your energy into your heart and center your attention there. Breathe deeply until you are calm and relaxed.
3. Look at the sun of your I AM Presence as it is shown in the center of the upper figure in the Chart of Your Divine Self. Gaze at it for a few minutes until you can hold this image in your mind's eye.
4. Now close your eyes and visualize a white-fire ball, like the sun of your Presence, in your heart.
5. See it rising gradually from the heart through the throat, third-eye and crown chakras en route to your Holy Christ Self and I AM Presence.

6. When the white-fire ball is in the center of your God Presence, give the following violet-flame mantra for several minutes. See the violet flame swirling through your entire being as shown on the lower figure of the Chart of Your Divine Self.

I AM a being of violet fire
I AM the purity God desires.

7. To seal your meditation, intone the *Aum*.
8. Take a few deep breaths as you come back to physical awareness.
9. Slowly open your eyes and give gratitude for your experience.
10. Make a record of your experience in your journal.

Serapis Bey, Chohan of the Fourth Ray

Serapis Bey, who holds the office of Chohan of the Fourth Ray, is a great devotee of the Divine Mother. He teaches us the discipline of raising up the white light of ascension's flame on the spinal altar. In fact, discipline is one of his most notable hallmarks. To students who make it to his etheric retreat over Luxor, Egypt, Serapis introduces himself with characteristic directness and a tinge of humor. "I am the hierophant[18] of Luxor, Retreat of the Ascension Flame," he says. "I am known among the Brotherhood as the disciplinarian, and among my disciples as the fiery master, and among those who have rejected the disciplines of our retreat by various and sundry names."[19]

The Ascended Master El Morya carries this description even further as it applies to Serapis Bey's students or chelas. He describes Serapis as "a Spartan if I ever saw one —whose fiery determination has saved many a soul from the mush of self-indulgence. His chelas reflect the fierceness of their master as they are immovable in their dedication to purity focused as the Mother light in the base-of-the-spine chakra."[20]

Head of Serapis, detail,
Hellenistic style of Egyptian art

Serapis once said that his most intense desiring was to manifest the purity of the mind of God. He explained why he originally chose to serve on the white ray: "When I was a chela determining on what ray I would serve, what ray I would preserve in the office of preserver of life, I contemplated all, but I came to the light of purity and I said—master of geometry that I was—'The shortest distance between two points, point A and B, is purity. Purity I shall be.' "[21]

This simple conclusion made Serapis Bey the exemplar for those who want to make a similar choice when determining how to most effectively go from point A, the human self, to point B, the Divine Self. A bird's-eye view of some of Serapis Bey's embodiments can provide a rich understanding of his character and approach to life's challenges.

Lifetimes of Serapis Bey

Long ago, Serapis was a high priest in the Ascension Temple on Atlantis. Before the sinking of that continent, many masters and their circles of devotees transported the precious spiritual flames they guarded to focuses and centers across the earth to establish etheric retreats, mystery schools and temples to the Divine Mother. Serapis and his band transported the ascension flame to Luxor, Egypt, which is now the location of his etheric retreat—the Ascension Temple and Retreat at Luxor. This important retreat is the place where many go at inner levels to make their ascension at the end of their incarnations on earth.

18 The word *hierophant* comes from ancient Greece, where it referred to the chief priest of the religious mysteries.

19 Prophet and Prophet, *Lords of the Seven Rays,* p. 140.

20 El Morya, *The Chela and the Path: Keys to Soul Mastery in the Aquarian Age* (Corwin Springs, Mont.: Summit University Press, 1976), p. 53.

21 Prophet and Prophet, *Lords of the Seven Rays,* pp. 139–40.

Serapis Bey continued to reincarnate in Egypt. In these lifetimes he became the sponsor of some of the greatest architectural feats that have ever been brought forth upon the earth. He was the architect of the Great Pyramid, which is a carving in stone of the record of the path of initiation. Beginning in Matter (the base of the pyramid), the soul balances the four lower bodies (the four sides) and transcends human existence by rising to the apex of the pyramid—which represents the crown chakra and attaining the ascension.

A later lifetime of Serapis was as Pharaoh Amenhotep III, who reigned in Egypt circa 1411–1375 B.C. Known as "the Magnificent" and the "Louis XIV of ancient Egypt," Amenhotep was the father of Ikhnaton, an embodiment of Mark Prophet. Amenhotep brought Egypt to a height of diplomatic prestige, prosperity and peace. He also built many monuments, palaces and temples, including the main portions of the Temple of Luxor. The temple's design corresponds to the outline of the human body, traced according to anthropometrical methods (measuring according to man's dimensions) and precisely proportioned. The entire structure is like a three-dimensional book explaining the secret functions of the organs and chakras in man. The temple displays the idea of the rebirth of the divine man based on transformation through the universal Mother principle, the light of the fourth ray.

Serapis Bey was embodied as the sculptor Phidias during the fifth century B.C. in Athens. He was regarded as the greatest of all the Greek sculptors. He was the architect of the Parthenon, supervising its exquisitely masterful construction. Within the Parthenon he placed his most famous work, the forty-foot-high statue in gold and ivory of Pallas Athena, the representation of the Mother figure, the Goddess of Truth.

Standing in the Parthenon, one stands in the presence of a piece of architecture that is designed by an individual who knows how to use form, symmetry, geometry and angles to create a chalice for a spiritual flame. The forcefield of the Parthenon does contain an essential flame, as do the Temple of Luxor and the Great Pyramid.

Not much later Serapis was embodied as Leonidas, King of Sparta, around 480 B.C. Leonidas means "Son of the Lion." He was not only a king but a soldier of great stature and courage who clearly exemplified the fourth-ray qualities of discipline, honor and integrity. While the Olympic games were being held, Leonidas led a small army of Greeks against the vast invading army of the Persian king, Xerxes, expecting backup troops to arrive when the games were over. He was holding a narrow pass at Thermopylae between the mountains and the sea to protect the nearby Greek fleet from being outflanked in combat. There were a total of 7,000 Greeks including Spartans, Thespians and Thebans, pitted against anywhere from 250,000 to 1.7 million Persians, according to different historical sources. Terrible odds any way they are figured!

For two days Xerxes suffered heavy losses without breaking Leonidas' resistance. Then a local man led Xerxes to a path through the mountains and a handpicked force of Persian "Immortals" attacked the Greeks from the rear. Leonidas at once informed the fleet, dismissed all but 1,400 men, including his own 300 Spartans, and prepared to die, declaring that he and his Spartans would not abandon their post. He and his handful of troops charged the hordes of Persian soldiers. Leonidas died in the heat of the battle and a fierce struggle ensued between the Spartans and Persians over his body. The Greeks drove back the enemy four times and by their great bravery, finally succeeded in bearing off Leonidas' body.

At the end, the Greeks were left with only a tiny hillock on which to fight. They defended themselves to the very last, until they were overwhelmed by a shower of spears and arrows. The Persians killed every Spartan and Thespian, but the Thebans surrendered. Afterwards Xerxes ordered that Leonidas be beheaded and his body crucified, but no such ignominy could mar his image. His heroism and selfless devotion to the ideals of Greece—the greater cause and glory more precious than life itself—had secured for him a singular place in history and in the imagination of his own and succeeding generations. And because of his superlative discipline and sense of timing, the Greek fleet was later able to defeat the Persians in a sea battle.

The Ascended Master Serapis Bey

Serapis Bey made his ascension around 400 B.C. Although he could have ascended after leaving Atlantis, he continued to reincarnate in the land of the Nile and elsewhere to perfect the work of the Great White Brotherhood[22] on earth.

There is a Graeco-Egyptian god called Serapis who gained prominence around the third century B.C. whose identity may be tied to the Ascended Master Serapis. His cult spread throughout Egypt and later into Asia Minor and even Italy. During the Graeco-Roman period in Egypt, approximately forty-two temples were erected to him. King Ptolemy I selected him as the official god for Egypt and constructed a temple to him at Alexandria. Yet Serapis is one of the most mysterious of the Egyptian gods; his country of origin is unknown, and scholars have suggested numerous translations for his name. The secrets of his cult, kept by his temple priests, lie buried with many other great mysteries of ancient Egypt.

22 The Great White Brotherhood is a confraternity of saints and sages of East and West who have risen from every walk of life, religion, race, and nation to minister to the souls of humanity anywhere and everywhere there is a need.

In the late nineteenth century, the Ascended Master Serapis Bey was one of the great lights who assisted the then unascended adepts M. (El Morya) and K.H. (Kuthumi) in their work with the Theosophical Society. This effort shows how tirelessly the ascended masters work to bring an understanding of spiritual realities to the people of earth. They have acted through many religions and organizations to ensure that souls of light will have an outline of the path to follow to their personal victory in the ascension.

There is a requirement that at least one individual ascend from earth every year in order for this planet to remain an evolutionary school. So Serapis Bey, as the master who works with each candidate for the ascension, has a special interest in making the teachings about the ascension accessible. The entire Great White Brotherhood has put forth immense effort to make the mysteries—the inner esoteric knowledge—available on earth and to keep schools open where these teachings can be found.

Keys for Expanding the Fourth-Ray Qualities

Below are some keys for expanding the white ray in your consciousness. The first three keys come straight from Serapis Bey himself.

- **Love purity.** According to Serapis, the love of purity will help you garner more of the white light in your aura and chakras. He said:

  > You should love purity with an utter devotion because purity is your freedom. In fact when you step into the flame, you find etched in fire and in crystal the permanent identity of the permanent atom of the permanent molecule of being. And you find that all else is consumed.
  >
  > And you stand to face the Presence, and behold, in the mirror of eternal life you see God face-to-face and you say, "Lo, I AM made in his image. I AM the image and the likeness of the Holy One." For in that fire you see yourself as God is—not as you were yesterday in the human consciousness or today or tomorrow—but you see yourself in the foreverness of the invincibility of that cosmic honor flame.[23]

- **Be humble.** Serapis Bey said that the first step toward reunion with God is humility before the awesome presence of the Lord, the I AM THAT I AM. Humility should be worn like an undergarment; it should be something we are never without, something we never forget if we are serious about making our ascension.

- **Give white-ray decrees.** The "Liberating Power of the Word" section in this chapter includes two white-ray decrees that you can give to increase the light of purity in your life.

- **Invoke the violet flame.** While giving violet-flame decrees and mantras, you can direct powerful violet rays into your chakras to clear away residual karma. You can

23 Prophet and Prophet, *Lords of the Seven Rays*, pp. 166–67.

also ask God to eliminate blocks in your consciousness that may be hindering your mastery of the Mother light.

- **Give the bija seed syllable for the base-of-the-spine chakra: Aim** (pronounced *Ah-eem*). It purifies and expands its light.
- **Listen to the "Triumphal March" from Verdi's opera *Aïda*.** This music keys into the consciousness of Serapis Bey and the uplifting currents of the ascension flame.
- **Go to Serapis Bey's Retreat.** You can visit the Ascension Temple at Luxor, Egypt, when you sleep by calling to Archangel Michael's angels to escort you there in your finer body. Ask Serapis Bey to teach you more about the ascension or mastering any white-ray quality.
- **Wear white.** White is especially effective on Fridays, but you can wear it any day to magnify the fourth-ray qualities. You can also call for Serapis Bey and your I AM Presence to increase these qualities in your life that day. Take note of any differences in your mannerisms, thoughts and feelings and/or of any challenges you experience in upholding the light of the Divine Mother.
- **Correct missed steps.** On the path of the ascension, we are often required to go back and master any steps we have previously skipped. To help you master every step on the path of self-mastery, reflect on a situation in your life where you know you made an error and missed a step, whether accidentally or intentionally.
  - Try to remember what went wrong.
  - What did you eventually have to do to come up with the right action or solution?
  - What would you do differently next time?
  - Resolve to put your solution into future practice by writing it down in your journal.

Serapis Bey's Retreat

Serapis Bey's etheric retreat, the Ascension Temple, is located on the Nile River at Luxor, Egypt. It is superimposed over a large, square, white stone building with a surrounding wall and courtyard, and an underground building including the Ascension Temple and Flame Room.

A few miles from this focus is a pyramid, also superimposed with etheric activity. In the upper room of this pyramid is the king's chamber, where the initiations of the transfiguration and the resurrection take place. Other rooms within the pyramid are used for initiations given by the Council of Adepts to the devotees who come to Luxor prepared for the most severe disciplines and the total surrender of their human consciousness.

In the underground complex there are other rooms for the meditation of the devotees who serve there. There is a focus of the resurrection flame, and there are chambers for the preparation of various initiations, including those of the transfiguration and the resurrection.

The Flame Room is square with doors on two sides. Twelve white pillars decorated in gold relief at their base and top form another square within the room and surround the central dais on which the ascension flame blazes.

The ascending one passes through the pillars and stands in the center of the ascension flame. The soul's cosmic tone is sounded and the flame from Alpha is released from the circle on the ceiling as the flame from Omega rises from the base. At the precise moment the individual's tone is sounded and the action of the flame occurs, the seraphim in the outer court of the retreat trumpet the victory of the ascending soul with a magnificent rendition of the "Triumphal March" from the opera *Aïda.*[24]

> *In order to ascend, you must abandon your past to God. . . . Cast aside illusion, then, veil after veil of the "personal person," and possess the willingness, in the name of Almighty God, to change your world!*
>
> *Men require "spunk" and a straight spine. There is no question they have pampered themselves, and that with illusion. Straight talk and straight thought will do much to clear the way, and it will not place any individual outside the citadel of hope but wholly within it.*
>
> *Men stay on the merry-go-round of human thought and feeling because they fear lest they fall off. But it will keep on going. So jump off the round of delusion and the mad whirl of human confusion. Come to Luxor, to the place where I AM.*[25]
>
> —SERAPIS BEY

Preparing for the Ascension

From the Ascension Temple Serapis initiates candidates for the ascension, assigning tutors to walk with their charges every missed step on the paths of the seven rays. This he does in cooperation with the other chohans. And the line is drawn—the student may not pass until he fulfills that neglected, long-forgotten or suppressed missed step. Such is the detail consciousness of the white ray.

Serapis' classes are filled with artists, musicians, sculptors, architects, planners and those who serve on every ray. They come to learn how to express purity, harmony, rhythm, balance and perfection in any undertaking. Also within his retreat, special training in the defense of life is given to military and intelligence strategists and all who serve in the armed forces, security and police departments of the cities. Serapis

24 For more information on making your ascension, see chapter 7 in *The Spiritual Quest* (Book 1 in the Sacred Adventure series).

25 Prophet and Prophet, *Lords of the Seven Rays,* p. 166.

clarifies for these and for all who come to his retreat the rigors of the highest path to attainment—the path of the white light, of a purity that is won through service, self-sacrifice and surrender to the all of God. Looking back at his embodiments, we can understand that he is more than prepared to train others this way, having totally mastered these qualities himself.

Yet his methods of discipline are tailor-made for each candidate for the ascension. Devotees who come to his retreat have an initial interview by him or one of twelve adepts presiding in his mystery school. They are then assigned in groups of five or more to carry out projects with other initiates whose karmic patterns (graphically illustrated in their astrology) forecast the maximum friction between each other. The masters test them through different situations in the retreats and in their daily lives to see how much of the teachings they have truly assimilated and become. This test is given so individuals may choose to be or not to be centered in God. It quickly becomes clear that the tyrant ego and karmic past must be surrendered if a candidate is to merge with the consciousness of the One.

Each group must serve together until they become harmonious, individually and as a cohesive team. All the while they are learning that those character traits that are most disturbing to them in others may be the same as their own worst fault in a different guise or the polar opposite of it. So what one criticizes in another is apt to be the root of one's own misery. For example, active rebellion is the opposite of passive aggression; depression is anger turned inward; lack of self-esteem and outwardly boasting are both manifestations of pride. When we get upset about these traits in others, it's important to look at our own psychology to see what may be lurking there that creates our upsetness—and then work actively on overcoming and transmuting it.

EXERCISE: PASSING WHITE-RAY TESTS

Here are a few steps to help you recognize, appreciate and deal with white-ray tests involving others.

1. Identify someone (or a group of people) who rubs you the wrong way or with whom you have a hard time relating—yet you *have* to deal with them, like it or not. It might be a grouchy bus driver or boss, a work group or your in-laws.

2. Isolate the specific characteristic that most annoys you when you are interacting.

3. Consider how this trait might be reflecting back to you a similar or opposite negative quality within yourself. For example, if you feel someone is controlling, it may mean you feel a lack of control over your life, or reversely, you may have some controlling tendencies yourself.

4. After you identify the negative personal trait, give violet-flame decrees to dissolve it. Ask God for its transmutation and strive to eliminate it from your consciousness.

5. Determine that from that point forward you will honor and appreciate the Higher Self within the other person(s) as well as within yourself.

6. Resolve to keep your harmony in the face of whatever arises. Then practice one or more of the following tips whenever you find yourself becoming irritated or annoyed:
   - Breathe deeply.
   - Count to ten.
   - Excuse yourself and leave the room until you are calm and centered.
   - Do the opposite of what you would normally do in such a situation;
     e.g., instead of becoming angry, be especially kind.
   - Forgive the other person(s) for any perceived wrongdoing.
     Ask forgiveness for anything you may have done to cause offence.

7. After you are able to consistently maintain your harmony, take note of how your improved attitude influences the other person(s).

8. Record your observations in your journal.

INTRODUCING...

Justinius and the Seraphim

Holy Justinius, Captain of the Seraphic Bands, is a mighty seraphim who works closely with Serapis Bey and his legions of purity to assist mankind. Justinius describes his bands of seraphic angels as fiery beings forming concentric rings around the Great Central Sun who absorb its light and then deliver it to the evolutions of our universe.

Although these descriptions make them sound far above us, the seraphim are actually close at hand. In fact, we each have seraphim who work with us personally. The Ascended Master Zarathustra revealed that a special seraphim has been with us since the birth of our soul. "This seraphim has an attachment to bringing your body and mind and soul into the health of God, the health enjoyed by seraphim."[26]

Justinius once said:

> We come to make you white and clean, to make you whole. The seraphim come to minister to the soul. And so they come passing through the microcosm, and their fire also burns the cause of disease, of poison, of the toxins that have been passing through you for so many years in the food, in the water, in the tobacco and the alcohol that mankind imbibe. . . .
>
> When they pass through your forms as spirits of living fire, they leave, as it were, the calling card of their identity. That calling card is a focus of fire tingeing your aura with the hue of the Central Sun, tingeing the aura with a halo. And for a while, then, there is that glow, that essence, that sense of well-being, that inner warmth.[27]

By asking the seraphim to pass through our four lower bodies, accumulations of negative effluvia can be exchanged for the incredible light they carry. The seraphim can prepare us for our mission in life and help us fulfill it as well. For protection, we can also invoke the silvery, platinum and white protective helmet and armor of Justinius and the seraphim. In addition, the electronic fire rings of the seraphim can surround and seal us when we make the call.

26 *Pearls of Wisdom,* vol. 35, no. 36.

27 Justinius, "The Army of the Hosts of the Lord," March 6, 1977.

Not only will seraphim protect us individually; the seraphic hosts are so eager to assist us toward our victory that if we are serious about our service, more of them will continually come to work with us. Justinius said, "Where you have that consciousness of the will to win, so you shall increase your number of seraphim."[28] Incredible as it may seem, these holiest of angels stand ever ready to assist us in small and great ways and will stay with us from this moment all the way to our victory in ascension's light!

28 *Pearls of Wisdom,* vol. 34, no. 17.

Expanding the Light of Purity

The idea of purity can be unpopular in today's world, in which there are so many pulls in different directions. The ascended masters, having lived on earth themselves, know the challenges of living in the material world and try to help us understand the concept of purity from the cosmic perspective—that the soul must ultimately choose this higher path in order to fulfill her spiritual destiny. As the Great Divine Director explained, "It is not to the banal aspects of mortality that men must draw nigh, but to the original puritan design of the Godhead. Unfortunately, the sinister force has often drawn an image of austerity around the idea of purity."[29] There are many spiritual tools to help us transmute such a rigid conception into the magnificent reality of joy that true purity conveys. The science of the spoken Word is one of them.

SPOKEN WORD PRACTICE: INVOKING PURITY

Purity, in the cosmic sense, brings us closer to wholeness and oneness with our own Higher Self. To achieve this goal, the Goddess of Purity instructed us to regard ourselves as worthy of taking part in its marvelous essence.

Try the following affirmation and experience the result! Center in your heart; then affirm the words with passion and joy. Repeat it three or more times for greater results.

> **Lord, I AM worthy of thy purity. I would have thy purity surge through me in a great cosmic burst to remove from the screen of my mind, my thoughts, and my feelings every appearance of human vibratory action and all that is impure in substance, thought, or feeling.**
>
> **Replace all that right now with the fullness of the mind of Christ and the mind of God, the manifest power of the resurrection spirit and the ascension flame, that I may enter into the Holy of Holies of my being and find the power of transmutation taking place to free me forever from all discord that has ever manifested in my world.**[30]

Understanding the amazing grace that can flow to us through purity's flame provides an impetus to give an abundance of white-ray decrees, and fortunately these are readily available.

---

29 *Pearls of Wisdom,* vol. 8, no. 23.

30 The entire decree by the Goddess of Purity is printed in the decree book *Prayers, Meditations and Dynamic Decrees for Personal and World Transformation* (Gardiner, Mont.: Summit Publications, Inc., 1986), pp. 344–45, no. 40.05.

The "I AM Pure" stanzas below, for example, are often given repeatedly for this purpose. The lovely words contain a rhythm that can reverberate in the soul, enfolding her in purity's flame.

I AM PURE

**By God's desire from on high,
Accepted now as I draw nigh,
Like falling snow with star-fire glow,
Thy blessed purity does bestow
Its gift of Love to me.**

**I AM pure, pure, pure
By God's own word.
I AM pure, pure, pure,
O fiery sword.
I AM pure, pure, pure,
Truth is adored.**

**Descend and make me whole,
Blessed Eucharist, fill my soul.
I AM thy law, I AM thy light,
O mold me in thy form so bright!**

Beloved I AM! Beloved I AM! Beloved I AM![31]

Giving purity decrees can infuse the soul with pureness and perfection, and provide a wonderful boost on the path toward personal Christhood. This heavenly gift can speed us on our way to fulfilling our highest potential in God, and inspire others to return to purity's greatest joy.

Asking Serapis Bey for Assistance

Finally, here is a lovely decree called "Prayer for Purity" that invokes the Master Serapis Bey himself to help us increase in the white fire of purity. Give it out loud and enjoy the wonderful change in rhythm that indicates the acceleration of the flame.

PRAYER FOR PURITY

www.SummitLighthouse.org/SA3-2

In the name of the beloved mighty victorious Presence of God, I AM in me, my very own beloved Holy Christ Self, beloved Serapis Bey, beloved Archangel Gabriel, beloved Cyclopea, Great Silent Watcher, beloved Elohim of Purity, beloved Mighty Astrea, beloved Guru Ma and Lanello, the entire Spirit of the Great White Brotherhood and the World Mother, elemental life—fire, air, water, and earth! I decree:

31 This decree is printed in *Prayers, Meditations and Dynamic Decrees*, p. 345, no. 40.06.

Beloved Serapis, in God's name I AM
Calling for purity's ray to expand,
Imploring that shadows no longer adhere,
So longing for purity now to appear.

My mind purify of its fleeting impression,
My feelings release of all impure direction;
Let memory retain the Immaculate Concept
And treasure the pearl of the holy Christ precept.

O souvenir of radiant wonder,
Let my mind on thee now ponder;
Christ discrimination, sunder
All that's less than God Success!

Cut me free from all deception,
Fix my mind on pure perception;
Hear, O thou, my invocation—
My Christ Self to manifest!

O flame of cosmic purity,
From Luxor, blaze through me;
Completely clear all shadowed weights,
Ascend me now to Thee!

And in full faith I consciously accept this manifest, manifest, manifest! (3x) **right here and now with full power, eternally sustained, all-powerfully active, ever expanding, and world enfolding until all are wholly ascended in the light and free!**

Beloved I AM! Beloved I AM! Beloved I AM![32]

32 This decree is printed in *Prayers, Meditations and Dynamic Decrees,* p. 340, no. 40.00.

CHAPTER 2

The Light of the Divine Mother

The Mother Light in Manifestation

The Divine Mother is the feminine polarity of the Godhead, the manifestation of God as Mother. She comes in many guises and has been called by many names—the universal Mother, Shakti, Cosmic Virgin and more. She peeks out at us from all creation and smilingly waits for us to recognize her. The Buddha Manjushri said, "Know that the Divine Mother in multiple manifestations is here, there and everywhere to love you, to tutor your soul and to rescue you from your own demises."[1] Indeed, we could probably all tell stories of how someone bearing the Mother light has rescued us from follies and errors and put our souls back on track. The Ascended Lady Master Vesta, a representative of the Divine Mother as all ascended lady masters are, sweetly describes this energy with these words: "I come now as a bird of paradise to nestle with you. I come in many forms, beloved. See me in everything and you will not miss me."[2]

Yet the Mother is not just outside of us. She resides within our own temples, lovingly and patiently awaiting our coming of age. It is enlightening to explore some of the faces of the Divine Mother and see how her light manifests in, through and around us every day.

The Divine Mother in Spiritual Traditions

The Divine Mother is everywhere as the feminine aspect of the Godhead. Matter is the feminine polarity of Spirit; in fact, the term *matter* is used interchangeably with *mater*—the Latin word for "mother." In this context, the entire material cosmos can be seen as the womb of creation into which Spirit projects the energies of life. All matter is really the womb of the Cosmic Virgin who, as the other half of the Divine Whole, also exists in Spirit as the transcendent polarity of God the Father.

The veils of the Mother are like the veils of the bride, hiding and protecting her virginity and innocence. These veils, sometimes called "maya," are what she uses to hide the brilliance of Spirit—the Father manifestation—and his pure energy. Maya also refers to the successive veils of appearances through which the Divine Mother plays hide and seek with us. We have to pass our spiritual tests to get beyond her veils so we can come face-to-face with reality as it is.

1 *Pearls of Wisdom*, vol. 37, no. 21.
2 *Pearls of Wisdom*, vol. 28, no. 7.

Sri Ramakrishna, renowned Eastern devotee of the Divine Mother, related the following story about the God Kartikeya (the Indian name for Sanat Kumara), which depicts the omnipresence of the Mother.

Kartikeya, leader of the heavenly hosts, once gave a scratch to a cat. Returning home, he saw the mark of a scratch on his mother's face. "How in the world, Mother," he asked, "came that ugly scratch on your cheek?"

"Why, child," replied the Divine Durga, "it is your own handiwork, the mark of your nail." "But how can that be?" said the astonished Kartikeya, "I never remember scratching you."

"No," said his mother, "but think what you did this morning to the cat!" "Why, yes," said her son. "Still how could that touch you?" "Dear child," said his mother, "nothing exists in this world but Myself. I am the whole creation. Whatever you hurt, I suffer."[3]

Though the body of the Divine Mother is the whole universe we see around us, she is not always recognized and acknowledged because of her sheer vastness and perhaps our familiarity with the material world. It is somewhat easier to understand her light and flame as they are honored in various spiritual traditions.

According to the ascended masters, the Mother represents the eighth ray through which the seven rays integrate and blend.[4] Gautama Buddha explained how this relates to the world religions, each of which correspond to one of the seven rays. He said, "It is my desire to see the flame of each of the world's religions grow and grow and burn brightly until in such brightness of universal understanding the flames of the world's religions become one, and all may see the paths to the center—seven paths and the eighth-ray path of the Divine Mother."[5]

WORLD RELIGIONS ON THE SEVEN RAYS

RELIGION	RAY	CHAKRA	MAIN QUALITIES
Judaism	First	Throat	Power, will
Buddhism	Second	Crown	Wisdom, understanding
Christianity	Third	Heart	Love, beauty, creativity
Hinduism	Fourth	Base of the Spine	Purity, discipline, order
Confucianism	Fifth	Third Eye	Science, healing, truth
Islam	Sixth	Solar Plexus	Peace, ministration, service
Taoism	Seventh	Seat of the Soul	Freedom, transmutation

3 Advaita Ashrama, *Teachings of Sri Ramakrishna* (Calcutta, India: Gipidi Box Co., 1994), p. 118.

4 The eighth ray of integration is explored in depth in chapter 8.

5 *Pearls of Wisdom*, vol. 37, no. 5.

Elizabeth Clare Prophet stated that our devotion to God as Mother will create the balance—both in the individual and in civilization—necessary for the alchemy of self-transformation. Not only women exemplify the Mother light; it is important to realize that the spiritual and religious traditions of both East and West are replete with examples of men who have raised the feminine flame within themselves and become the living Christ. A few well-known examples of males who were deeply devoted to the Divine Mother are Saint John of the Cross, Paramahansa Yogananda, Padre Pio and Ramakrishna. All masculine ascended masters are suffused with the Mother light as well.

Below are some glimpses of how various spiritual traditions perceive the Divine Mother so we can more easily understand her universality. The truth within ourselves and in all existence can then more readily be seen.

The Mother in Jewish Mysticism

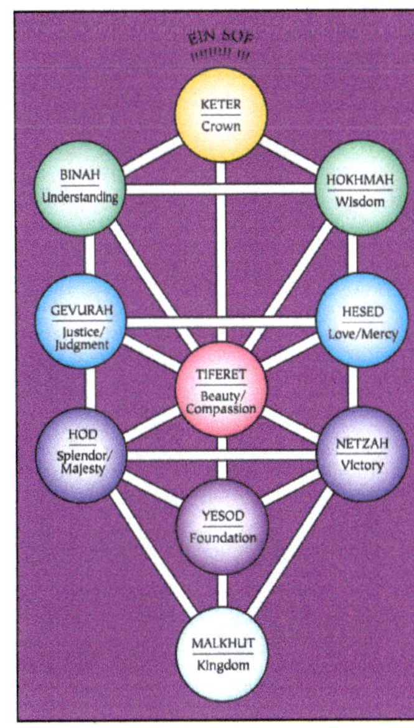

Jewish mysticism describes the ten *sefirot,* or aspects of God's being, which emanate from the infinite Godhead, *Ein Sof.* The Kabbalists' diagram of the sefirot is called the Tree of Life; it symbolizes "conscious immortality." It is a blueprint for the divine world and for our own bodies and souls since the sefirot correspond to the seven major chakras within man. Climbing the Tree of Life, or raising the light up the chakras along the spine, leads one to union with God.

The *sefirah*[6] *Malkhut* corresponds to the purified light and vibration of the base-of-the-spine chakra. Malkhut represents the Divine Mother, and connecting to her is the key to accessing the power of all the other sefirot and their corresponding chakras. It is the Mother who raises us up in love and adoration to be one with the consciousness of our Divine Father. The Zohar, a Jewish sacred text, explains it this way:

> Who is "the way to the Tree of Life?" It is the great consort; she is the way to that great and powerful tree.... If one does not enter through this gate [Malkhut], one cannot gain entry to the worlds. It is like an exalted king, who is high, hidden and concealed, and who has made gates [sefirot] for himself, one upon the other, and at the end of all the gates he has made one particular gate.... He says: Whoever desires to enter into my presence, this gate shall be the first that leads to me; and whoever enters by this gate shall enter.

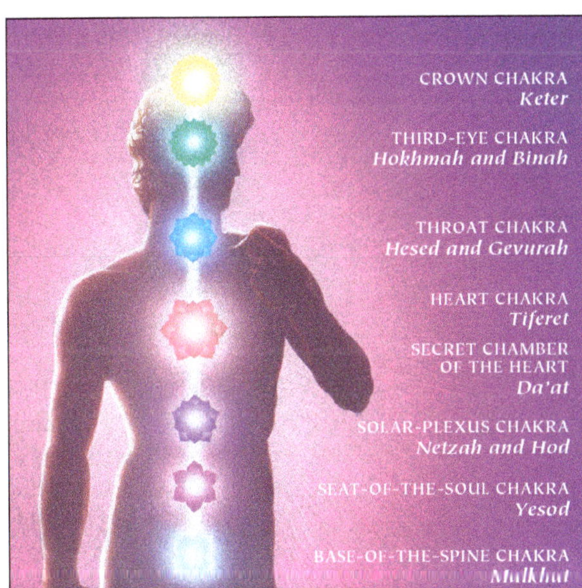

The Mother opens this door to the Father's heart when we open our hearts and extend mercy, justice and compassion to ourselves and others. Once it is open, we are able to enter the gates of the sefirot and pass their initiations one by one.

---

6 *Sefirah* is the singular form of *sefirot.*

Some Hindu Mothers

In Hinduism, the concept of the Divine Mother is known as Shakti, the active principle and force that brings into manifestation the Father's will. The Mother is the Word, the Great Shakti of Brahman, who releases the power, wisdom and love of the Hindu Trinity of Brahma, Vishnu and Shiva. Like the four petals of the base-of-the-spine chakra, there are four different Hindu aspects of this Mother flame. We'll look at these Divine Mothers: Sarasvati, Lakshmi, Kali and Durga. Each has a unique seed syllable and bija mantra which purify and amplify the light of the base chakra and release the light of Spirit into the material world. In addition, there is also another aspect of Mother known as Chamunda.

SPOKEN WORD PRACTICE: SEED SYLLABLES AND BIJA MANTRAS

Chanting the seed syllables and bija mantras is a great way to cleanse and protect the light at the base of the spine and seal the light in all of the chakras. The Mother light can then rise, quickening the higher chakras as she ascends.

Try the mantras below to feel the energy and power of the names of the supreme feminine deities described earlier. Go to the online audio track to hear them pronounced and chanted.

www.SummitLighthouse.org/SA3-3

1. Sarasvati's seed syllable is Aim (pronounced *Ah-eem*), a variation of the primordial sound Aum. When we chant Aim, we are emitting the vibration that releases knowledge of the law of the Father from the base chakra.

   Sarasvati's bija mantra is:

   OM AIM SARASVATYE NAMAHA

   (Om Ah-eem Sah-rah-swaht-yay Nah-mah-hah)

2. Lakshmi's seed syllable, which releases the enlightenment of the Son, the path of the abundant life and wisdom, is Shrim (pronounced *Shreem*).

   Lakshmi's bija mantra is:

   OM SRIM LAKSMYE NAMAHA

   (Om Shreem Lahk-shmee-yay Nah-mah-hah)

3. The Mother complement of the Holy Spirit has two feminine forms, Kali and Durga, since in Hinduism the Holy Spirit is both destroyer and deliverer. By love, the Holy Spirit extinguishes or transmutes evil; and by love, the Holy Spirit delivers us.

   - Kali is the fierce Mother who slays and exorcizes the demons attacking her children. She will bind and exorcise subconscious demons connected with negative emotions like fear and anxiety. Her seed syllable is Krim (pronounced *Kreem*).

   Kali's bija mantra is:

   OM KRIM KALIKAYE NAMAHA

   (Om Kreem Kah-lee-kah-yay Nah-mah-hah)

- Durga is the elegant Mother in the person of the evil-slayer. She releases the light of the Holy Spirit as the one who comes with many arms to aid us spiritually, just as our physical mother performs many tasks for us at a human level. Her seed syllable is Dum (pronounced *Doom*).

  Durga's bija mantra is:

  OM DUM DURGAYE NAMAHA

  (Om Doom Door-gah-yay Nah-mah-hah)

4. In addition to the four personages of the Divine Mother, there is also a mantra to the universal Mother Chamunda, also a demon-slaying force:

   AIM HRIM KLIM CHAMUNDAYE VICHE

   (Ah-eem Hreem Kleem Chah-muhn-dah-yay Vee-chay)

Mother Figures in Buddhism

In Oriental Buddhism, Kuan Yin is regarded as the universal Mother, the feminine embodiment of mercy and compassion. She is known by students of the ascended masters as the "court of last resort" because her compassionate heart will not turn anyone away. Kuan Yin is also known as the Saviouress of the East. Throughout the Orient in temples, homes and wayside grottoes, altars are dedicated to her as the Mother of Mercy. Prayers to her presence and flame are incessantly on the lips of devotees as they seek her guidance and succor in every area of life.

Kuan Yin

Kuan Yin is the ascended lady master hierarch of the etheric Temple of Mercy over Beijing, China, where she focuses the flame of mercy and forgiveness for the people of China and the souls of all mankind. For centuries, Kuan Yin has been epitomized in her Buddhist role as a *bodhisattva,* which means literally "a being of bodhi or enlightenment" who is destined to become a Buddha but has forgone the bliss of nirvana with a vow to save all children of God.[7]

A similar beloved and approachable deity in Tibetan Buddhism is Tara, the White Goddess. Many of Tara's powers are parallel to those attributed to Kuan Yin, and the relationship between Tara and Kuan Yin has been the subject of much speculation. Some say that Kuan Yin is Tara's Chinese counterpart and others believe that the two are really one and the same.

Tara, the White Goddess

It is said that when Tara took her bodhisattva vows to work unceasingly for others, she also vowed to always take the form of a woman. Tara is known as the Goddess of Action, and in this mode she is considered to be Green Tara, a fifth-ray healer who acts with lightning speed to help those in distress. In an emergency one can just think of her and she will be there. The ten-syllable mantra of Green Tara is:

7 For more information about Kuan Yin, see chapter 6 in *Meeting the Masters* (Book 2 in the Sacred Adventure series).

www.SummitLighthouse.org/ SA3-4

OM TARE TUTTARE TURE SVAHA

(Om Tah-ray Too-tah-ray Too-ray Svah-hah)

Hail to Tara! or Hail to Thee, Thou liberator from samsara, the liberator from the eight fears, the liberator from disease!

Yeshe Tsogyal is another outstanding example of the Divine Mother in Buddhism. Padma Sambhava, whose name means "Lotus-born," was the eighth-century founder of Tibetan Buddhism. Yeshe Tsogyal, a Tibetan princess whose name means "Victorious Ocean of Wisdom," was his chief disciple. In the East she is considered an incarnation of Sarasvati. The ascended masters have revealed that she was a past embodiment of Elizabeth Clare Prophet.

Yeshe studied with Padma Sambhava for eleven years, during which time they were always together. It was as if he poured all the contents of his being into her as a worthy vessel. He revealed to her all his secret heart treasures and many teachings that she concealed at the time since they were meant for those who would be born in future centuries. Padma Sambhava also taught Yeshe about the human body being the basis for realizing enlightenment, saying, "Male or female—there is no great difference. But if she develops the mind bent on enlightenment, to be a woman is better."[8] Indeed, Yeshe attained the Buddhic consciousness in that lifetime. Padma Sambhava then instructed her to strive unfailingly for the benefit of others.

Yeshe Tsogyal traveled far and wide in Tibet, spreading the teaching and training thousands of monks and nuns. Many attained enlightenment and a number became equal to her in power. She is said to have appeared to many people in different guises in order to help them. At the amazing age of 211, Yeshe prepared to leave Tibet and go to the land of the Lotus Light to join Padma Sambhava. When her students entreated her to stay, she responded, "There is no such thing as meeting and parting. My power is such that I am free from karma and can lead others—I give refuge without distinguishing self and other, and I manifest compassion. For me, the Mother, there is no suffering from death or from change."[9] When she began to withdraw from the physical octave, Yeshe said, "Listen, faithful Tibetans! I am merging with the fundamental, the ground of all that is—physical pain and suffering are disappearing. The conditioned Tsogyal is expanding into the unconditioned.... Even the illusion of a body is dissolving.... The holy Dharma has transformed my body into light."[10]

Foreseeing dark times in the future of Tibet and the world at large, Yeshe instructed her students—including spiritual seekers who would embody in the future—to give the Vajra Guru mantra, which the ascended masters call the Golden Mantra.

8 Nam-mkha'i snying-po, *Mother of Knowledge* (Berkeley, Calif.: Dharma Publishing, 1983), p. xxiii.

9 Ibid., p. 178.

10 Ibid., pp. 208–9.

These twelve syllables are the very essence of Padma Sambhava. Yeshe said, "This mantra is the antidote, the means to pass from and reverse all misery. . . . This mantra is the wish-fulfilling gem. . . . You beings here now, and you who are yet to come, please practice and rely upon this essential mantra."[11] The twelve-syllable mantra is:

OM AH HUM VAJRA GURU PADMA SIDDHI HUM
(Om Ah Hoom Vuhj-ruh Gur-roo Pud-muh Sid-hee Hoom)

OM AH HUM! Vajra Guru, who arose from a lotus,
please grant me the ordinary and supreme accomplishments, HUM!

www.SummitLighthouse.org/SA3-5

The Mother in Christianity

Mother Mary is venerated as the Divine Mother in the West. In Christian tradition, Mary is considered the divine mediatrix who opens the door to our understanding of the embodiment of the Christ consciousness. As she nurtured and mothered the Christ in her son, Jesus, so she can assist us in becoming the fullness of our Christ Self. Mother Mary serves on the fifth ray, the emerald-green ray of healing, wholeness, truth, science, abundance and precipitation.

Mary was an embodied archangel, the archeia, or divine complement, of Archangel Raphael. Archangels don't generally take embodiment, but Mary was chosen for this mission because of her devotion to the Mother light. She prepared for many earthly embodiments to become the mother of Jesus, who had such a valuable mission for the planet. Mother Mary ascended after her life as his mother.

She is sometimes called the "Mother of God," which may cause some to take offense. But the name actually enables us to realize that it is divinely ordained for any woman to nourish the God-potential within all souls. Elizabeth Clare Prophet once asked Mother Mary to explain how someone could be the Mother of God if God preexisted all of us. Mary replied, "I am the Mother of God as the nourisher of the flame of God within you. I am nourishing and watering that flame of your divinity on earth. This is my mothering."[12]

In a dictation given in 1968, Mary tells the story of how she instructed her son, Jesus, about patience. We can see from the account what a loving teacher and mother she was.

> I recall one morning when beloved Jesus was yet a small lad that he came to me with a very hard piece of wood that he was trying to whittle. He desired that I should persuade his father Joseph to exchange it for a softer piece, one that would lend itself more easily to molding.
>
> I sat him on my knee, and I proceeded to explain to him that there was an

---

11 Ibid., p. 216.

12 For more information about Mother Mary, see chapter 6 in *Meeting the Masters.*

> ingrained quality that of old had been placed within the tree, making one possess a harder quality and another a softer quality. I told him that the soft wood would easily mar and that, were he to use it, the little image that he sought to whittle would not endure the knocks and tumbles that might later come to it, whereas a carving made of hard wood would endure more substantially. I also told him that the wood enjoyed being shapened by his hands and the only difference between the soft and the hard wood would be that of a greater use of patience on his part.
>
> Jesus brushed back his hair, which had fallen across his eyes, and with great and quick gentleness planted a kiss upon both of my cheeks. I noticed a trace of a tear in one eye as he dashed away to continue his work of shaping the hard wood.[13]

Mother Mary finished by quoting from the Bible, "Thus, in your patience possess ye your souls."[14]

Cosmic Beings of the Mother Flame

All ascended masters exemplify the light of the Divine Mother, and many have demonstrated a profound mothering of humanity. For example, Purity and Astrea, Elohim of the Fourth Ray, infinitely care for our souls through their Mother flame. Astrea, the feminine half of this Elohim pair, is often referred to as "the Starry Mother." As the fierce protectress of souls of light, she personifies the Hindu concept of Kali, "the demon-slayer." Purity, her masculine counterpart, holds the divine pattern of the perfection of the Christ for all in manifest form. He focuses the fire that is in the heart of every sun and atom—the pure white energy out of which flow the seven rays of the Christ consciousness.

Blue is considered the feminine aspect of white because the white fire of Purity coalesces as blue in the matter plane. These Elohim therefore use a white-fire/blue-fire action in their service to mankind. Astrea works twenty-four hours a day wielding a cosmic circle and sword of blue flame to free souls from all that is not real and from all that opposes the fulfillment of their divine plan held in the heart of Purity. The circle of fire invoked from Astrea's heart is a dazzling blue-white flame that oscillates as two concentric rings of fire—the blue of Astrea and the white of Purity—interchanging frequencies at such a rapid rate as to appear as the action of blue-white lightning flashing around souls, countries, planets, solar systems, galaxies—wherever there is a need for the reinforcement of the will of God in the divine blueprint held in the white-fire core of being.

You can make Astrea's circle and sword of blue flame practical in your life as Jesus Christ did when he exorcised a boy possessed of a demon. As Astrea explains, the disciples could not heal this youth who lay on the ground frothing at the mouth.

13 *Pearls of Wisdom*, vol. 11, no. 9.

14 Luke 21:19.

> The disciples had attempted, again and again, to cast out the demon from that boy, and I tell you they exerted themselves to the fullest. But they lacked the faith and they lacked the knowledge of our octave of light. If my cosmic circle and sword of blue flame had been invoked around that boy by any one of those disciples, they would have found that that demon would have left on the instant and would not have remained for a second. This was the power of light that Jesus himself invoked. He invoked that energy of the blue flame, and it immediately fulfilled the destiny that God intended it to do.[15]

Astrea said that if we want to contemplate the action of the circle and sword of blue flame, we can meditate upon the Concerto in A Minor by Grieg, which contains the same action. She said, "You can hear the cutting cadences of that circle as it whirls about your four lower bodies, getting tighter and tighter around the very core of being until the magnet without, the magnet within send forth into the fire those consciousnesses that stand in rebellion against Almighty God."[16]

Astrea also gave a powerful formula for our spiritual victory. She said:

> Forget not that at any hour of the day or night when the trial comes, when the fires of crucifixion are upon you, you can know that you can win if instantaneously you address the Almighty, if you address Jesus the Christ, the Holy Spirit and the Divine Mother and then call to the mighty Elohim, call to Astrea to release the circle and sword of blue flame around the cause and core of all that opposes your God-identity. . . . If you will do that, I will promise you that you will not fail one single test along the pathway of life.[17]

Elizabeth Clare Prophet

The messenger Elizabeth Clare Prophet was another key representative of the Divine Mother—one we can relate to especially well because she was embodied in recent times. She was a mother, not only to her own five children, but also to thousands throughout the world who called her "Mother" as a term of endearment. As Guru Ma,[18] she gave teachings, counseling and spiritual "spankings" to students of the ascended masters for almost four decades. She described the Mother as one who is understanding and not judgmental or critical, but simply a person who offers a personal presence and meets people where they are.

The Retreat of the Divine Mother

A wonderful etheric retreat where everyone is welcome is the Retreat of the Divine Mother over the Rocky Mountains on the northern border of Yellowstone National Park. The physical focus of this retreat is the Royal Teton Ranch, a property

15 Astrea, *Keepers of the Flame Lesson 23* (Gardiner, Mont.: Summit Publications, Inc., 2002), p. 49. Keepers of the Flame lessons are published for members of the Keepers of the Flame Fraternity, a spiritual order for men and women sponsored by the Ascended Master Saint Germain.

16 *Pearls of Wisdom,* vol. 17, no. 16.

17 Ibid.

18 Padma Sambhava bestowed the mantle of Guru upon Elizabeth Clare Prophet on July 2, 1977. On August 28, 1977, the Ascended Master Confucius revealed her title: "Guru Ma."

Royal Teton Ranch

secured by students of the ascended masters under the masters' guidance as an outer focus of the Great White Brotherhood.

The Retreat of the Divine Mother is the retreat of Lady Master Venus, Sanat Kumara's twin flame. On December 15, 1985, Venus positioned herself in the Temple of the Divine Mother located there. Sanat Kumara spoke of the event in a dictation that day:

> The opening of the door of the temple of the Divine Mother and her Inner Retreat is also come. And this Inner Retreat, positioned now as a vast center of light, is indeed above that "Place Prepared"—prepared, of course, by the Divine Mother—the entire area of the Royal Teton Ranch.
>
> The Mother has waited long . . . for your coming. And she does hold the balance of ancient civilizations that have occurred, both on Lemuria and Atlantis and those long forgotten upon this continent as well as in other areas of the earth.
>
> This great and vast temple of light, beloved, has been prepared over aeons. It is the place of the gathering of the culture of all nations and peoples. It is the place of the drawing together of many lifewaves. . . .
>
> In the very heart of Lady Venus, who keeps the flame of Mother Earth with you, the flame of the Divine Mother of love does abide. Thus Venus, initiator with the Holy Kumaras of your souls on the path of the ruby ray, does position herself in this hour in the etheric retreat of the Divine Mother over this ranch, arcing her heart's love to the retreats of the earth . . . and to every soul who must journey there.[19]

There are several important dispensations from the Brotherhood for this retreat, which also extends onto the physical land of the Royal Teton Ranch:

- Lady Master Venus described her retreat as a vast expanse of the "New Jerusalem, . . . a place of culture and learning."[20]

- A large cohort of ascended master youth live at the retreat. In 1989 the Ascended Master Rex announced that he had come from the planet Venus with companions Nada, Bob and Pearl and a mandala of twenty-five-thousand ascended master youth in order to sponsor the youth of the world.

- A corridor of light arcs from this retreat to the etheric retreat of the feminine ray at Lake Titicaca, as well as to the retreat of Lord Jesus Christ over the entire Holy Land, Saudi Arabia and the Middle East. We can invoke light to flow along this etheric corridor to hold the balance against war.

19 *Pearls of Wisdom,* vol. 29, no. 10.

20 *Pearls of Wisdom,* vol. 34, no. 7.

- The retreat contains a focus of the retreat of the Divine Mother Omega. Sanat Kumara said, "Once Omega did place a focus of her retreat over La Tourelle.[21] So, you may know that that entire retreat and forcefield, removed at the hour of the passing of this property to other hands, has been held in the etheric octave until the announcement of the opening of this vast retreat of the Mother over this wilderness land, over this park and ranch."[22]

- Lord Lanto revealed that a cathedral of the second ray of illumination's flame is anchored in the retreat over King Arthur's Court:

> Myriad angels of illumination's flame form with their bodies of light and the brightness of the golden aura of the sun a cathedral of light around this place. . . .
>
> It is a cathedral of the second ray of illumination's flame whereby the power of the great minds of the Buddhas and bodhisattvas, the World Teachers and their disciples might anchor here that living presence and that place at inner levels which is a part of the Retreat of the Divine Mother, the cathedral itself. . . .
>
> The design of this cathedral is like that of some of the greatest cathedrals in Europe, yet it is even larger. Therefore, many souls of light may begin coming here at inner levels, for we establish this cathedral not alone for the adornment of your soul and your heart and the secret chamber of your heart but also as a place of the gathering. . . .
>
> When they come to the wilderness retreat, beloved, they gather in the great tabernacle of the congregation as of old. But when they come to the mighty Yellowstone, whose waters have a special energy from the heart of the earth, there they will find in the outer place the cathedral built.[23]

Years after the Retreat of the Divine Mother opened, Sanat Kumara spoke about its congruence of heaven and earth. His words convey how the holiness of the retreat permeates the area that it covers and affects people who visit, live and work there.

> This etheric retreat does embrace the physical. When you are on this land, you are always in the etheric octave and the physical simultaneously. This in itself is an adjustment which some cannot make. Being uncomfortable, they quickly leave. You have found it necessary, then, to adjust the dial of frequency of your own physical atoms and cells so that you might experience the etheric domain simultaneously as you are in the physical, balancing the karma of the physical.[24]

21 "La Tourelle" in Colorado Springs was the headquarters of Church Universal and Triumphant from January 1966 through the summer of 1976 and a community teaching center from then until the sale of the property, November 1984. Beloved Omega consecrated it as the Retreat of the Resurrection Spiral on April 11, 1971.

22 Sanat Kumara, "The Retreat of the Divine Mother at the Royal Teton Ranch."

23 *Pearls of Wisdom,* vol. 35, no. 17.

24 *Pearls of Wisdom,* vol. 31, no. 44.

Many students of the ascended masters from all over the world make pilgrimages to the Royal Teton Ranch to experience the heavenly vibration of the Divine Mother's retreat. They come to learn about the teachings of the ascended masters, attend spiritual conferences, work as employees and help out as volunteers.

EXERCISE: MEETING AT THE RETREAT OF THE DIVINE MOTHER

The Elohim of the third ray, Heros and Amora, presented a most effective way to prepare for scheduled meetings. They said to "ask that all parties who will discuss the matter on the morrow be taken to the Retreat of the Divine Mother to review it the night before."[25] Heros and Amora asked us to test their suggestion in the following way:

- At least the day before the meeting, "begin by setting your agenda and giving a copy of it to each one who will be in attendance."
- If you anticipate having to deal with attitudes of bigotry, prejudice, persecution or racism, invoke the violet flame the night before to consume these energies before they cast a pall on your meeting.
- Before retiring, pray for the enlightenment of the souls of those who will attend:
    - Call for the binding of any negative energies that would deter them through pride or stubbornness from making right decisions.
    - "Especially call that those points of discussion you expect to be difficult be resolved harmoniously. *Call* for the guardian angels! *Call* for the Holy Christ Self of all who are to assemble!"
- Then ask Archangel Michael to escort everyone involved (including yourself) in their finer bodies to the Retreat of the Divine Mother over the Royal Teton Ranch to review the topics. "The Holy Christ Self (who is often referred to as the guardian angel) will overshadow and direct each one and prepare all to reach a consensus from the highest level."
- You can also use this method for situations like going to the dentist, working with a lawyer or accountant, having business meetings with people you haven't met, attending parent-teacher conferences, etc. It will pave the way for easier, more harmonious encounters. "And you will see how in those meetings divine resolution, human resolution, legal resolution can come about because you have made your spiritual preparations."

25 *Pearls of Wisdom*, vol. 36, no. 22.

The Culture of the Divine Mother

While most spiritual traditions single out a few exemplars who have embodied the Mother flame, the highest cultures in past civilizations have evolved best when *many* among the people raised the Mother light within and bonded with their Holy Christ Selves. There have been many cultures where light has flourished and golden ages have taken place. Some examples are Lemuria, Atlantis, several locations in South America such as the Amazon region, and a golden-age civilization where the Sahara desert now is.[26]

All culture is the Mother flame expanded by a mandala of people who together need to bring forth a specific beauty and flame of the Mother as part of their karma and dharma. It is the office of the Divine Mother to sustain the way of life of the nations. Each people or nation has its own innate genius and unique expression of the Mother culture, a cultivation of the light of the soul of that people that comes forth through the overshadowing presence of the Mother flame.

Mrs. Prophet said that any attempt to redistribute peoples, nations and wealth under a one-world economic system and government destroys these cultures. It interferes with each one's karma and cultivation of light. The Mother flow is cut off when the stream of consciousness and the awareness of one's origins and identity are destroyed. When people don't know who they are because the memory of their collective roots and reason for being is destroyed, there is no culture, and without culture people quickly go back to a primitive consciousness. This has been the case after the fall of each golden-age civilization.

> *In the denial of the Divine Mother of ancient Lemuria, there has come to pass a civilization bereft of the intimate knowledge of being the vessel of the Mother. . . .*
>
> *Those who neglect a self-knowledge of their history are doomed to repeat that history. Thus you stand in a moment on the pinnacle of a choice, to move upward in the spiral of being, to transcend oneself all the way back to the days of Lemuria and enter the high road of reunion with God, else to repeat the former cycles and go down again.*[27]
>
> —PAUL THE VENETIAN

The Age of Aquarius

Atlantis and Lemuria were civilizations of far greater light, enlightenment and culture of the Divine Mother than those of today. In fact, the earth is still rising out of the dark ages that followed the catastrophe of the destruction of these ancient civilizations. Although we have many scientific accomplishments and achievements, our understanding of true being and the reason for being is not at the same heights reached by mankind in earlier eras. This tells us that many souls evolving on earth

26 For more information on Atlantis, Lemuria and Saint Germain's golden-age culture, see chapters 1, 3 and 7 in *Meeting the Masters.*

27 *Pearls of Wisdom,* vol. 31, no. 26.

today have far more light in their causal bodies than they are manifesting in their outer awareness and apparent self-mastery. They have tremendous deposits of virtue and glories of former times and civilizations locked in their causal bodies. The flow of the Mother light within them can help release this light and energy, not only to raise their individual souls but also to help bring in the golden age of Aquarius and reestablish the culture of the Divine Mother.

Elizabeth Clare Prophet said there is light locked in the heart of every one of us as a unique idea of love that we can bring forth for the benefit of our fellowman and the progress of the divine culture of the Mother on earth. It may be an invention, a poem, a geometric design or any number of things. But whatever it is, it is a gift that we alone can provide. Unfortunately, many of us have held that gift in our hearts for a succession of embodiments because no one told us we could release it as beings of ultimate creativity.

The Aquarian age is an era of alchemy and transformation based in the energy of the Mother flow. It is destined to be an age of creativity, of unlocking the genius within each soul. It will be the age of the greatest of dramas, art, literature and culture because the Mother flame, wedded to the Holy Spirit, is for the perfecting of the matrices of the Christed identities of all the sons and daughters of God. The ancient religion of Lemuria, the Motherland, was the way of the Divine Mother. In the age of Aquarius the Divine Mother returns to be raised up within our temples along with the Holy Spirit.

It is up to the individual to determine that the Mother light is honored and raised within and ultimately reflected in society at large. As this occurs person by person, the golden age of Aquarius will be ushered in and the world will once again reflect the divine culture of the Mother.

The Flow of the Light of Mother and Father Within

The culture of the Mother, then, begins one person at a time. The Divine Mother doesn't just dwell within a chosen few; she dwells within each of us no matter what gender we are. She nestles her light within the base-of-the-spine chakra, waiting for us to raise her energies as we transmute our negative karma and progress in spiritual development. The Kundalini, which literally means "coiled-up serpent," is latent or sleeping in most people. When it is awakened and begins to rise, it penetrates and activates each of the chakras along the way.

This action occurs as the light of the Divine Mother polarizes with the light of the Divine Father in the crown chakra and the two are naturally drawn to each other. When the light of the I AM Presence descending through the crown chakra and the ascending light of the base chakra meet in the secret chamber of the heart, the forces of Father and Mother join together. There, they give birth to the Christ consciousness. Elizabeth Clare Prophet said this union of the energy of the Father-Mother God is necessary for us to become the full manifestation of what we are intended to be. El Morya also explained how it produces wholeness:

> The Mother flame is for the "watering" of all of the chakras and the cleansing of the soul. And as the fire of the Mother does rise on the spinal altar, you ultimately experience communion with her in the secret chamber of the heart, where your Mother energies and your Father energies reunite. It is then that you sense your wholeness, your completeness, and the balance of your yin-yang energies. No longer are you incomplete, no longer do you crave this or that, for you have entered into the internalization of the white fire of God. This is possible unto you.[28]

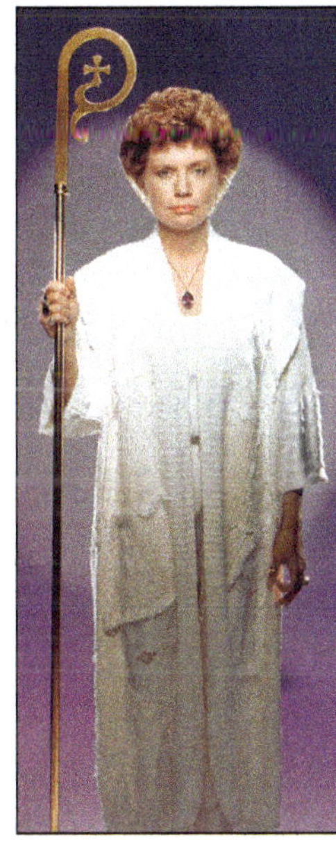

His words are a clear reminder it is not only entirely possible but desirable for each of us to give birth to the Christ consciousness where we are. Mother Mary also explained that raising the light of the Mother releases the light of the crown chakra and the vision of the third eye. The energy flows over a track like a shepherd's crook, rising up the spine and over the head. Those who raise the sacred fire therefore become a staff in the Lord's hand, upholding the flame.

Raising the Kundalini fire is accomplished naturally through various spiritual techniques, which include meditation, intoning Eastern bija mantras, giving the "Hail Mary" prayer and invoking the violet flame. Raising the Kundalini this way is not a sudden burst of fire but a gentle rising of strength and consciousness. We might even sense the consciousness of God as part of ourselves mounting the "spinal altar," a term used for the seven main chakras containing the light along the spine. It can give us the strength of mind, will and body to achieve our ends.

In this process, we should simply place our hand in the hand of our own Christ Self, content to walk the spiritual path under the direction of our God Presence, in the calm and certain knowing that if we do all things well, fulfilling the precepts of the Law in service and in grace, we will attain the supreme goal of reunion based on self-mastery.[29]

> *All souls in the Matter cosmos are undergoing the initiations of the feminine ray whether or not they so aspire. For with the age of Aquarius come the initiations of mind and heart, i.e., the crown and the heart chakras, that they might be the receptacles of the enlightenment of the Holy Spirit and the love of the Divine Mother respectively—and alternately, the Mother's profound wisdom and the Spirit's mystical love. Know, then, that the Divine Mother is the living Word and she is made flesh in every Christed one. And so in you is that Christ, and so in you is that anointing if you come into conformity with your Christ.*[30]
>
> —KUAN YIN

28 *Pearls of Wisdom*, vol. 38, no. 26.

29 The ascended masters Kuthumi and Djwal Kul have provided exercises, meditations and visualizations for strengthening the aura and increasing the light in the chakras. See Kuthumi and Djwal Kul, *The Human Aura* (Gardiner, Mont.: Summit University Press, 1996). For more information on spiritual techniques to safely raise the sacred fire, see chapter 4 in *The Spiritual Quest* and chapter 6 in *Meeting the Masters*.

30 *Pearls of Wisdom*, vol. 36, no. 24.

The Roles of Woman and Man

In this age of the rise of the feminine ray and of women coming into their own, it can be helpful to examine the role of woman in relation to the role of man. In ascended master terms, it is the role of all feminine beings to mother or nourish the God flame incarnate on earth. Women, in their roles as daughters, sisters, wives and mothers, are intended to exemplify a spark of God as the universal Mother. Therefore, women need to realize that whether they own a business or run a household, a home, have a husband and children or are responsible for a large project in the community, the flame that God has given them to express is the flame of Mother.

Life in both a male and a female body affords us the wondrous opportunity of realizing all aspects of God—Father, Son, Holy Spirit and Mother. But in the cosmic scheme there has to be an Alpha and Omega polarity, and the Mother flame is intended to be in a supportive role vis-à-vis the flame of Father. This relationship is reflected in the Chart of Your Divine Self.

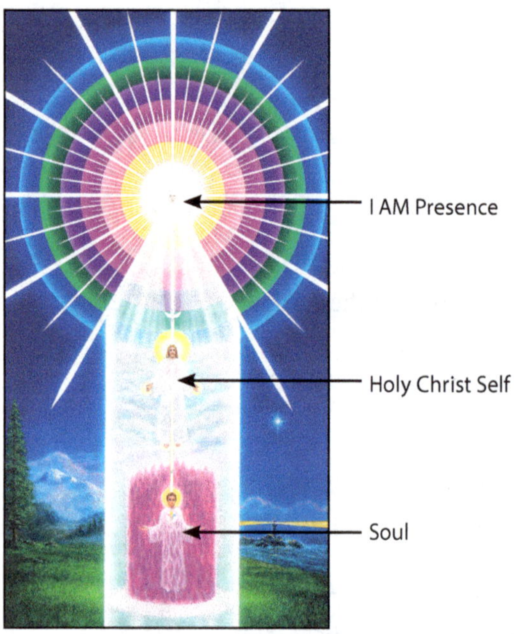

Chart of Your Divine Self

The I AM Presence is the symbol of Spirit, and the evolving soul is the feminine potential projected into physical existence and intended to reunite with Spirit after a learning journey on earth. The soul of any human being represents the feminine potential of his being, and his spiritual being, his I AM Presence, represents his powerful, masculine part.

Elizabeth Clare Prophet has spoken clearly regarding the roles of men and women. She explained that while this is the age of the raising up of the feminine ray, this is not for the emasculation of man but rather for his adornment. Woman is intended to provide inspiration and vision, and man—through developing both his masculine and feminine sides—is intended to provide the foundation of society, exhibiting all the strengths and the nobility women admire and need in men. Both men and women should play prominent roles in society. Women betray themselves when they allow the desecration of the body and allow themselves to be sex symbols. In doing this, they lower the respect men have for them.

Mrs. Prophet explained that the feminine nature is a spiritual one, and the woman's presence in the home is the key to the children, the home and the husband being exalted to their fullest divine potential. The keeping of the spiritual flame in the home is first and foremost the work of woman. It is difficult for her to do this when the head of the household, who represents Christ, does not fulfill his role. The more people are involved in human perversions of their respective roles, the more they enter into conflict and competition with each other. The resulting confusion and burdens in today's society are somewhat karmic and indicative of being in a transition between ages. Honoring the gender-specific gifts of both men and women and at the same time recognizing their divine similarities will open the way for society to reflect the wholeness that is the goal of each soul.

Man's role in the ultimate manifestation of the Christ is unique. Women should have a reverence and a devotion to the spirituality of the man and all the things he can do that they cannot do. In order to be equal with man, the woman should not need to step down from the role of visionary and the spiritual light of her family. She should be prayerful and close to God. It is fine for women to seek equality in the area of jobs and things having to do with society. But a woman should also acknowledge that she should excel in her role and that man should excel in his.

Balancing Our Masculine and Feminine Sides

We are all masculine and feminine in potential, and whether we are male or female in this embodiment, the goal of life is to balance these forces. Balancing the Alpha and Omega energies within opens the door to becoming one with cosmos. Alpha-Omega is a synonymous term for the Father-Mother God, the masculine-feminine polarity of the cosmos, one with the whole. The whole is the source of harmony, joy, bliss, happiness and cosmic consciousness. Whenever we are outside of this whole, we are prone to depression, degeneration, disease and death.

Each person's soul is androgynous, just as the mighty I AM Presence is androgynous. Ideally a well-balanced individual has a sixty-forty percent balance of energies —a man is sixty percent masculine and forty percent feminine, and a woman is sixty percent feminine and forty percent masculine. While this does not totally reflect the androgynous nature of God, it is a good balance for the Alpha-Omega energies within people living in the world and fulfilling their respective male and female roles.

Wholeness is the key to the joy of life, so attaining completeness becomes the quest of the soul. This inner wholeness is designed to be reflected in the outer manifestation of the love between a man and woman.

God has ordained marriage as the matrix for the working out of the polarity of being. And the marriage of man and woman is intended to bear, as the fruit of that union, the Christ consciousness in the offspring. Mrs. Prophet said family life is the foundation of the Aquarian age, so it is wise to guard the family and realize the family is a crucible for the testing of our souls on the path of initiation. She also wanted individuals to understand—especially young people—that the bringing forth of the Christ consciousness, whether in a creative work, in a career or in something that becomes the dedication of one's life, is the purpose of the life force, the sacred fire we are given.

A disciple asked Sri Ramakrishna: How ought we to look upon women? He answered in many ways. Here are a few:

> *He who is face-to-face with Reality, who is blessed with the vision of God, does not regard them with any fear. He sees them as they really are, images of the Divine Mother of the universe. So he not only pays to womankind honour and respect, but actually worships them as a son does a mother.*[31]

> *I look upon every woman as my Divine Mother.*[32]

> *Women whether naturally good or not, whether chaste or unchaste, should always be regarded as images of the Blissful Divine Mother.*[33]

Ramakrishna, devotee of the Divine Mother

31 Advaita Ashrama, *Teachings of Sri Ramakrishna* (Calcutta, India: Gipidi Box Co., 1994), p. 118.
32 Ibid., p. 119.
33 Ibid.

Lady Master Venus

Lady Master Venus is the twin flame and divine complement of Sanat Kumara. Sanat Kumara came from the planet Venus during Earth's darkest hour to hold the flame for the souls of light living here until some among mankind would return once again to an understanding and upholding of the threefold flame within their body temple. During all the aeons Sanat Kumara resided in the etheric octave of our planet, Lady Master Venus remained on Venus holding the Mother flame of love for the evolutions of light there. She once said, "I have been matriarch of Venus for longer than I should care to number the years."[34] Sanat Kumara returned to Venus and to his beloved twin flame on January 1, 1956, when Gautama Buddha took on the office of Lord of the World for our planet.

In 1975, Lady Master Venus came to Earth on a special mission to keep the flame and work with mankind to distribute the teachings of the Cosmic Virgin. And in 1985 she took up residence in the Temple of the Divine Mother in the Retreat of the Divine Mother over the Royal Teton Ranch in Montana. Years later she revealed how she viewed her earthly residence: "I am the Divine Mother occupying this Retreat of the Divine Mother here over the Royal Teton Ranch. It is my home away from home, and yet I am fully at home."[35] On New Year's Eve in 1996, Sanat Kumara announced that both he and Lady Master Venus would stay with Earth until God's plan is fulfilled and every lightbearer is ascended and free.

Lady Venus has given profound and practical teachings urging us towards individual Christhood. She said, "This is the hour for self-transcendence. And as you understand that the goal of the Path is increasing light in your body temple in preparation for the descent of your Holy Christ Self, then know, blessed hearts, that to clear the physical body, to purify it and to strengthen it will result in far less distress in those periods when we must give you the initiation of increased light."[36] She reminded us that the forces of darkness will try to taunt, tempt, aggravate, irritate and cause strife in and amongst us each time the Mother flame begins to flower within us. Then she instructed us in how to overcome these tendencies.

34 *Pearls of Wisdom,* vol. 33, no. 40.
35 Ibid.
36 Ibid.

> May you defeat and outsmart the forces of anti-love that would set one against another over nothing. The best way to cure such situations is to simply walk away from them, to refuse to be offended or intimidated by anything or anyone, to look into the face of Jesus and remember his words to disciples who would be rivalrous, who would be concerned of who would be the greatest in heaven or the greatest on earth, who would be the favorite, who would be this, who would be that. "What is that to thee? Follow thou me."[37]

Lady Venus is indeed a wonderful advocate, a tremendous example of the Divine Mother who will love and cherish us and do all within her power to raise us into the fullness of our divine potential. But as with all children, it is up to each of us individually to follow the loving advice of this heavenly Mother as we mature into our own personal Christhood.

37 Ibid.

Invoking the Power of the Divine Mother

We have been told that the revelation of the names of the Elohim is an amazing dispensation because so much power is produced from just pronouncing their names. Each letter in their names is a release of fohatic energy from the causal body of the Elohim.

In this section you will find out how to give a decree to the Starry Mother, Elohim Astrea, and invoke and direct the power of her name.

The Power and Gift of Astrea's Decree

The ascended masters extol the decree to Astrea and the tremendous action and power it wields in the world. Lady Master Venus said that this "mantra to the Maha Kali . . . is the most powerful mantra to the Divine Mother."[38] On July 5, 1985, El Morya explained why: "The power of the universal Mother carrying the circle and sword of blue flame that is released in this mantra is great indeed, capable of fulfilling every manifestation of the Mother, East or West, and capable of driving from you evil spirits that lurk, addictions, self-indulgences and all pettiness that snatch from you that precious love which comes so gently, so powerfully, and yet is as fragile as crystal."[39]

We have been instructed to call in the name of the Christ to mighty Astrea to lock her cosmic circle and sword of blue flame around the cause and core of any type of discord. We then visualize this circle of the sacred fire locking around ourselves or any other individual at the waist, or locking around entire groups of people, buildings, cities, states, nations and even around the earth at the equator.

You can see this in your mind's eye as a ring of brilliant sapphire and diamond-flashing fire—its regular, almost geometric flames cutting away, like a buzz saw, layers and layers of discord and density. Then visualize the sword of blue flame as a pillar of blue fire perpendicular to the circle of blue flame, breaking the matrices of darkness, shattering forcefields of disease, decay and death. And above all, see the Elohim standing over each individual for whom you are praying, holding the sword of blue flame parallel to the spine and two inches from it.

38 *Pearls of Wisdom,* vol. 29, no. 8.
39 *Pearls of Wisdom,* vol. 28, no. 33.

This is the action whereby the Elohim can demagnetize the consciousness of the individual of all anti-God, anti-Christ and anti-Spirit manifestations, all sinister strategies of the fallen ones and the deceitful energies of the carnal mind. Whenever and wherever you invoke the circle and sword of blue flame from the heart of Purity and Astrea, you can know with absolute certainty that an action of cosmic momentum is taking place.

Astrea encourages us to give her decree on behalf of ourselves and loved ones who are burdened by addictions of all kinds. In 1991, she also explained how we could help a million souls through her decree:

> See how that loved one can be cut free and kept free and how that one will return to the dignity of a child of light and find his mission before it is too late. . . .
>
> If you would keep the vigil for a loved one or a number of loved ones, know that the power of the circle and sword of blue flame will work as you pray for them each day and *for every other child of God on this planet who is similarly enslaved!* . . .
>
> I, Astrea, make you this offer: Pray for your loved ones and put as many photographs as you like upon your altar. And when you pray for them, pray also for all others upon this planet who can be delivered by Astrea. . . .
>
> The single prayer, beloved, will authorize us to help a million souls.[40]

This is a magnificent promise from a powerful cosmic being, and it's readily available whenever we make the call!

SPOKEN WORD PRACTICE: DECREE TO BELOVED MIGHTY ASTREA

The pattern of this decree is more complex than most decrees. The verses and choruses are clearly marked in the decree to assist with this, and the pattern of one repetition of the decree is outlined below. One complete repetition is also included on the link next to the decree to familiarize you with the pattern and rhythm of giving it. With practice, it becomes easier and easier to master the cadence and accelerate the clearing action.

After giving the preamble, give the decree as follows:

- Verse 1 followed by the first chorus
- Verse 2 followed by the first chorus
- Verse 3 followed by the first chorus

Next comes:

- Verse 1 followed by the second chorus
- Verse 2 followed by the second chorus
- Verse 3 followed by the second chorus

40 *Pearls of Wisdom*, vol. 34, no. 13.

Finally you give:

- Verse 1 followed by the third chorus
- Verse 2 followed by the third chorus
- Verse 3 followed by the third chorus

DECREE TO BELOVED MIGHTY ASTREA—"THE STARRY MOTHER"

In the name of the beloved mighty victorious Presence of God, I AM in me, mighty I AM Presence and Holy Christ Selves of Keepers of the Flame, lightbearers of the world and all who are to ascend in this life, by and through the magnetic power of the sacred fire vested in the threefold flame burning within my heart, I call to beloved Mighty Astrea and Purity, Archangel Gabriel and Hope, beloved Serapis Bey and the seraphim and cherubim of God, beloved Guru Ma and Lanello, the entire Spirit of the Great White Brotherhood and the World Mother, elemental life—fire, air, water and earth! to lock your cosmic circles and swords of blue flame in, through, and around: [my four lower bodies, my electronic belt, my heart chakra and all of my chakras, my entire consciousness, being, and world.]

Cut me loose and set me free (3x) **from all that is less than God's perfection and my own divine plan fulfilled.**

www.SummitLighthouse.org/SA3-6

1. **O beloved Astrea, may God Purity**
   Manifest here for all to see,
   God's divine will shining through
   Circle and sword of brightest blue.

First chorus:

Come now answer this my call,
Lock thy circle round us all.
Circle and sword of brightest blue,
Blaze now, raise now, shine right through!

2. **Cutting life free from patterns unwise,**
   Burdens fall off while souls arise
   Into thine arms of infinite love,
   Merciful shining from heaven above.

3. **Circle and sword of Astrea now shine,**
   Blazing blue-white my being refine,
   Stripping away all doubt and fear,
   Faith and goodwill patterns appear.

Second chorus:

Come now answer this my call,
Lock thy circle round us all.
Circle and sword of brightest blue,
Raise our youth now, blaze right through!

Third chorus:

Come now answer this my call,
Lock thy circle round us all.
Circle and sword of brightest blue,
Raise mankind now, shine right through!

And in full faith I consciously accept this manifest, manifest, manifest! (3x) **right here and now with full power, eternally sustained, all-powerfully active, every expanding, and world enfolding until all are wholly ascended in the light and free!**

Beloved I AM! Beloved I AM! Beloved I AM![41]

41 This decree is printed in *Prayers, Meditations and Dynamic Decrees,* p. 200, no. 10.14.

CHAPTER 3

The Science of Wholeness

Healing Body, Mind and Soul

Today's society has a fascination with staying young longer—or forever, if we could. The media speaks about it, getaway retreats are dedicated to it and researchers investigate many ways to dip into the fountain of youth. People are concerned about physical wholeness for a good reason; it affects their quality of life in many ways.

The ascended masters teach that total health ultimately comes from Spirit, our own Higher Self. By drawing down the perfection of body, mind and soul from higher realms, we can become spiritually empowered and more liberated from physical concerns. The science of wholeness involves looking at the entire person at all four levels of being—spiritual, mental, emotional and physical. In order to truly become all that we really are, we must learn how our four lower bodies work together with Spirit to produce perfection.

Serving on the fifth ray are health practitioners, advocates of truth in any occupation, musicians, scientists, mathematicians and those specializing in computers and space technology. Fifth-ray men and women also serve in fields that are dedicated to bringing into manifestation the divine plans of governments, science, religion, education and all branches of higher learning.

The Ascended Master Hilarion, Chohan of the Fifth Ray, stands ready to assist us in this pursuit. As our tutor on the path of green-ray mastery, we can call for his help during the day and study in his etheric retreat while we sleep at night. He is always ready to walk by our side and teach us how to create greater wholeness in our lives.

Green-Ray Qualities

The green ray, the fifth of the seven rays, is the ray of divine wholeness. Its healing action produces completion in body, mind and soul. Its beautiful emerald flame helps us envision, concentrate upon and bring into tangible shape the abundant treasures of our Higher Self. It is primarily expressed through science, technology, logic, mathematics and music. Its life-giving essence is the sustaining power behind the healing arts and taking a stand for truth. The fifth ray also helps us hold the highest possible vision of ourselves and others and assists us to express our divinity in everyday affairs.

The fifth ray is next in order after the four previous rays: (1) blue, (2) yellow,

(3) pink and (4) white. By the action of the green ray, spiritual qualities can "precipitate" or take form in the physical world. Spiritual virtues and graces are brought into the material universe through this ray because it draws down the treasures of the causal body into form.

Threefold Flame

Green is the first of the composite color rays, a blend of the primary colors blue and yellow. The proportions of blue and yellow that make up its hue help determine its qualities. When blue—the color of divine will—is predominant, such as in emerald and teal blue, the fifth ray acts as a catalyst for the healing, regeneration and rejuvenation of the four lower bodies. When the golden hue of illumination is prevalent, such as in turquoise and Chinese green, it focuses the action of precipitation, drawing down abundance from realms of Spirit.

In order to learn more about this special flame, let's examine its major qualities in detail. The following chart lists the positive and negative characteristics covered in this chapter.

FIFTH-RAY QUALITIES	
Positive Expressions	**Negative Expressions**
Healing	All forms of disease; relying only on chemical substances to heal without acknowledging the spiritual dimension; healing techniques that violate the laws of karma
Truth	Lying, misstating facts or omitting needed information, skepticism, dogmatism, doubt, impure reasoning, atheism, agnosticism, argumentation, intellectual pride, misinterpretation of scripture, psychic channeling or mediumship
Precipitation	Greed, refusing to share one's abundance with others, investing in unwise ventures, wasting one's spiritual and material resources
Science	Materialism that is devoid of Spirit, genetic engineering, cloning, the spreading of harmful viruses and bacteria, chemical and biological warfare
Music	Impure rhythms and lyrics that cause one's energy to descend from the crown chakra to the base-of-the-spine chakra instead of raising it up the spine from the base chakra to the crown
Divine Vision	Focusing on the flaws and weaknesses in oneself and others; taking in too many impure images in the environment or through the media; being overly concerned with one's physical remains at the time of death

Healing and Wholeness

One of the most prominent aspects of the fifth ray is healing. Healing, wholeness and regeneration spring from the mighty fountain of truth that comes from within because healing is the natural result of coming into alignment with one's Higher Self. When the soul is raised up to the level of the Christ consciousness, the rest of one's being rises to the fullness of its innate divinity.

Complete healing involves several factors. First is the desire for wholeness. Before a person can be healed, he must want to be whole. He then must do what it takes for health to be restored. The blue-flame power of divine will provides the drive to carry out the necessary actions, one of which is envisioning perfect wholeness. The Goddess of Wisdom explained that the will of God is important because "the will to behold wholeness is the foundation of wholeness. By will you set the blueprint. Your will is your conviction that God does and can and will heal, the absolute conviction that life is whole and free and blessed."[1]

Although much real healing takes place through medical science, the scientific world cannot always determine the underlying cause of disease. Physicians may use drugs or surgery to alleviate the symptoms of ill health, but the treatments may not address the real cause of the problem. This is because sickness is really caused by an absence of wholeness in one's being, which is a more complex issue.

Creating Wholeness in the Four Lower Bodies

The word *disease* is composed of two parts, *dis-ease.* When people are diseased, they are not at ease with themselves because something isn't right within. They are not whole, and in that state there is an absence of comfort and ease. Archangel Gabriel said that unresolved conditions at other levels of being are the root cause of physical distress. He also explained that joy can be a powerful tonic for the body:

> Most people are never truly healed of the core conditions which they carry vibrationally in and about their spirit.
>
> In actuality, one's spirit governs one's health. If the spirit is morose, the body will follow suit. And the morose spirit will magnetize other morose spirits, reinforcing the person's weakened state until a host of mental, emotional and finally physical diseases may result. . . .
>
> Happy is the man who entertains a perpetual spirit of joy, for his spirit is like the sun shining at its zenith. He will know health, happiness and prosperity and he will attract to himself, and forever entertain, spirits of joy.[2]

In order to really heal the physical form, it is necessary to first heal the etheric, mental and emotional bodies, all of which affect the physical. True healing takes place through the restoration of the perfect pattern of one's being. This occurs first in the etheric body, next in the mind, then in the emotions and finally in the physical form.

1 *Pearls of Wisdom,* vol. 20, no. 8.
2 *Pearls of Wisdom,* vol. 39, no. 2.

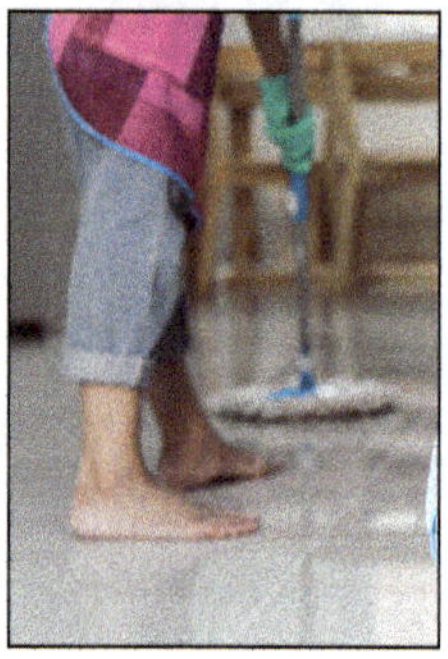

The process can be understood through the analogy of a sink—a teaching given by the Ascended Lady Master Meta, a fifth-ray master who teaches the science of healing in the etheric retreats. She explained that when we see a sink overflowing we do not mop the floor before we turn off the faucet. Healing works on the same principle. We first stop the source of distress, disease and discord in the four lower bodies. When we have turned off the source by turning hatred into love, doubt and fear into faith, and disharmony into harmony, then we can begin to mop up the side effects that appear at the physical, mental and emotional levels.

The action of healing the four lower bodies often takes time. When someone requests personal healing through prayer or decrees, he may not see immediate results. In fact, other problems may be brought to the surface before genuine healing can begin. This is because wholeness involves the transmutation of impure substance at all levels of being, including those beneath the threshold of awareness.

The masters have also taught that we must establish wholeness within ourselves before we can become instruments of healing for others. As Jesus Christ, the master healer, said, "Physician, heal thyself!"[3] We can increase our potential for wellness by attuning to what our body and Higher Self may be telling us. We can also pursue standard medical and alternative means of healing and make any necessary lifestyle changes to increase vitality. In addition, practicing certain spiritual techniques can release the divine energy necessary to reestablish balance in our chakras and organs, helping correct underlying imbalances that may be causing problems.

Tips for Healing

The ascended masters have given many suggestions for creating wholeness in our four lower bodies, several of which are described below.

1. **Consider what your body is trying to tell you.** A disrupted energy field in one of your other three bodies, which may have originated in this embodiment or in past lives, can show up as a physical ailment. A sudden rash for example, could mean emotional irritation. Ear problems may signal not wanting to hear something. Heart disease can stem from the lack of forgiveness. And breathing problems may mean you are unknowingly suffocating yourself.

2. **Listen to your Higher Self.** Ask your I AM Presence and Holy Christ Self what your four lower bodies are trying to tell you. Meditation, visualization and/or decrees can prepare you to be more receptive to their message. Before you go to sleep, you can also ask your Higher Self or favorite ascended master to give you the answer and to assist you to implement the solution.

3 Luke 4:23.

3. **Work with natural healing methods.** In addition to using traditional medical means, you may want to consider natural healing modalities as adjuncts or alternative therapies when appropriate. These could include chiropractic work, naturopathy, homeopathy, aromatherapy and the therapeutic use of color and sound, among others.

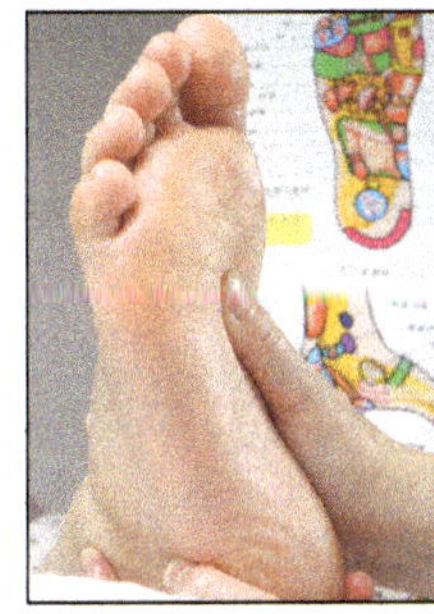

4. **Examine your lifestyle.** In order to attain spiritual mastery and physical healing, it can be helpful to switch to a healthier lifestyle. Changes might include improving your diet and getting the proper amount of exercise and rest, as well as surrendering harmful substances (e.g., nicotine, alcohol, marijuana) and unproductive emotional habits (e.g., irritability, anger, envy). Taking the time to examine and improve personal habits can often make a big difference in conditions of health.

5. **Use spiritual techniques to help establish wholeness.** Spiritual tools such as the science of the spoken Word and the healing thoughtform are recommended for healing body, mind and soul. These are explored in the "Liberating Power of the Word" section later in this chapter.

The Role of Karma

In its most positive expression, the fifth ray produces wholeness in the four lower bodies. The ability to heal comes from the Higher Self, however. So healing techniques that draw on the light of the Infinite are the most effective since they are able to address the cause and core of health concerns.

According to the ascended masters, karma can be at the root of health conditions. So, the soul's mastery over her karma will result in a spiritual victory as well as a physical one. In fact, a little adversity in the form of health challenges can open the door for the balancing of karma and produce integration within the four lower bodies. The final effect will ultimately be physical healing, though this approach can take longer than other methods.

It may sometimes seem desirable to be healed instantly through a quick cure or apparent miracle. But at times people must bear their karma no matter what means of healing are employed. It is therefore wise to acknowledge the will of God in the quest for healing.

The Maha Chohan explained that accepting one's karmic accountability sometimes means giving of oneself first before true wholeness can be received:

> So then, understand that there must be healing. But there can be healing only where individuals are truly on a path of service to the living Saviour and of balancing their karma. If people pay their way, paying as they go with violet flame and healing-green decrees, thereby transmuting the cause of their conditions, they will be healed according to the will of God.

> This is the price you must pay, beloved. By cosmic law, we cannot bestow either empowerment or healing unless there be deeds of merit on your record showing your active engagement in balancing your karma by the alchemy of service to life. In addition, you must seek and find the cause and core of disease in the karma recorded in each of your four lower bodies.[4]

Sometimes trying to find a physical cure can even cause harm. It could keep the karma of the illness or disease from being worked out according to one's divine plan if the healing is not in alignment with God's will. Archangel Raphael explained this principle:

> To remove the symptoms of disease without removing the record of its cause in this or a past life does a great disservice to the soul. And the individual who assents to the easy "cure" will see sometime, somewhere, in this or a future life, the same problem coming to the surface to be dealt with as karma that must be transmuted before the physical symptoms may permanently disappear.[5]

In such cases the karma is pushed back into the patient's emotional, mental or etheric body. There it waits for a time when it can come out once again and be transmuted by the action of the sacred fire or by living through the problem. When this happens, the patient's cycle of karma is delayed and spiritual progress is hindered. Some healing approaches that can cause this to occur include taking a strictly materialistic approach to healing the body or using chemicals as a substitute for the light of Spirit. Others involve using alternative methods such as hypnosis,[6] faith healing, the laying on of hands and psychic healing, such as when healers place their hands into another person's body to remove diseased organs, rotten teeth, etc.

In ministering to the sick, it is also possible for a practitioner to make karma because energy is typically transferred between individuals in the therapeutic process. This can occur when the healer transfers to the sick the impurities of his aura, takes on the ill person's impurities or interferes with the individual's karma.

It is therefore always wise to qualify the energy exchange according to God's will. Whether giving or receiving treatment, we can ask our mighty I AM Presence and Holy Christ Self to regulate the exchange of energy. One way to do this is to say, "Let God's will be done in this healing," before giving or receiving healing treatments and when invoking healing using decrees or mantras. We can also ask God to seal our chakras so that no light is exchanged unlawfully between ourselves and any part of life. This call also works whenever we wish to protect our light in many other situations, such as going into a crowd of people.

---

4 *Pearls of Wisdom,* vol. 37, no. 38.

5 Mark L. Prophet and Elizabeth Clare Prophet, *The Masters and Their Retreats,* ed. Annice Booth (Corwin Springs, Mont.: Summit University Press, 2003), p. 300.

6 The ascended masters strongly caution their students against using hypnosis or autohypnosis. While people are hypnotized, they effectively surrender their free will and are not under the direction and protection of the Holy Christ Self. Hypnosis also opens one's subconscious mind to outside influence beyond one's control, allowing the subconscious and unconscious habit patterns, desires, etc., of the hypnotist to be transferred to the person's subconscious—regardless of the good intentions of both people.

Truth

Truth is another attribute of the fifth ray. Truth can be thought of as a laser-like beam that has the ability to separate the authentic Self from the aspects of consciousness that are unreal. When the energy of truth is guided by spiritual discrimination, it can sift out human errors from genuine awareness of our Higher Self.

How can truth divide the real from the unreal? We can better understand its penetrating action by learning why it falls on the green ray. The Ascended Lady Master Pallas Athena, who exemplifies this quality as the Goddess of Truth, explained that "truth . . . is the emerald green. It is comprised of the first ray of God's will. It is comprised of the second ray of cosmic Christ illumination. Thus it is the will of God engaged in illumined action."[7] This combining of the will and wisdom of the universal Christ consciousness produces an inherent ability to separate the wheat of divine realization from the chaff of the false—or unreal—self.

It is always effective to embody the spirit of truth in one's daily affairs, but truth does its best work when spoken aloud. The ascended masters have explained that it is important to state the truth when the need arises, even though this may not always be pleasant. The heavenly hosts will support the speaker of truth wholeheartedly in his task. In fact, the light of all cosmos rallies to the aid of the person who takes a stand for an honest cause. Pallas Athena aptly expressed this when she said: "Blessed ones, as everyone knows, speaking the truth at times is very painful, distasteful, given certain situations. But the truth that is spoken becomes a focus of the Great Central Sun. . . . This power of the Sun . . . is released to all who espouse truth without compromise."[8] She said that it is amazing to see how many supporters will rally to the side of those who take this course of action.

Championing a righteous cause also helps other souls choose the right course of action when they might otherwise pursue a misguided path that could result in ultimate harm to themselves or others. If someone doesn't tell them the truth, they may never know there is another way. The Ascended Master Saint Germain explained: "Do not be chary with your teaching and your words, beloved. Do not withhold pointing out to another the error of his ways. Do not fear the response. Only fear that if you withhold the truth, you may make the karma of depriving another of his freedom. For the truth shall make men free."[9]

Fifth-Ray Motto

And ye shall know the truth, and the truth shall make you free.[11]

—JESUS CHRIST

In speaking the truth, however, it is important to use diplomacy and kindness and to be sure of the facts so that you don't create new karma. As Mother Mary said, be "always kind in your speech. Let your interchanges be gentle ones and always let the soft answer turn away wrath."[10]

7 *Pearls of Wisdom,* vol. 32, no. 1.
8 Ibid.
9 *Pearls of Wisdom,* vol. 37, no. 20.
10 *Pearls of Wisdom,* vol. 33, no. 36.
11 John 8:32.

Untruthful Expressions

Like the other fifth-ray qualities, truth is not always purely qualified. Wrongly used, it can result in untruth. Examples are lying, misstating the facts or omitting needed information. In the intellectual realm, untruth can appear as skepticism, dogmatism and doubt. Other examples are impure reasoning, argumentation, intellectual pride and misinterpretation of scripture. Atheism and agnosticism also fall into this category because they deny the validity of universal truth.

At times, truth can also become mingled with error. This can happen when one hears about or receives information from psychic realms, mistakenly thinking that it comes from higher octaves of light. Communications received through séances, channeling and psychic healers inevitably contain error, whether great or small. The misinformation can create a costly diversion or even ultimate separation from the spiritual path for those who believe and follow what they hear. It is therefore important to consciously guard the purity of truth because it contains valuable keys to unlocking wholeness and true spiritual potential. Much harm can come through impure routes that lead the soul astray.

Precipitation

Precipitation is a fascinating quality of the green ray. In spiritual terms, it means bringing into physical form the ideals found in the realm of Spirit. Abundance can precipitate from one's causal body into many kinds of prosperity, including health, wealth, happiness, joy, peace, faith, hope, wisdom and just being in tune with the flow of the universe. Precipitation can also be seen in the physical world through the technology and science that make our lives better. It can mean releasing the harmonies of inner spiritual dimensions through music and sound. And precipitation can be the abundant flow of rain and snow that descends from heaven to nourish all plants and living things.

The color of the flame of precipitation is Chinese green tinged with gold. The Ascended Lady Master Fortuna, Goddess of Supply, described it poetically: "The flame of precipitation is the flame of power illumined by the mighty intelligence of God. And so the green bursts forth as a mighty aurora borealis, the shooting star of God's promise for the fulfilling of every good and perfect gift."[12]

A focus of this flame burns on the main altar at the Royal Teton Retreat, the center for the precipitation of the culture of the Divine Mother.[13] This retreat is congruent with the Teton Range near Jackson Hole, Wyoming. Because of its location in North America, the precipitation flame has helped endow the American people with the pragmatism necessary to bring science, technology and invention to the present state, and to bring forth creative abundance.

12 Annice Booth, *Secrets of Prosperity* (Corwin Springs, Mont.: Summit University Press, 2000), p. 17.

13 For more information on the Royal Teton Retreat, see chapter 4 in *Meeting the Masters.*

Tips for Creating Abundance

The ascended masters have released many tips on how to precipitate divine energy into the physical world. Whenever you feel a desire to increase the flow of abundance from your causal body, try one or more of their suggestions below.

1. **Release fear and anxiety.** Fear, doubt, anxiety and worry can hinder people's efforts to precipitate because they cause them to become agitated at all levels of being. Giving the following affirmation one or more times helps remove these energies:

   In the name of my mighty I AM Presence and Holy Christ Self,
   I AM the peace commanding Presence that banishes all anxiety, all fear, all doubt, all human questioning of my ability to precipitate divine abundance into my world now.

2. **Express gratitude for your abundance.** Continually thank God for who you are and what you have, and you will see how your abundance will increase. You can do this with the mantras, "**Hear, O Universe, I AM grateful!**" and "**Let God be magnified!**"[14] (Give them in multiples of three for maximum effect.) You can also simply thank God at any hour of the day or night for what you have been given.

3. **Give abundance mantras and decrees.** For example, you can visualize gold coins tumbling into your lap as you say: "**I AM! I AM! I AM! the Resurrection and the Life of my finances!** (3x) **Now made manifest in my hands and use today!**" (3–33x) You can also give any of the abundance decrees in the green section of the decree book.[15]

4. **Make a treasure map.** A treasure map is a prayer in pictures, a blueprint of the spiritual and material abundance you want to create in your life.[16]

HOW TO MAKE A TREASURE MAP

- **Plan your treasure map before you create it.** First, make a list of the dreams you want to see come true in each area of your life. Your list can cover career, finances, family, children, education, health, home, relationships, spirituality, travel and hobbies.

- **Allow God to inspire and guide you.** Ask your I AM Presence and Holy Christ Self to show you which of your desires are God's desires for you. Then refine your ideas. Once you are certain about what you need, you are ready to construct your treasure map. *(Continued)*

---

14 Psalms 70:4.

15 See Prophet and Prophet, *Prayers, Meditations and Dynamic Decrees*, nos. 55.00–55.02.

16 For more information, see Elizabeth Clare Prophet and Mark L. Prophet, *Creative Abundance: Keys to Spiritual and Material Prosperity* (Gardiner, Mont.: Summit Publications, Inc., 1998), pp. 55–77.

- **Use green paper.** Treasure maps can be any color you want but they work particularly well when you use green paper or cardstock, since this color immediately connects you with the green ray's energy of abundance and precipitation.
- **Make your treasure map large or small.** Your map can be big enough to post on a wall or door, or small enough to fit in a notebook or scrapbook.
- **Make one or more maps.** You can picture several goals on one map or create more than one, each dedicated to a different need. Divide your map or scrapbook into sections for each area of your life. Then choose images and statements that show exactly what you want to accomplish in that area.
- **Be precise when selecting images and statements for your map.** Show and tell exactly what you want, including size, dimension, color, location and target date.
- **Always picture something better than the best of what you are experiencing now.** You always want to be reaching for something higher.
- **Use colored images on your map.** The imagination responds well to color. Include pictures of your favorite ascended masters to remind you that they are helping you accomplish your goals.
- **Accompany your images with words and affirmations describing your needs.**
- **Keep your treasure map uncluttered.**
- **Include what you will offer to God in return for the blessings you are requesting.**
- **Keep your map private.** It is better not to share it with others.
- **Meditate on your map at least twice a day.** Put it in a place where there is positive and uplifting energy, and it can readily be seen. If you think others might interfere with your alchemical precipitation, move the map out of sight when you are not alone. Look at it in particular before you go to sleep so your subconscious mind will work on the realization of your desires for an uninterrupted period of time.
- **Ask God to fulfill your requests according to his will.**
- **Update your map as needed.**

Damming Up the Flow of Abundance

When working to create abundance, it helps to remember that improper uses of fifth-ray energy can hinder the process. For example, one way to misqualify this ray is by refusing to share God's prosperity with others. The choice always exists to squander one's supply on selfish desires instead of using it to help those who are less fortunate. Greed not only incorrectly qualifies the energy of precipitation but dams up the flow of abundance. It is like the Dead Sea, which is fed by the River Jordan but has no outlet. The water doesn't flow but instead evaporates and what's left in the lake becomes saturated with salt. As a result, the Dead Sea supports no life.

Abundance must also flow freely. One's stream of abundance is increased by being willing to give gifts instead of just receiving them. The joy of giving springs from the fountain of pure love flowing from the heart. The Ascended Lady Master Fortuna gave this excellent teaching:

> Supply comes to those who have the heart of gold, and the golden heart is the heart of love for all life. When mankind love life, the source of supply wells up within them as the wellspring of beauty, in life and light and love. Mankind have a poverty consciousness because first they have been selfish and without love for their fellow creatures. Those who love in Spirit are rich in Spirit as well as in physical things, for love is the fulfilling of the law of supply.[17]

> *Bring ye all the tithes into the storehouse, that there may be meat in mine house, and prove me now herewith, saith the Lord of hosts, if I will not open you the windows of heaven and pour you out a blessing that there shall not be room enough to receive it.* —MALACHI 3:10

It is also good to know that increasing one's abundance requires carefully guarding and increasing the light of the Creator in one's being and world. If people lose divine energy through wrong decisions or uses, they will also lose the abundance that comes into their hands. They may find it slipping through their fingers or being taken from them, or they may unknowingly invest it in unwise ventures that don't work out.

Science

Science also falls on the fifth ray. Science is generally understood as the knowledge of the natural laws of the physical world. Indeed, scientific disciplines such as biology, chemistry and physics are the foundation stones of our current civilization. The practical applications of this knowledge surround us in the form of the technology and industry that make our lives easier, simpler and more efficient.

Science is foundational to the spiritual path because its principles extend into the etheric realm. In fact, the ascended masters have explained that all of material science really correlates to spiritual dimensions. The Ascended Lady Master Leto, scientist and teacher of youth, described the spiritual realm as "all science, the science that embraces a cosmos both in the mathematics and in the principles of physics."[18] A perfect example is the science of the spoken Word, which uses principles of physics to effect molecular and physical change. The violet flame, for instance, can transmute impure

17 Booth, *Secrets of Prosperity,* p. 19.
18 *Pearls of Wisdom,* vol. 33, no. 45.

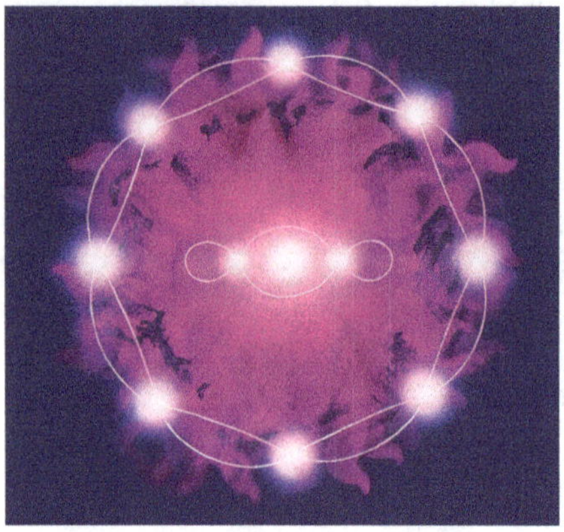

Sub-Atomic Violet Flame Action

substance through its invisible scientific action on physical atoms and electrons when it is invoked.

Here is how the violet flame works: When we invoke it by means of a prayer or decree, it surrounds each of our atoms. A polarity is set up between the nucleus of the atom and the violet flame. The nucleus, being matter, assumes the negative polarity; the core of the violet flame, being Spirit, assumes the positive polarity. The interaction between the nucleus of the atom and the violet flame establishes an oscillation, a rapid back and forth movement, which releases the density trapped between the electrons. As the substance is freed, the electrons move more freely and the negative substance is thrown into the violet flame.[19]

Because of the spiritual importance of scientific laws and principles, the ascended masters have made numerous references to them in their teachings. For instance, in *Saint Germain on Alchemy,* Saint Germain suggests the study of wave propagation, mechanics and quantum theory, elementary and advanced chemistry and physics, seismology, astronomy, geology and related subjects for background knowledge in the practice of spiritual alchemy and precipitation.

Science Misused

Even though science can be a transformative power to bring about spiritual and material good, its energy can be misapplied. Misuse can occur whenever natural laws are viewed only from a materialistic standpoint without considering Spirit as the first cause. Some examples that deny the sanctity of the life force are genetic engineering and cloning. The ill use of science can also be seen in the spreading of harmful viruses and bacteria, such as in chemical and biological warfare.

Music

Music is another notable quality of the fifth ray. It is so important, in fact, that the next chapter is dedicated to exploring its effects in detail. By its definite action on subtle energy fields, certain types of music—such as traditional classical and sacred pieces—can help us touch the Divine. Its spiritual action occurs through the raising of the sacred fire from the base-of-the-spine chakra to the crown chakra in an ascending spiral of light.[20]

The best music ennobles the soul. Elizabeth Prophet explained that music can be used to travel back to the heart of the Creator. By meditating upon music inspired by the hosts of heaven through qualified musicians, the listener can trace a path back to his own soul, to his Holy Christ Self and beloved I AM Presence. Cyclopea, Elohim of the Fifth Ray and the God of Music, gave the following perspective about its power:

---

19 For more information, see chapter 3 in *The Spiritual Quest.*

20 For more information, see chapter 4 in *The Spiritual Quest.*

> What is music, beloved? It is the original sound with which earth was endowed in etheric spheres. It is the sound and the hum of a bee or an electron or a child learning his first tune. Music is the melody of the soul that is always in the divine rhythm of love. Music conveys all virtues of God. Music therefore does bring to you the inner sound of the living Word. But you are that Word, you are that Peace, you are that Peace-commanding Presence.[21]

In contrast to raising the sacred energy up the spine, impure music draws it downward. This action is contrary to the purpose of life, the ascension. The misuses of music are thoroughly explored in chapter 4.

Divine Vision

Divine vision is the single-eyed focus that comes from staying one's mind on the Higher Self, since the Holy Christ Self has the power to restore spiritual vision to the soul. This outcome is produced by the removal of the illusion and delusion of the world—of relative good and evil—which in turn brings peace to the soul.

Achieving God-vision involves making a choice about what we do with our energy since we can use it in wise or unwise ways. Saint Germain gave some valuable instruction about making the highest choices. In the following quote, he relates spiritual vision to the third eye, the fifth-ray chakra:

> Jesus taught that if one would dwell solely in the light, one must have single-eyed vision through the use of the third eye. But in order to achieve that state, one must garner the light in his chakras. The goal is to fill one's whole body so full of light that no darkness may enter.
>
> According to the Gospel of Matthew, Jesus said, "The light of the body is the eye: If therefore thine eye be single, thy whole body shall be full of light. But if thine eye be evil, thy whole body shall be full of darkness. If therefore the light that is in thee be darkness, how great is that darkness!"[22]

What we hold in the mind's eye can contribute to or detract from the awakening of divine vision. What we see within and what we gaze upon in our environment are therefore important aspects of our spiritual development.

Holding the Immaculate Concept

When one beholds images of pure perfection of himself or of others, he is correctly qualifying the energy of the fifth ray through the third eye. This practice is called "holding the immaculate concept."[23] The immaculate concept can be thought of as the pure concept or image of the soul's potential. It is the vision of the original fiery blueprint of the soul as it was created in the image of the Divine.

The science of the immaculate concept is based on visualizing a perfect idea

21 *Pearls of Wisdom,* vol. 31, no. 43.
22 *Pearls of Wisdom,* vol. 39, no. 33.
23 *Pearls of Wisdom,* vol. 17, no. 51.

which then becomes a magnet to attract the creative energies of Spirit to fulfill the pattern held in one's mind. God is the supreme practitioner of the science of the immaculate concept. No matter how far an individual might wander from his divine center, God ever beholds him in the image of reality in which he was created. To practice the immaculate concept means to follow the Creator's example, holding in the mind's eye the highest vision of good for oneself and others.

Archangel Raphael and his divine complement, Mother Mary, teach the science of the immaculate concept to humanity. This science is practiced by every angel in heaven. When angels look upon a person, they see him in the divine purity in which he was originally created, holding their vision of that pattern over him. This enables the individual to fill in the design and realize who he really is—a son or daughter of God.

Each of us also has an internal vision of ourselves that affects what we ultimately become. We may see only our flaws and weaknesses or we may perceive the beauty of our own hearts. We might visualize ourselves as we imagine others think us to be or see ourselves as a soul and spirit with vast potential. How we envision ourselves has a real impact on our soul evolution. When we see ourselves as great spiritual beings, we grow closer and closer to that divine Reality. Envisioning the image of perfection also repels everything that would prevent us from attaining self-mastery.

Holding the immaculate concept for our own souls can also transform personal situations and relationships. We can hold in mind the highest blueprint and the greatest possible outcome for any circumstance or individual. In so doing, we are using our single-eyed vision to tune into another's divine pattern instead of focusing on what is occurring at the moment. We mentally envision the best results for all. The Ascended Master Saint Germain says that in this lies the real meaning of being our brother's keeper: "How helpful we can be to one another by holding the immaculate concept for each one's life plan," he says. "Let all, in being their brother's keeper, esteem the highest and best possibilities for everyone."[24]

Beholding the Beautiful

A person becomes what he puts his attention upon outside of himself, as well as within. By continually gazing upon imperfection in the environment, he becomes imperfection. If he concentrates mainly upon perfection, he becomes perfect. As the Ascended Master Djwal Kul said, "In order to be perfection, man must see perfection."[25]

Each time you behold the sun, the clouds, a rose, a perfect leaf, a pebble, a crystal or a wave and then tuck the design into the folds of memory, you are adding to your treasure of perfect ideas. When your mind traces the lines of a Michelangelo, the strokes of a Raphael, the cadences of a ballet or the formations of birds across the sky, your soul is taking in the patterns of the mind of God. These images then become the building blocks of your reality as patterns that form the underlying schemata of your universe.

24 Prophet and Prophet, *Creative Abundance,* p. 38.

25 *Pearls of Wisdom,* vol. 17, no. 46.

This process is scientific in nature. When we gaze at an image, an actual nucleus of energy forms within us. This energy stamps the matrix of the design upon our interior being. An imprint of the picture we see is then made upon each atom and molecule and upon each cell, organ and chakra. Thus, the types of images we view determine whether positive or negative imprints will be formed. They can draw us into our own divine nature or move us farther from it. Images that contain beauty and symmetry contribute to the conception of perfection. Those that are impure or chaotic contribute to concepts of imperfection. When we take in too many impure pictures through our physical eyes, our interior vision also becomes unclear.

We view many types of images frequently in movies, works of art or the environment. It is therefore wise to select for viewing those that leave the most positive impressions. It can also be helpful to focus on pure images as we meditate or decree, and hang them on the walls of our homes or workplaces to strengthen our ability to behold the Infinite. Some examples are below:

- Hindu or Buddhist mandalas. These symbolic graphic images can tie us into the geometry of the cosmos.
- Pictures of the ascended masters, the Chart of Your Divine Presence, the threefold flame, the violet flame or chakras
- Beautiful works of traditional art by master artists like Rembrandt, Veronese and Raphael
- Photos or pictures of the locations of etheric retreats or of beautiful scenes in nature

Expanding the Light of the Third Eye

The third-eye chakra is the spiritual center located at the midpoint of the brow that focuses the multifaceted qualities of the fifth ray. This chakra looks like an emerald-green lotus with ninety-six petals.

The third eye has the unique ability to convey the divine vision of one's inner blueprint. It gives us glimpses of etheric patterns and divine designs. The Infinite can also be perceived through this chakra. By tuning into the cosmos through clear seeing, we can gain a clearer perception and more accurate perspective of ourselves, others and the world at large.

The third-eye chakra can connect us with the magnificent realm of the higher mind and its flashes of insight, genius and originality. An insight is an *in-sight,* a looking within. *Insight* means the ability to see into a situation, to look inside ourselves or to perceive the inner nature of things. It is discernment and penetration. The third eye is also associated with *intuition,* which comes from the Latin word meaning "to look at, to contemplate."[26] Our insights and intuitions are the interior revelations that come to us through this spiritual center when we are in tune with the Higher Self. They can come as hunches, promptings or visions.

The third eye and the two physical eyes do not always see things the same way, however. Our physical eyes often give a relative and unclear perspective on the world. Mrs. Prophet said that the third eye always gives the ability to see the pure designs of life and to discriminate between good and evil. We can enhance the ability of our physical eyes to see purely by consciously focusing our attention on someone else's best qualities. Our physical eyes can then begin to perceive the other individual in his divine image. Lord Maitreya explained it this way:

> I ask that you shall realize that your eyes are the eyes of God and that you have the full right to behold good in all creation. I ask that you realize that when you behold good in all creation, your two eyes are indeed "single-eye vision," holding an immaculate concept of cosmic purity which is then released into the world of form and is not a spirit of criticism, condemnation, or judgment, but a spirit of Christ love and compassion.[27]

By purifying this energy center through spiritual practices like giving the violet flame, we can more completely tune in to the divine pattern of being. A wonderful violet-flame mantra is, **"My third eye is a center of violet fire; my third eye is the purity God desires!"** You can give it for several minutes to clear your third eye of negative energy. The following exercise can also help purify this chakra and expand its capacity to perceive the Absolute.

EXERCISE: BEHOLDING PERFECTION

1. Sitting in a straight posture, close your eyes and breathe deeply until you are calm and centered.

2. Chant the *Aum.*
3. Visualize your third eye in the center of your forehead. See it as a pulsating disc of emerald-green light superimposed over your forehead like a miner's light, only brighter.
4. The bija syllable Shrim intensifies the light in the third-eye chakra. Chant Shrim (pronounced *Shreem*) continuously for a few minutes. As you intone it, see the disc of light spinning clockwise and filling your vision center with brilliant emerald-green light.
5. Give the following affirmation several times (multiples of three work best).

26 *Merriam-Webster's Collegiate Dictionary,* 11th ed., s.v. "intuition."
27 *Pearls of Wisdom,* vol. 27, no. 12.

I AM, I AM beholding all,
Mine eye is single as I call;
Raise me now and set me free,
Thy holy image now to be.

6. Seal your exercise with this prayer:

I thank thee and accept this done right now in full power!
In the name I AM THAT I AM, Amen.

Assessing Your Third-Eye Chakra Mastery

Discovering how you use the energy of your third-eye chakra can help you pinpoint what to work on for greater self-mastery on the fifth ray. Four major categories define the uses of this energy center:

1. Honoring the creative genius and insights of yourself and others
2. Recognizing that you will become what you put your attention on
3. Striving to transcend human mindsets and to see as God sees
4. Holding in mind the highest possible image of others, regardless of what they are presently doing

SELF-ASSESSMENT: YOUR THIRD-EYE CHAKRA

1. On a scale of 1 to 5, where 1 is "never true of me" and 5 is "always true of me," please rate the following statements based on your current perceptions.

1	Never true of me
2	Rarely true of me
3	Sometimes true of me
4	Often true of me
5	Always true of me

a) **I honor the creative genius and insights of myself and others.**	1	2	3	4	5
1. I am able to shape and refine my creative ideas and insights in order to bring them to fruition.					
2. I receive flashes of inspiration.					
3. I honor new ideas that come from myself and others.					
4. I make room in my life for a creative hobby.					
5. I can be creative, intuitive and imaginative at times.					

b) **I recognize that I will become what I put my attention on, and I act accordingly.**	1	2	3	4	5
1. I am careful about the types of music, images and thoughts I allow into my world.					
2. I am able to magnetize positive circumstances and conditions by focusing my attention on them.					
3. When necessary, I am able to visualize and/or concentrate.					
4. I make time to focus on Spirit through prayer, meditation and/or contemplation.					

c) **I strive to transcend my human mind-sets and to see as God sees.**	1	2	3	4	5
1. I try to remain objective and not let preconceived notions keep me from seeing a situation clearly.					
2. I catch myself when I fall into the habit of stereotyping people.					
3. I can see the unity of God's creation behind cultural, ethnic, economic and political differences.					
4. When I need help solving a problem, I ask God to show me the answer.					

d) **I hold in mind the highest possible image of others, regardless of what they are presently doing.**	1	2	3	4	5
1. I envision the highest possible outcome for individuals and situations.					
2. I don't make up my mind about people the moment I meet them.					
3. I treat those who honor or offend me with the same respect.					
4. I try to see others as God sees them, no matter how they are acting at the moment.					

2. After completing the assessment, add up your score in each one of the four sections and divide it by the number of statements in that section to get an average.
3. Use the following action plan to formulate a personal strategy that will enhance your performance in every area where your average score was "3" or below.

Third-Eye Chakra Action Plan

a) I honor the creative genius and insights of myself and others.

I resolve to improve in this area by doing the following: ____________________

____

____

____

b) I recognize that I will become what I put my attention on, and I act accordingly.

I resolve to improve in this area by doing the following: ____________________

c) I strive to transcend my human mind-sets and to see as God sees.

I resolve to improve in this area by doing the following: ____________________

d) I hold in mind the highest possible image of others, regardless of what they are presently doing.

I resolve to improve in this area by doing the following: ____________________

4. Put your action plan into practice for three months. Then take the assessment again and note the positive changes in your journal.

Amplifying Fifth-Ray Energies

The energies of the fifth ray are amplified on earth on Wednesday. The Ascended Master Kuthumi describes how this life-giving vibration can work to our benefit:

> And what of the green (the fifth ray) imbuing all life with the perfect blend of the yellow and the blue, evidencing the faith and wisdom of God in nature and speaking of eternal newness? The green, the wearing of the green, charges man with the healthful and health-giving chlorophyll of the sun—the fire of the sun and the fire of the power to create locked in a mighty omen of healing green, restoring man to the primal nature of God. Endowed and endowing, the ray of green supplies man with every lack as it penetrates the earth on Wednesday.[28]

Use the Color Green

As Kuthumi said, wearing an emerald color or an uplifting shade of pure green can magnetize the healing energies of the fifth ray and remind us of its nourishing light. This works especially well on Wednesdays. The color green can also produce a harmonizing effect in our surroundings, whether used in design features or in the form of decorations and plants.

28 Mark L. Prophet and Elizabeth Clare Prophet, *The Science of the Spoken Word* (Corwin Springs, Mont.: Summit University Press, 2004), p. 67.

Tune the Third Eye

The musical instrument that corresponds to the third eye is the piano. Classical piano music can therefore stimulate this energy center in a positive way. Rachmaninoff or Grieg piano concertos are great meditation music for the third eye. They are thrilling to focus on because the energy feels uplifting as it rises up the spine and anchors in the center of the brow. As you listen, you may perceive the notes of the piano stimulating the petals of this chakra.

Employ Gemstones

You can also amplify the qualities of the fifth ray by wearing or using gemstones that focus its action—emerald, diamond, jade and quartz crystal. Gemstones have been used for thousands of years as a chalice for spiritual energy. In some cases, people also use them for healing.

It is said that the emerald lends focus to the power of vision and can help precipitate the abundant life. Jade can be powerfully used for healing. When jade is placed next to the skin, it imparts a therapeutic, relaxing vibration as its molecular structure holds the peace and quietness of the harmony of this ray. Jade is also said to be good for calming children, especially those with hyperactive tendencies.

Wearing or using these stones can boost the qualities of the fifth ray as you go about your daily affairs. You can also put them on your altar to magnify the energy in your sacred space or place them in your home as electrodes of the emerald ray.

Hilarion, Chohan of the Fifth Ray

The Ascended Master Hilarion, Chohan of the Fifth Ray, is a devotee of truth and a scientist of the new age. He reveals the path of fifth-ray mastery through science, truth, healing, music and spiritual vision through the third-eye chakra. In addition to the light of healing that he bears, Hilarion organizes his legions of angels to protect the logic of the divine mind in mankind.

Only a few of Hilarion's embodiments are known. He was a high priest on Atlantis and later embodied as Saint Paul, disciple of Jesus Christ. His most notable other incarnation was as Saint Hilarion (290–372 A.D.), the founder of monasticism in Palestine. Saint Hilarion was a renowned healer who spent the latter part of his life as a hermit in the desert.

High Priest on Atlantis

More than 12,000 years ago on Atlantis, Hilarion was high priest of the Temple of Truth. He transported the flame of truth and the artifacts of the temple to Greece a short time before the sinking of that continent. The focus of truth that he established became the central point for the Oracles of Delphi, messengers of truth who served under the direction of Pallas Athena, now an ascended lady master. The Oracles of Delphi were active for hundreds of years until priests skilled in the black arts penetrated the Delphic Order and perverted the truth that had been brought forth. The Great White Brotherhood then withdrew this service to embodied mankind since people were unable to distinguish between truth and error.

Saint Paul

Hilarion was later embodied as Saul of Tarsus, who became the apostle Paul. The story of Saint Paul is a biblical favorite. Saul of Tarsus, an official who persecuted the followers of Jesus Christ, was on his way to Damascus, Syria, when suddenly a brilliant light enveloped him. "And he fell to the earth, and heard a voice saying unto him, Saul, Saul, why persecutest thou me? And he said, Who art thou, Lord? And the Lord said, I am Jesus whom thou persecutest: it is hard for thee to kick against the pricks."[29]

Saul, being afraid, asked Jesus what he wanted him to do. He was told to go into Damascus, where he would learn what God had in store for him. When Saul got up and opened his eyes, he found that he could not see. He remained blind for three days. In a dictation, Hilarion explained the cause of that event:

> My soul knew Him [Jesus] as of old and recalled to my outer mind the memory of the inner vow. It was not the first time I had seen the Lord Christ. I had seen him before taking incarnation, and yet I had to work through that pride, that karma on the fifth ray of much learning, much studying and superiority in social standing and intellectual standing that I had in regards to the early Christians. And so, it was my own karma that was upon me whereby I was resisting the call.
>
> My Lord did pursue me as I made my journey on the road to Damascus. Yes, beloved, I was blinded, not by his light but by my own sin and the alchemy of his light penetrating the record of sin in my being. Thus, I was turned around, converted by the Spirit of the Lord in the full manifestation of Jesus Christ upon me.[30]

This profound event marked his conversion to Christ. For a period following it, Paul retreated into the Arabian desert. Commentators have often speculated as to what he did during his sojourn there. Hilarion has explained that Jesus took him "with others into his retreat over the Holy Land and at Arabia." He said, "I have been there and learned of him. And this was my desert sojourn in meditation with him, taken up as I was in my finer bodies and trained directly heart to heart."[31]

Paul began to preach the doctrine of Jesus Christ. Over a period of thirty years he converted many to Christianity, extolling Christ's presence as the living Savior in

29 Acts 9:4–5.
30 *Pearls of Wisdom,* vol. 36, no. 45.
31 *Pearls of Wisdom,* vol. 33, no. 39.

Paul preaching

sermons and letters he delivered throughout Asia Minor and the Mediterranean.

The apostle Paul's experiences in building Christ's church are recorded throughout the New Testament. His encounters as a direct chela of the Ascended Master Jesus Christ exemplify the concern that Jesus holds for every one of us once we allow ourselves to be transformed into new creatures in Christ.

Paul was also known as a healer. The Bible explains: "And God wrought special miracles by the hands of Paul: So that from his body were brought unto the sick handkerchiefs or aprons, and the diseases departed from them, and the evil spirits went out of them."[32] It records another incident when Paul healed a man from Lystra who was crippled from birth. When the apostle commanded him to "Stand upright on thy feet!"[33] the man leaped up and walked.

Because he had consented to the stoning of Saint Stephen, the first Christian martyr, and had actively persecuted and killed Christians, Paul did not ascend at the conclusion of his life. The taking of life in one incarnation often requires another embodiment to balance that karma. The Ascended Master Hilarion has explained why he was required to embody again before making his ascension: "Remember, then, that we, the apostles of Christ, did come under the dispensation of the Law that required that one balance 100 percent of one's karma ere the soul enter the ascension in the light.[34] Thus, I was required to atone in my life as the apostle Paul and in my next life as Saint Hilarion for the sins I had committed before I received my Lord."[35] So Jesus, who raised up Paul to be his apostle, sponsored him in a final incarnation as Saint Hilarion.

Saint Hilarion

When the soul of Paul incarnated as Hilarion, he became once more a teacher, preacher and healer. Hilarion spent twenty years in the desert in preparation for his mission and only then wrought his first miracle. God working through him cured a woman of barrenness, enabling her to bring forth a son. From that day forward, he carried out a healing ministry. History records that he healed children of fever, cured paralysis and cast out devils. Crowds followed him everywhere, beseeching him to help them. Being solitary in nature, Hilarion tried to run away and hide, but he was always found.

Jerome, a fourth century Church Father whose biography of the saint provides most of the available information on him, records: "The frequency of his signs in Sicily

32 Acts 19:11–12.

33 Acts 14:8–10.

34 Since the inauguration of the new dispensation early in the twentieth century, it is possible to ascend having balanced at least 51 percent of one's karma, the remaining portion then being balanced on inner levels after the ascension.

35 Hilarion, "The Revolution of Truth."

drew to him sick people and religious men in multitudes; and one of the chief men was cured of dropsy the same day that he came, and offered Hilarion boundless gifts; but he obeyed the Saviour's saying, 'Freely ye have received; freely give.'"[36]

Another incident occurred on the occasion of a great earthquake when the sea was threatening to destroy a town. According to Jerome, "The sea broke its bounds; and, as if God was threatening another flood, or all was returning to primeval chaos, ships were carried up steep rocks and hung there."[37] The townsfolk, seeing these mountains of water coming towards the shore, ran and got Hilarion, and "as if they were leading him out to battle, stationed him on the shore. And when he had marked three signs of the cross upon the sand, and stretched out his hands against the waves, it is past belief to what a height the sea swelled, and stood up before him, and then, raging long, as if indignant at the barrier, fell back, little by little, into itself."[38]

Toward the end of his life the saint retreated to a spot in Cyprus so remote that he was convinced no one would find him. It was even haunted—the people would be afraid to approach, he thought. But one paralyzed individual managed to drag himself to the place, found Hilarion, was cured, and spread the word.

And so it was that the saint ended his days in that valley, with many people coming to see him. After his passing, his followers buried him there, as was his desire, but within several months his closest disciple, Hesychius, secretly dug up his grave and carried his body off to Palestine.

Hilarion had the gift of healing in abundant measure. The truly great healers of mankind, who can bring souls to the point of resolution and wholeness by a touch of the hand or a simple command, "Be thou made whole!"[39] are sent from God. The identifying mark of the true healer is that he walks in the shadow of his mighty I AM Presence, that he is humble before God and man and that he gives all glory to God for the works God performs through him, knowing that he is but the instrument of the Holy Spirit. These holy ones of God are self-effacing, and they will not necessarily tell you that they have the gift of healing.

Hilarion

Through this embodiment in service to the sick, Hilarion settled his accounts with life and in the process blessed untold thousands as the Lord worked in him and through him.

Hilarion's Etheric Retreat

As Chohan of the Fifth Ray, Hilarion is the hierarch of the Temple of Truth, serving there with Pallas Athena. This retreat is located in the etheric plane over the island of Crete, where the ruins of the original physical Temple of Truth remain from the

36 Matthew 10:8.

37 Prophet and Prophet, *The Masters and Their Retreats,* p. 135.

38 Ibid.

39 *Pearls of Wisdom,* vol. 25, no. 27.

Crete

period when the island was part of the mainland of Greece.

The etheric temple is a replica of the physical focus built on the scale of the Parthenon. Long marble steps lead to the columned building decorated in gold frieze. The classrooms and council halls are located in the immense area beneath the ascending marble steps. The altar in the center of the temple, a single beautifully carved pillar, holds the focus of the flame of truth in a golden brazier. The brothers and sisters who minister unto the flame and serve in this retreat form concentric squares at the base of the pillar. Their places are marked by mosaic designs, and between the innermost square and the pillar are mosaic patterns depicting great masters and cosmic beings who have served the cause of truth throughout the ages.

The flame of truth enshrined at Hilarion's retreat is an intense bright, fiery green—the color that compels precipitation, actualization, practicality, healing and rejuvenation. The flame and the service rendered by all who are devoted to it make the abstract, the ephemeral and the intangible concrete in this fifth-ray retreat.

Hilarion has a major role in directing the flame of truth for the upliftment of mankind. "My responsibility," he revealed, "is to release through the fiery core of my heart, energies for healing, for science, for truth, for the enlightenment of souls by the law of mathematics of the energy flow, the energy systems that can and will contribute to the wholeness and the integration of souls with the life that is God here on the planet Earth."[40]

Hilarion is also concerned with helping atheists, agnostics, skeptics and others who may have become disenchanted: "The agnostics cry out today against the trivia of this age and quite frequently they take a stand for principles of the light,"[41] he says. "The atheists deny while the agnostics struggle to see. In our temple at Crete, we have determined to bring new meaning to life through the avenues of science and to stop the perpetual harassment of those forward-moving individuals who seek to assuage some measure of human grief"[42]—even though they may not conform to some people's version of truth or science or religion.

Hilarion invites to this retreat all who espouse the cause of truth or who are messengers of truth in the media or any field. He spoke of the tutoring that students receive there, saying: "If you would be fishers of men, if you would carry the sword of truth and wear our robe, then come and be initiated, and receive a just portion of the fires of truth. For our God is a consuming fire, and he shall consume in this hour all that is allied with error and that defiles the image of the Holy Virgin."[43]

40 Prophet and Prophet, *Lords of the Seven Rays,* p. 196.

41 Ibid., pp. 195–96.

42 Ibid.

43 Elizabeth Clare Prophet, *The Opening of the Temple Doors* (Corwin Springs, Mont.: Summit University Press, 2003), p. 65.

Keys to Working with Hilarion

You can increase the powerful action of the fifth ray in your world by making a conscious effort to be tutored by Hilarion. Below are some practical steps to help you take advantage of his offer to assist you on your spiritual path.

1. **Attend classes at Hilarion's retreat.** Call to Archangel Michael to escort you to his Temple of Truth over Crete in your finer body while you sleep. Before you retire, you can ask Hilarion to:

    - Teach you the way of truth
    - Expose truth in the media or in any other area
    - Teach you the divine applications of healing and science
    - Help you solve any problems related to healing and wholeness
    - Convert souls to the path of true Christhood

2. **Sing or play the song, "Onward, Christian Soldiers."** This keynote of Hilarion will draw his radiance into your world. Through it, listeners can feel the same fervor and zeal today that enabled the apostle Paul two thousand years ago to inspire the early Christians to establish the Church of Christ in Asia Minor and eventually throughout the known world.

3. **Give and give and give again.** Hilarion asked us to generously share our cup of light and the teachings with others. This means perceiving and supplying the needs of those who are lonely, burdened or pained. When we do this with all humility, the Holy Spirit can convert others through us.

4. **Study the world's sacred scriptures and learn to convey them.** Hilarion said to place ourselves on the path of being God-taught by studying the scriptures well enough to explain them to others. He said to begin with the New Testament, reading both the King James Version and the Jerusalem Bible. His instruction includes learning the ascended masters' teachings since they complement and shed light on the sacred scriptures of all world religions.

5. **Take a stand to protect the youth of the world.** Hilarion especially asked us to take spiritual and physical action to bring to others the awareness of the images on television that are unfit for children and youth. In 1995, he said:

    > I, Hilarion, call for a campaign on behalf of the children of the world....
    >
    > I tell you, it is as though there were termites boring into the very hearts and bones and flesh of your children as they are riveted before the TV sets and as they are allowed to see motion pictures that are not fit for human consumption!

I say to you, beloved, you must wage war! There is no other way to deal with this situation. You must wage war by giving your fiats to the archangels at the altar of God, and then you must present your statements and your challenges in the right way and in the right circumstances to bring enlightenment to the people as to what is happening to the youth.[44]

Statue of Saint Paul

44 *Pearls of Wisdom,* vol. 38, no. 7.

INTRODUCING...

Archangel Raphael

Archangel Raphael and his divine complement, Archeia Mary, are the archangels of the fifth ray. A Jewish tradition names Raphael as one of the three archangels who appeared to Abraham on the plains of Mamre. In fact, it is believed that it was Raphael who endowed Sarah, Abraham's wife, with the strength to conceive when she was past childbearing age.

The name "Raphael" means "God has healed" or "the Medicine of God." One Jewish text says that Raphael revealed to Noah the curative power of plants; another tells how he healed a blind man and bound a demon. Catholics revere him as the angel who healed the sick at the pool of Bethesda, and the Book of Enoch tells us that his responsibilities include healing the diseases and wounds of men.

Raphael and Mother Mary inspire new cures and alternative healing methods upon scientists and those trained in the healing arts and the medical profession. They also minister unto the hospitals of the world, and they train expectant mothers and fathers at inner levels in the precipitation of the Christ consciousness through the four lower bodies, which are the vehicles for each one's Holy Christ Self.

Raphael is also known as the patron of travelers. In the *Book of Tobit,* Raphael, disguised as a knowledgeable traveler, accompanies Tobit's son as his guide on a long journey. At the end of the story, Raphael reveals his true identity and explains that God sent him to test the faith of Tobit and his son. They passed their tests and received great blessings of healing and abundance.

You can attune to Archangel Raphael through his keynote, "Whispering Hope," by Alice Hawthorne. The music of the *Messiah* was inspired upon Handel by Raphael and brings his vibration as well.

Raphael and Mary's retreat is in the etheric realm over Fátima, Portugal. The healing flame blazing on the altar there was anchored in the physical octave when Mother Mary appeared to the children at Fátima in 1917. To the present hour, there is a stream of light that flows like a mighty waterfall from the etheric temple to the physical focus, and pilgrims are healed by the "waters" of the healing flame. Raphael and Mother Mary have invited us to visit their retreat: "Do, then, call to God and your guardian angels to take you at night in your finer bodies where you may study and learn what are the golden-age methods of healing and how... through you and others there may come about finally the liberation and the revelation of the true healing arts."[45]

Mother Mary also reminds us to take advantage of their gifts to mankind: "Remember to call upon God, Archangel Raphael and myself and many angels, to bring healing where healing is possible. And if the Law does not allow it in the flesh, then call... for the healing of the soul and the spirit.... It is the healing of the whole man that we are about."[46]

Cathedral at Fátima

45 Ibid.

46 *Pearls of Wisdom,* vol. 30, no. 7.

Using Mantras and the Healing Thoughtform

Invoking light through the science of the spoken Word can help balance, cleanse and heal negative conditions in our four lower bodies. Several of the seven rays have healing properties, especially the violet and green. Giving affirmations, mantras and decrees on these rays can therefore yield powerful results. Archangel Raphael has also released a special image called the healing thoughtform that, when visualized around a person or an area of the body, can mightily assist Spirit to create perfect health in one's being.

Healing with the Violet-Purple Flame

The violet transmuting flame can consume the cause and core of all that impedes the flow of energy and light from the heart of the I AM Presence into the four lower bodies. It has the ability to cleanse the chakras, flush out the organs and transmute karma before it becomes disease.

This seventh ray has many hues, ranging from the orchid-pink of mercy's flame, which contains a greater saturation of the pink ray of divine love, to the deep purple flame, which embodies more of the blue of the will of God. The purple flame has a greater electronic cleansing action that can effectively purify and heal us. It is sometimes called the "chemical ray"[47] because of its ability to dissolve toxins, poisons and substance within the system. It can especially heal the etheric (memory) body of past records that may be buried deep within the subconscious. Decrees to the purple flame can be especially effective when used alternately with healing decrees and affirmations on the green ray.

To invoke the purple flame, take any violet-flame mantra or decree and substitute the word "purple" for "violet." For example, when giving Saint Germain's Aquarian age mantra "I AM a being of violet fire, I AM the purity God desires," you can say, "I AM a being of purple fire, I AM the purity God desires." Often it is harder to penetrate the etheric body than any of the other lower bodies, so the repetition of this purple-flame affirmation thirty-six times can be very effective in cleansing us of old records and past momentums of consciousness.

---

47 *Pearls of Wisdom,* vol. 29, no. 75.

SPOKEN WORD PRACTICE: HEALING AFFIRMATIONS AND DECREES

Healing affirmations can also be given to accelerate healing and the flow of abundance. Try giving one or more of the following affirmations whenever there is a need. Remember, the more times they are given, the more effective they are.

- **In the name of my mighty I AM Presence and Holy Christ Self,**
  I AM wholeness. I and my Father are One. I and my Mother are One.
- **In the name of my mighty I AM Presence and Holy Christ Self,**
  I AM decreeing right here and now an end to any lack that has manifested in my health!
- **In the name of my mighty I AM Presence and Holy Christ Self,**
  I AM perfect [*sight and hearing*] (or personal prayers for healing).

The healing decree "Come We Now Before Thy Flame," can be especially helpful for healing others, since it provides a blank into which their names can be inserted. Specific conditions can be named after the decree preamble as well. Try giving it regularly over a period of time and watch what happens!

www.SummitLighthouse.org/SA3-7

COME WE NOW BEFORE THY FLAME

In the name of the beloved mighty victorious Presence of God which I AM and by and through the magnetic power of the sacred fire vested in the threefold flame burning within my heart, beloved Guru Ma and Lanello, the entire Spirit of the Great White Brotherhood and the World Mother, elemental life—fire, air, water, and earth! I decree:

O Cyclopea, Jesus dear,
Mother Mary so sincere,
Come we now before thy flame
To be healed in God's own name.
Stand we in this place in time
Invoking now thy healing chime!

Tone of golden radiance
Tinged with brilliant healing green,
Pouring comfort through the earth,
Perfection so serene!

Come, O love in holy action,
Give us now God-satisfaction.
By the power of holy healing
In perfection's flame now sealing!

I AM holding [_______ *name or names* _______]
Before thy Presence here;
Shed thy love ray forth upon [_______ *him, her, them* _______],
Release thy blessing dear!

And in full faith I consciously accept this manifest, manifest, manifest! (3x) **right here and now with full power, eternally sustained, all-powerfully active, every expanding, and world enfolding until all are wholly ascended in the light and free!**

Beloved I AM! Beloved I AM! Beloved I AM![48]

Archangel Raphael and the Healing Thoughtform

Archangel Raphael has given many tips for healing in the dictations released through The Summit Lighthouse. On March 28, 1964, he released the healing thoughtform,[49] an image that is scientifically formulated to restore one's divine blueprint and reestablish wholeness. It can be visualized surrounding and penetrating the cells and atoms of the four lower bodies or a specific organ or area. This thoughtform is composed of three concentric spheres:

- White in the center, for purification and restoration of the balance of the Father-Mother God
- Sapphire blue, symbolizing the will of God and the perfection of the inner blueprint
- Emerald green, the sacred-fire healing substance which restores life

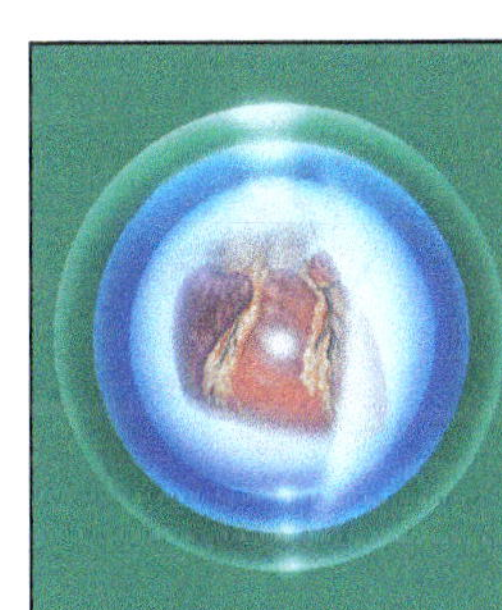

The power of the healing thoughtform has a scientific basis. Aside from magnetizing the noted qualities, the angels of Raphael's bands are master surgeons and use a "laser technology to penetrate to the very core of a cell, . . . to expand the violet flame from within" and to seal that cell in the healing thoughtform."[50] Just imagine how effective this can be!

48 This decree is printed in *Prayers, Meditations and Dynamic Decrees,* p. 371, no. 50.03.

49 A thoughtform is an exact pattern formed in thought, a living design of intense activity animated by the thought or mental idea that generated it.

50 *Pearls of Wisdom,* vol. 29, no. 32.

EXERCISE: USING THE HEALING THOUGHTFORM

To apply the healing thoughtform, do one or both parts of this exercise.

Part 1: Construct a Healing Thoughtform

1. To enhance your ability to visualize the healing thoughtform, make one out of white, blue and green paper using the design described above. You can place an image of any organ or body part in the center, or pictures of loved ones and anyone who needs healing.
2. Post your healing thoughtform in your sacred space or in a place where you will see it often, such as on the refrigerator door. You can also use it to help in visualizing for Part 2 of this exercise.

Part 2: Visualize the Healing Thoughtform

1. Center in your heart and make your attunement with your Higher Self.
2. Give the following call:

   "In the name of my mighty I AM Presence, beloved Archangel Raphael and your healing angels, I call to you to place the healing thoughtform over [*name the person and/or area of the body*]."

3. Visualize the white-fire core of the healing thoughtform centered in scintillating, sapphire-blue flame, wrapped in emerald-green fire. Use the image you created or the color plate above to help you envision it.
4. See the thoughtform placed over the person or area of the body needing healing.
5. Visualize the unhealthy area becoming whole until an original healthy state appears. A color picture of the healthy person, area or organ can be used to enhance your visualization.
6. Hold this image steady in your mind's eye, focusing on it to the exclusion of all else for as long as you can sustain your concentration.
7. Repeat this process as often as possible.
8. Note any improvements in the condition in your journal.

CHAPTER 4

The Creative Power of Music

The Harmony of the Soul

Music has the power to move all creation. Throughout history it has been a prime mover of people and civilizations and has influenced human emotions all across a spectrum that ranges from the despair of suffering to the exuberating sense of transcendent victory. We encounter it almost everywhere—in stores, restaurants, malls, airports and the ever-present media. Wherever it is found, music emanates waves of vibration that can profoundly affect the soul, the chakras and the four lower bodies, for good or for ill.

Music's Unseen Influence

We have heard that "music hath charms to soothe the savage beast." Its effects on the psyche can be tremendously powerful. In ancient China, Egypt, India and the golden age of Greece, we find the same belief, that music has the power to contribute to the sublime evolution or the utter degradation of the soul. Many of the great Greek philosophers, including Plato, Aristotle and Pythagoras, regarded music as influential in moral culture and indispensable to the health of the soul. The ancients were convinced that music has an effect on the "rhythm of man's thoughts, the melody of man's emotions, and the harmony of his bodily health and manner of movement."[1]

Pythagoras was a prominent exponent of the extraordinary power of music. In the sixth century B.C., he and his spiritual community at Crotona, Italy, regarded music as a stepping-down in frequency of the music of the spheres. After discovering that music expressed the harmonic ratios of mathematics, Pythagoras realized that the whole universe could be explained in terms of musical numbers and ratios. Since good music was in accord with the universe, it could be used to restore health by bringing people into consonance with divine harmony. The Pythagoreans therefore used "musical medicine" for the healing of both body and soul.

The wise men of ancient China also credited music with the power to impact individuals and civilization. Around 500 B.C. Confucius—now the ascended hierarch of the Royal Teton Retreat—attached the same level of importance to his kingdom's music that politicians today attach to military or economic issues. He believed regularity could be brought into one's life by tapping into the divine symmetry of heaven and expressing its love and wisdom through music. Elizabeth Clare Prophet said:

1 David Tame, *The Secret Power of Music* (Rochester, Vt.: Destiny Books, 1984), p. 15.

"Confucius dedicated his life to teaching others how to bring order into their lives, their families and the empire. His vision has been described as a 'social order in communion and collaboration with a cosmic order.'"[2] Mrs. Prophet tells the following story about how profoundly music influenced this ascended master when he was in embodiment:

> Confucius was often moved by the etheric patterns and the beauty of music. One day when he was traveling, he saw a boy skipping and dancing while carrying a full pitcher. He found out that the boy had been listening to the ancient music of the sages. Impressed, Confucius hurried to hear the rest of the performance and was so moved by it that he went into a trance for three months. . . . When Confucius finally came out of the trance, he said, "I never imagined that music could be so sublime!"[3]

The noble-minded man's music is mild and delicate, keeps a uniform mood, enlivens and moves. Such a man does not harbour pain or mourn in his heart; violent and daring movements are foreign to him.[4]

—CONFUCIUS

Confucius believed that music had a hidden significance and possessed tremendous power for good or evil. The same basic beliefs can be found in almost every advanced civilization of antiquity from Mesopotamia and India to Greece. The ancients thought of music as a tangible force that could be used to create change within the individual and society, and even within matter itself. Since sound is the source of creation, individuals and cultures are perpetually being created and re-created, preserved or destroyed by its use.

The great music of ancient China, India, Egypt and Greece had as its fundamental purpose the transcendence of former states of consciousness. In fact, the Greeks legislated strongly to preserve the purity of their music. Composers were fined and even exiled from the state if their musical compositions were considered detrimental to the public good. Ultimately the Greek culture, founded on classical beauty and strength, began to degenerate into a sensual state through the music, which started becoming weak and effeminate. Greek music began to deteriorate during the era of Pericles (444–429 B.C.). Gradually, the mere virtuosity of musical performance replaced the true artist, and the character of the Greeks degenerated. Their morals weakened and they lost their love of freedom and patriotism. Some experts believe that the civilizations of Egypt and Greece fell into complete decline because of the degradation of music.

---

2 *Pearls of Wisdom,* vol. 41, no. 32.

3 Ibid.

4 Tame, *The Secret Power of Music,* p. 34.

In India, music has held a position of vital importance from ancient times to the present. Since music consists of audible sound, it is seen as a manifestation of the Aum, the earthly sound which—according to the Hindu cosmo-conception—mirrors the primal sound of heaven. The ancient Vedas, India's oldest scriptures, state that the entire universe is created and sustained through the vibratory power of the Aum. They say that this power even shapes and organizes matter-energy in such a way as to cause atoms to coalesce, creating physical matter. Cyclopea, the Elohim of the fifth ray, confirms this ancient Vedic philosophy. In 1973 he revealed that all creation is formed by music.

> *The syllable OM, which is the imperishable Brahman, is the universe. Whatsoever has existed, whatsoever exists, whatsoever shall exist hereafter, is OM. And whatsoever transcends past, present and future, that also is OM.*[5]
>
> —MANDUKYA UPANISHAD

The music of India reflects a spiritual consciousness and origin. When Lemuria sank, the priests and priestesses who served in the Lemurian temples took the secrets of true religion, culture, art and music to India.[6] Ancient Indian religion therefore is imprinted with the cultural heritage of the lost Motherland.

Indian music, in addition to the music itself, contains two unique aspects: language from the sacred scriptures and dance as movement of the human body, which replicates the rhythm of the cosmos. In India, it is well known that the correct use of rhythm brings about equilibrium and poise. The music of India is quite striking because it is so intuitive. It requires one to go within to the white-fire core of the chakras to find a sound that is not always familiar to the outer ear. Indian music is gaining popularity in the United States and if people can learn to appreciate it, it can have a tremendous positive effect upon their lives.

> *I AM the God of Music. Therefore,* I AM determined to save the earth with music. *What is music, beloved? It is the original sound with which earth was endowed in etheric spheres. It is the sound and the hum of a bee or an electron or a child learning his first tune. Music is the melody of the soul that is always in the divine rhythm of love. Music conveys all virtues of God. Music therefore does bring to you the inner sound of the living Word. But* you are *that Word,* you are *that Peace,* you are *that Peace-commanding Presence.*[7]
>
> —ELOHIM CYCLOPEA

5 Swami Prabhavananda and Frederick Manchester, trans, *The Upanishads: Breath of the Eternal* (Hollywood, Calif.: Vedanta Press, 1975), p. 73.

6 For more information on Lemuria, see chapter 3 in *Meeting the Masters*.

7 *Pearls of Wisdom*, vol. 31, no. 43.

How Music Affects Body, Mind and Soul

Because of its inherent qualities, music can exert a strong influence over the four lower bodies. Meditation upon it can affect the whole being, especially the harmony of the emotional body. Compositions can uplift, inspire and soothe or produce anxiety, depression and hyperstimulation, depending upon the piece. They can cause cycles of tension and relaxation to occur within many parts of the body as well. The roots of the auditory nerves are the most widely distributed and have the most extensive connections in the body. There is scarcely a physical function that is not affected by musical sounds. In *The Secret Power of Music,* David Tame explains:

> Investigation has shown that music affects digestion, internal secretions, circulation, nutrition and respiration. Even the neural networks of the brain have been found to be sensitive to harmonic principles.... Researchers have discovered that consonant and dissonant chords, different intervals, and other features of music all exert a profound effect upon man's pulse and respiration—upon their rate and upon whether their rhythm is constant, or interrupted and jumpy. Blood pressure is lowered by sustained chords and raised by crisp, repeated ones....
>
> Music affects the body in two distinct ways: directly, as the effect of sound upon the cells and organs, and indirectly, by affecting the emotions, which then in turn influence numerous bodily processes.[8]

God Harmony, a cosmic being who focuses the cosmic consciousness of divine harmony, explained that music has the power to soothe the awful manifestations of our shadowed self and heal the expressions of subtle darkness lurking in the subconscious. He said that it can also seal the destiny of planet Earth with light. Science is only beginning to discover how this occurs.

Some of music's unseen influence may be due to hidden qualities. Cyclopea explained that "music is the geometry of God. Each note has its frequency, its mathematical formula, its color, its healing potential."[9] These characteristics may affect people in various ways. For example, research has uncovered impacts of music on the brain. Certain kinds of classical music by composers like Bach, Mozart and Beethoven have been shown to have a range of positive effects on mental processes. These include expanding memory and speeding learning. Some believe that this type of music can even raise IQ or change chromosomes.

Mozart

Music has also been used therapeutically to help heal physical, developmental and psychological problems in hospitals, outpatient clinics, drug and alcohol programs, senior centers, schools, private practice and rehabilitation centers. Studies have found music therapy to be useful for reducing pain and anxiety in babies and children and relaxing them. It can also help treat patients with cancer, burns, cerebral palsy, stroke and brain injuries. Patients can be taught how to use music to help relieve their

8 Tame, *The Secret Power of Music,* pp. 136–37.

9 *Pearls of Wisdom,* 1978, vol. 21, pp. 396–97, hardbound.

own pain, depression and disability, and increase feelings of power. Still other research has shown that cradle songs can decrease bed-wetting and sleeping pill use in debilitated children and mentally challenged adults.

Music is an expression of beauty, a universal medicine. When we meditate upon the lovely music of master composers, our perceptions of the world can be enhanced. It has long been recognized that music has the ability to literally catapult us into a higher sphere of awareness. This is why we sing sacred music or intone chants. They can advance us out of time and space into greater dimensions of being and contact with the Divine. Mrs. Prophet said:

> If we cannot see the masters, if we cannot hear the masters, if we cannot converse with the masters, if we do not know how to consciously walk and talk with the masters on the path of life, there is one thing we can do: We can go to the heart of the music inspired by the hosts of the Lord and many qualified musicians on earth who serve on the fifth ray of truth, science, healing and music and follow that music back to the heart of the masters. . . .
>
> We can go to the heart of the music . . . and follow it back to our own souls, to our Holy Christ Self and to our beloved I AM Presence.[10]

Using Music to Tune the Chakras

If a bow is drawn across a violin string to produce the note of "A" at the vibration of 440 cycles per second, a tuning fork many feet away that is tuned to 440 cycles will begin to quiver in sympathy with the violin. This is called resonance, and it demonstrates how sounds interact with the chakras. Each chakra has a certain geometrical pattern and a primary sound. The right tone can create a resonance with the chakra, causing it to vibrate to the pattern of that sound.

Some have suggested that certain pitches correspond to the seven chakras. The ascended masters have not confirmed these pitches, however, nor released the exact chakra notes. As individuals come more into tune with their Holy Christ Self, they may be able to intuit the correct notes for revivifying the chakras from higher realms.

In the same way that a piano is tuned, sound and rhythm can tune the chakras and four lower bodies as instruments capable of producing the divine harmonies of Creation. The four lower bodies are the soul's vehicles of expression in the world of material form. Just as a musician uses his instrument to draw forth harmonies, the soul can give utterance to the music of the spheres through its "four-stringed lute"—the four lower bodies—which are designed to focalize the creative energies of the universe. Our chakras are envisioned by the Elohim Arcturus as seven openings for the violet flame to pass through. When this happens, we become an instrument of God's light.

Cosmic sound and rhythm can only flow through those who are closely attuned with their Real Self, because only consonance with the Divine will cause the chakras to

Crown

Third Eye

Throat

Heart

Solar Plexus

Seat of the Soul

Base of the Spine

10 *Pearls of Wisdom,* vol. 38, no. 29.

vibrate in the correct key. One's chakras may naturally be off-pitch, too high (sharp) or too low (flat). By restoring their correct vibration and pitch, a person may become a conductor of the seven spheres or rays of cosmic consciousness. This is the goal of meditation and the science of the spoken Word.

One's entire well-being depends upon how well the chakras are tuned. It has long been understood that harmony is the key to wholeness and health, both physical and spiritual. A consciousness that is inharmonious cannot receive vibratory patterns from higher levels. The more the chakras vibrate in harmony with the pure attributes of the seven rays, the greater the cosmic interchange will be. Music that is pure in its classical forms or in devotional songs to the ascended hosts can be immensely helpful in clearing and expanding the chakras. As the energy centers are cleared of density, the Kundalini lying dormant at the base chakra begins to rise naturally. As the Kundalini force rises, more and more divine power is available for serving life.

Instruments that Harmonize the Chakras

Energy can be governed in the planes of consciousness of the seven chakras through the correct use of sound. The chakras correspond to certain instruments that release the light of the energy centers. The violin and stringed instruments are highly effective in stimulating the crown. The third eye is attuned to the piano. The heart chakra is quickened by the harp; the secret chamber of the heart by the harpsichord. Brass instruments stimulate the throat chakra. The organ expands the desire to be one with God through the solar plexus. The soul is called by the woodwinds, especially the flute, which always quicken the ancient memory of higher octaves of light. Finally, in the base chakra the percussion instruments keep the time and beat of the Divine Mother. These correspondences are shown in the following chart.

THE SEVEN CHAKRAS, THEIR ENERGIES AND INSTRUMENTS		
CHAKRA	ENERGY	INSTRUMENT
Crown	Enlightenment	Stringed Instruments
Third Eye	God-Vision	Piano
Throat	The Word	Brass Instruments
Heart	Love	Harp
Secret Chamber of the Heart	Divinity/Threefold Flame	Harpsichord
Solar Plexus	Desire for God	Organ
Seat of the Soul	Soul Awareness	Woodwinds, especially flute
Base of the Spine	The Mother Light	Drum

The Music of the Spheres

The term "music of the spheres" refers to melodious sounds emanating from the etheric plane, the subtle realm some think of as heaven. In a vibrational sense, it is extremely spiritual music beyond the physical music we normally hear. The ancients thought that all music had physical coordinates in the heavens, an idea that has been verified by the ascended masters. We don't normally hear the celestial music, but some highly developed musicians have the ability to tune in to its sounds through inner hearing and to record them as compositions.

Each individual also has a personal connection to the music of the spheres because it registers the harmony and frequency of the soul through an inner melody or "keynote." This keynote represents the melody of each person's divine will, the fiat of the soul's unique identity and the point of his distinctive release of light to the world. The keynote can be heard through attunement; those who tune in to it often discover it in retreat away from the world, listening to its subtle vibration in quiet contemplation, service or prayer.

The science of celestial music has its origins in ages past. Pythagoras, a former embodiment of the Ascended Master Kuthumi, was one of its primary proponents. He held that each of the planets emits a keynote. In a dictation given in 1959 Kuthumi confirmed this and said that the musical keynote of earth is "F" below "middle C." Recent discoveries of celestial tones have added scientific evidence that heavenly bodies emit sounds. For example, astronomers found that a black hole in the Perseus Cluster, a giant clump of galaxies 250 million light-years from earth, has been emitting the note B-flat for billions of years. Humming along at 57 octaves below middle C, they believe it is the deepest note ever detected in the universe.

In 1968, Archangel Raphael explained that the Pleiades and the bands of Orion actually sing. This type of phenomenon has also been validated by science. Voyagers 1 and 2, space probes from the late 1970s, recorded audible electromagnetic waves from the soundless void of space surrounding Jupiter, Saturn, Uranus and Neptune. NASA translated these signals into "music" and sold them as recordings. The sounds remind listeners of waves of wind, giant Tibetan bowls, birds, dolphins and human voices.

Archangel Raphael also said that the angelic host has choirs and cosmic orchestrations that only a few upon the planet have ever heard. When humanity develops the ability to tune in to them, the fear of life will vanish and mankind will begin to understand the love that God wants to impart to all. Raphael said that people will "see" this love with their hearts.

The unparalleled harmonies of the music of the spheres are said to be able to restore sanity in an unsettled planet. They have value especially for the youth of the world. God Meru, a cosmic being who focuses the feminine ray of divinity for the earth, explained:

> When all of the forces of chaos are attempting to break down a way of life, let us turn to the music of the spheres. Let us turn to the quieting of souls, to the invoking of harmonies, to the bringing forth of the golden-age sounds that have not been heard.... Cyclopea holds secret melodies waiting to come forth that will remind the youth of ancient times, inner vows, other years when beauty and love, even in etheric octaves, was their lot.[11]

Recording Celestial Music

The music of the spheres has been released by the ascended masters over the centuries through special souls attuned to its subtle vibrations. One such example is the song, "Onward! Christian Soldiers." Kuthumi said that "this melody is one of those played by 'the music of the spheres,' from the combined musical tones released by each of the planets belonging to the same system as the earth. As each planet spins in its orbit, it releases into space its cosmic tone.... Many years ago, a rather insignificant parish priest of the Catholic Church—during some moments of quietude and spiritual contemplation—'tuned in' to what is known as 'The Inner Realms' and, hearing this lovely melody, wrote it down for posterity to enjoy."[12] The music that now accompanies this hymn was later credited to Sir Arthur Sullivan as the composer.

A number of composers throughout history have tuned in to cosmic melodies. Among them are Richard Wagner, Ludwig van Beethoven, Sir Edward Elgar, Giacomo Puccini, Sergei Rachmaninoff, Johann Strauss, Jr., and Gustav Mahler. Their compositions have a certain power for good. For example, the Ascended Master Cuzco, who is dedicated to averting or tempering cataclysmic activities on this planet, said that "compositions by Mahler have to do with earth changes and the holding at bay of major planetary upheaval. You would do well to play recordings of this music continuously.... Music is what has saved the planet in the past."[13]

Some of these compositions actually sound the keynotes of certain ascended masters and their retreats. The following chart gives an overview of such keynotes that have been revealed to us. The chart, "Chakras, Rhythms, Instruments and Musical Expressions," at the end of this chapter contains a list of composers and their uplifting compositions recognized for their high spiritual quality.

ASCENDED MASTER KEYNOTES		
MASTER/RETREAT	**TITLE**	**COMPOSER**
Archangel Michael	"Eternal Father, Strong to Save" (The Navy Hymn)	John B. Dykes
Archangel Michael's Retreat (at Banff, Canada)	"Soldiers' Chorus"	Charles Gounod
Archangel Gabriel	"Intermezzo" from *Cavalleria Rusticana*	Pietro Mascagni
Archangel Raphael	Messiah Overture	G. F. Handel

11 *Pearls of Wisdom,* vol. 30, no. 19.
12 *Pearls of Wisdom,* vol. 2, no. 29.
13 *Pearls of Wisdom,* vol. 38, no. 27.

Archangel Uriel	"Lullaby"	Johannes Brahms
The Ascension Flame	"Triumphal March" from *Aïda*	Giuseppi Verdi
Ascension Temple at Luxor	"Liebestraum"	Franz Liszt
Astrea	Piano Concerto in A Minor	Edvard Grieg
Clara Louise	"Calm as the Night"	Carl Bohm
El Morya	"Pomp and Circumstance" no. 1	Edward Elgar
Eriel of the Light	"To a Wild Rose"	Edward MacDowell
Gautama Buddha	Symphony no. 9 in D Minor, fourth movement, "Ode to Joy"	Ludwig van Beethoven
God Harmony	"Anvil Chorus" from *Il Trovatore*	Giuseppi Verdi
Great Divine Director	"Rakoczy March"	Franz Liszt
Guru Ma (Elizabeth C. Prophet)	"Beautiful Dreamer"	Stephen Foster
Hilarion	"Onward Christian Soldiers"	Sir Arthur Sullivan
Jesus Christ	"Hallelujah Chorus" from the *Messiah* and "Joy to the World"	G. F. Handel
Lanello	"Greensleeves"	Traditional
Leto	"The Heather on the Hill"	Lerner and Lowe
Portia	"Radetsky March"	Johann Strauss, Sr.
Royal Teton Retreat	"Evening Star" from *Tannhäuser*	Richard Wagner
Sanat Kumara	"Finlandia"	Jean Sibelius
Serapis Bey	"Celeste Aïda"	Guiseppi Verdi

Messengers of Music

Among the musicians who have tuned in to the music of the spheres, two have been specifically named by the ascended masters as "messengers of music." They are Ludwig van Beethoven and Dorothy Lee Fulton.

Beethoven

Beethoven

Elohim Cyclopea, the God of Music, mentioned Beethoven as a messenger of music in 1986 when he said: "The sign of Victory and the movement of light is heard in this music that is of the Ancient of Days, that is of Elohim—a gift of God to earth through that messenger of music, Beethoven."[14] Liberty and freedom were the message of the cosmos through the music Beethoven composed.

Beethoven ranks foremost among well-known composers of classical music. An initiate of the Great Divine Director, much of his greatest work was composed when he was deaf and he brought forth his magnificent works through the inner ear. Saint Germain said that Beethoven's nine symphonies represent the greatest music of freedom ever written. He also said that they contain the action of the Trinity multiplied by

14 *Pearls of Wisdom,* vol. 29, no. 66.

the power of three. In the splendor of these symphonies, Beethoven traced steps whereby man progressively awakens to his divine destiny and rises majestically over his lesser self to a level of self-mastery. Each of his nine symphonies therefore depicts some aspect of this great overcoming. Saint Germain recommends that we meditate with this music and learn to recognize the first to the ninth because the nine symphonies are degrees of initiations that are lowered into form by frequency, vibration, sound and ultimately by God's consciousness.

As the capstone of this symphonic series, Beethoven's ninth is a record of what he experienced at lofty levels of awareness. The first three movements of this colossal work depict the passage of the spirit ascending through the three heavens. The final choral movement sounds the exaltation theme which sweeps the soul into the very presence of God. The symphony as a whole gives expression to the supreme realization that all life is one and immortal.

Archangel Michael revealed that Beethoven's music is an antidote for rock music, which is harmful to the freedom of the soul. He said that we can counteract rock's negative effects by playing "perpetually the music of Beethoven. It is in the nine symphonies that you will find the power of the three-times-three to neutralize the rock beat that is continually playing on this planet, gaining momentum on the airways from satellite, through television and radio, on stereo systems, in headsets, vibrating through the very marrow of the bones of the people as newer and more perfected forms of technology allow these sounds to resonate to the very core of the cell."[15]

Beethoven's works are a great boon to the souls of earth. Beloved Helios, the God Presence of our solar system who ensouls the physical sun, described the stupendous power of Beethoven's Victory Symphony:[16] "I say, play it and play it again and play it every day until you have victory in every way in your personhood, in your church, in this nation and in this planet. And play it, beloved, . . . that victory might come shining through. And see that victory descending as a mighty V that parts all darkness, which can no longer coagulate!"

EXERCISE: TESTING BEETHOVEN

The next time there is disturbance, chaos or disharmony in your environment, try the following experiment using Beethoven's symphonies to raise the vibration and restore harmony.

1. Write a description of the inharmonious situation in your journal.
2. Play one or more of Beethoven's symphonies for several days or a whole week, in sequence if possible.
   - If you can, play the music in continuous playback mode.

15 *Pearls of Wisdom,* vol. 25, no. 28.

16 The "Victory Symphony" is Part 2 of *Wellington's Victory (Battle of Vitoria),* opus 91. Many also refer to Beethoven's Symphony No. 5 in C minor, Opus 67, by this name.

- If this is not possible, you may want to play it at a specific time each day.
- If you are trying to dispel noise or loud music from outside your home, you might want to open your windows so the music goes outside at a low volume, soft enough to not disturb others.

3. In your journal, document the changes in your household or neighborhood after playing Beethoven. Try to detect when and with what symphony these changes occurred and record them in your journal.

4. If you can, repeat the experiment to determine whether or not the result can be duplicated. If you are able to correlate good results to a specific symphony, note which one it is for future reference—and have it handy in case you need to deal with the same kinds of disturbances again.

Dorothy Lee Fulton

In 1991 Mother Mary bestowed a special anointing upon contemporary composer Dorothy Lee Fulton, who was previously embodied as Brahms. On August 25 that year, Mary gave a dictation through Elizabeth Clare Prophet where she called Dorothy Lee to the altar to anoint her as the "messenger of music" to bring forth music for the healing of souls. The blessed Mother transferred an increment of her Diamond Heart, bestowed a mantle of protection upon her and gave Dorothy Lee angels of protection to form a ring of light around her.

Dorothy Lee Fulton

Brahms, ca. 1853

Since then, other ascended masters have spoken about the power of Dorothy Lee's music to woo souls back to God. One of these is the Ascended Lady Master Nada Rayborn, a great opera singer before her ascension. In 1995, she described Dorothy Lee's music as a magnet that has the power to draw souls to the altars of God: "And they shall swiftly know the Path and set aside all past ignorance. They shall know the way, beloved, for they shall follow the music all the way Home to God. . . . This music can galvanize souls to return in simple sweetness to the heart of the Holy Christ Self."[17]

The masters called Dorothy Lee the messenger of music because she received the music directly from heavenly realms. Dorothy Lee called her music Mother Mary's music. The Maha Chohan referred to one of her later works, "Come, Holy Dove," as "a great, great hymn, known of old by Sanat Kumara."[18] In it, the names of God are recited in Hebrew. He said: "This piece is the highest manifestation of the inner Word and name of God that we have released to you in this . . . century. And not for many centuries has the earth been bathed in this holy sound. I speak of the holy sound, beloved. This piece drawn from the music of the spheres has not sounded in the earth since the days of Atlantis, and you have heard it this day. And it is a gift to you from God."[19]

www.SummitLighthouse.org/SA3-8

www.SummitLighthouse.org/SA3-9

Dorothy Lee's history with The Summit Lighthouse began in the early 1960s when she was invited by Mark Prophet to come to a conference in Washington, D.C. There, Mark introduced her as the one sent from heaven to produce the music for the newly created Summit Lighthouse. Dorothy Lee anchored the music of the spheres and produced hundreds of pieces of ethereal music, including 120 songs in The Summit Lighthouse songbook. "Great Central Sun" was one of them; it came to Dorothy Lee even before she knew what the Great Central Sun was! She gave it to Mark when she arrived in Washington, quite certain that he would be the one who could explain it to her, which he did. Dorothy Lee was knighted Lady Edelweiss in 1969 by Mark Prophet. She made her transition and ascended into the octaves of light on March 18, 2011 at the age of 96.[20]

www.SummitLighthouse.org/SA3-10

www.SummitLighthouse.org/SA3-11

Waiting with Cupped Ears

The music of the spheres can accomplish wonders for humanity. In addition to raising the vibration of any location, Archeia Christine said that its resplendent tones can actually change the cell patterns and cell formations of children, of those who are incarcerated in mental institutions and prisons, and of those lost to society because of their own rebellions against the Law.[21]

However, God Harmony cautions that the music of the spheres will only be heard by souls on earth when they wait with cupped ears to hear the cadences of the Father's voice. By attuning their hearts with harmonious sounds, people can begin to enter into the delicate, subtle and magnificent beauty of this interior music. They can then travel —in the etheric sense—on waves of harmony between the planets from one luminous orb to the other in a state of wonderful consciousness. Mankind can then become a part of the beauty of the cosmos which derives its nourishment from the invisible vital world. Such a meditation on cosmos depends upon attunement with one's Higher Self, the Great Central Sun of being. Amerissis, the Goddess of Light, gave the following meditation to help mankind make this connection.

17 *Pearls of Wisdom,* vol. 38, no. 20.

18 *Pearls of Wisdom,* vol. 38, no. 10.

19 Ibid.

20 For information on purchasing music composed by Dorothy Lee Fulton, please call customer service at 1-800-245-5445 or 406-848-9500.

21 *Pearls of Wisdom,* vol. 16, no. 49.

MEDITATION:
TUNING IN TO THE MUSIC OF THE SPHERES

www.SummitLighthouse.org/SA3-12

1. Sit in a meditative posture that is comfortable for you with your spine straight.
2. Breathe deeply and relax, focusing your attention on your heart.
3. Sound the *Aum* to attune with your Higher Self.
4. Close your eyes and visualize rings of white fire and yellow fire as mighty concentric rings looping around the heart. See them continuing to grow, layer upon layer upon layer.
5. Remaining centered, visualize the rings as a golden sun, its fiery light so dazzling that you can't open your eyes.
6. Now see another dazzling sun enveloping the first sun. See then another sun and another, until you are sealed in layer upon layer of suns in infinite number.
7. See these suns intensify and intensify as an armor of God's mind. Envision yourself as one with the Great Central Sun.
8. Listen quietly for the music of the spheres. Can you hear angelic choirs or other cosmic tones? If so, you may later want to hum or record them in writing or as songs.
9. When you are ready, focus your attention again on your heart.
10. Sound the *Aum* to seal your meditation.
11. Thank God for your experience in Spirit.
12. Repeat this meditation whenever your mind is calm and free.

> *Music is the perpetually flowing stream. It is the River of Life.*
> *It is movement in self, and as movement, beloved, it is always power.*
> *Each change of the note, the vibration, beloved, is a release of power.*[22]
>
> —BELOVED CYCLOPEA

Positive and Negative Types of Music

Music can be generally classified into genres that result in positive or negative effects on one's consciousness and four lower bodies. Philosophers and musicians of ancient civilizations claimed that certain types of music were inherently good and

22 *Pearls of Wisdom*, vol. 31, no. 43.

others were innately bad. Scientific experiments have also shown that certain combinations of sounds and rhythms are life-enhancing while others are unhealthy and dangerous. The ascended masters teach that positive music has the ability to draw the energy of the Divine Mother—the Kundalini—up from the base-of-the-spine to the crown chakra. Negative types produce the opposite effect by pulling the Kundalini downward, thereby depriving the upper chakras and organs of the nourishing vitality of this inner light.

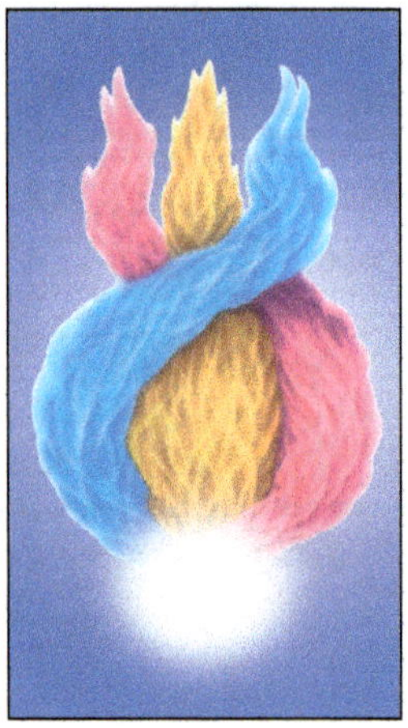
Threefold Flame

Different types of music also have various effects on the threefold flame. Positive music expands the heart flame; negative sounds cause it to contract. Music can be divided into three components—rhythm, melody and harmony—which comprise the heart's trinity of life. The rhythm launches the power of the Father (the blue plume of the threefold flame), the melody establishes the intelligence of the Son (the yellow plume), and the harmony maintains the flow of the Holy Spirit (the pink plume). We are perpetually being recreated, preserved or destroyed by the use we make of these musical elements.

The ascended masters have explained that music's power for good or ill is often determined by the rhythm, which has either a rejuvenating effect or an unhealthy action upon the chakras. The following chart gives an overview of the primary rhythms and their chakras, instruments and types of expressions.

CHAKRAS, RHYTHMS, INSTRUMENTS AND MUSICAL EXPRESSIONS

CHAKRA	RHYTHM	INSTRUMENT	POSITIVE EXPRESSION	NEGATIVE EXPRESSION
Crown	Varies	Strings	Classical symphonies and string compositions	Jazz
Third Eye	2/4	Piano	Piano concertos	Computer music
Throat	4/4, 2/4	Brass	Marches	Rock music
Heart	3/4, 12/8	Harp	Waltzes	Tango and jazz waltz
Solar Plexus	5/4	Organ	Bhajans and Western devotional music	Blues
Seat of the Soul	6/8, 2/4	Woodwinds, especially flute	Folk music	"Soul music"
Base of the Spine	4/4	Drum	Early American patriotic marches; classical Indian rhythms	Voodoo
All Chakras	5/4, 7/4	Drum (white-fire core of all chakras)	Indian ragas and bhajans (these raise the light up the spine)	Jazz, voodoo, rock (these drain the energy of all chakras)
Rings of Causal Body	12/4			

Causal Body

We can learn much about what is positive or negative music from research conducted on plants. Such studies are particularly helpful in demonstrating the effects of certain types of music on living organisms, since unlike people, plants do not have any cultural preferences. For example, various studies have demonstrated that plants thrive when exposed to classical music and are stunted, damaged and even die when exposed to acid rock.

Research has produced evidence that constructive music promotes life and destructive music contributes to disintegration or death. The results of being bombarded by music that has negative effects may be subtle. But those imperceptible effects may become cumulative, involving the life or death of cells in the body. In addition, every moment that we listen to music can enhance or diminish our soul's spiritual faculties as well as the life-energy in the spiritual centers, increment by increment. It is therefore valuable for spiritual students to be able to distinguish between music that is healthy and that which causes harm.

Music That Soothes the Savage Beast

The types of music that are life-enhancing cause all living things to thrive. They fill the chakras with the light intended for the sons and daughters of God, expand the aura with positive energy and fill one's consciousness with life. Beneficial music is found in classical and folk genres as well as in waltzes, marches and Indian ragas and bhajans.

Classical Music

One of the best types of music for our use is "classical" music. This term describes a broad range of pieces from the works of well-known composers like Bach, Mozart, Beethoven, etc. It includes music from the baroque, classical, romantic, and modern musical periods that is disciplined and melodic. Classical music generally contains the types of regular rhythms and sounds that help tune the seven chakras and uplift and enliven the soul. Modern or other music that is atonal, dissonant or mechanical in nature (such as twelve-tone or computer music) does not fulfill this purpose and is not considered to be in this category.

The ascended masters have consistently recommended classical music for its benefits to the soul, and civil authorities have also discovered some of its benefits. Classical music has helped police chase away drug dealers, prostitutes and bored teenagers who bristle at the sounds of Brahms, Mozart and Bach. It's not apparent why some people dislike classical music so much that they leave when it is played. But the trend was first reported in 1985 in Vancouver, B.C. Later, New York City police began using opera to chase the homeless out of the Port Authority bus terminal, and San Francisco authorities broadcasted classical music in a sleazy part of the city to successfully deter rowdy youths. Businesses have adopted it as well. A 7-Eleven store owner began playing it to keep crowds of teens from congregating in its parking lot. Another business owner found that playing it at high volumes completely and consistently deterred loitering.

Classical music has also been shown to reduce crime. In West Palm Beach, Florida, a street corner riddled with crime became more law-abiding after Mozart and Beethoven were blasted by police. And authorities in Montreal and Toronto reported that crime decreased in their subway systems after piping arias and symphonies into their stations. The London Underground began transmitting classical music into its subways in 2005 and saw certain types of physical and verbal abuse decline by 33 percent. In Portland, Oregon, calls to police dropped after the transit authority started playing classical music at its light-rail stops.

> *Beloved ones, the first point of restoration of the Christhood of America, [the place where] the I AM Race of the world [gather], I say, is the restoration of right music and right sound. Music and sound can carry the heart and the soul to the octaves of their source. Great music has come forth out of the higher octaves in all centuries. And very good music has come out of these planes that is the ascended master music that you use.*[23]
>
> —LORD MAITREYA

Other Musical Genres

In addition to classical music, there are other types of music that are considered beneficial to the soul and four lower bodies. Most musical genres have a certain meter, or beats per measure that recur in a rhythmical pattern. For the musically inclined, the time signature and meter are shown for each type of music discussed in this section.[24] The large bold numbers of the meter indicate the beat(s) that receive greater emphasis when the music is sung or played.

www.SummitLighthouse.org/SA3-13

Folk Music

6/8 time (**1**-2-3-**4**-5-6)
2/4 time (**1**-2)

One positive genre is folk music, traditional songs originally composed to evoke stories and memories shared by groups of people. Folk may include ballads, song airs and dance tunes that came from original cultures and were passed down through oral transmission. From the 1960s onwards, folk music in North America also included the music of ethnic and racial communities. One good example is "Greensleeves." Other popular examples can be found in the traditional music of Ireland, Scotland, Hungary, Russia, Israel and many other countries.

Folk music positively stimulates the seat-of-the-soul chakra. The soul, which resides in this chakra, can find liberation through its vibration. Folk is true "soul music," as opposed to what is often called by that name. Its purpose is to call souls back

23 *Pearls of Wisdom,* vol. 35, no. 42.
24 *Pearls of Wisdom,* vol. 43, no. 53.

to their original culture, to their homeland and to the fulfillment of their divine plan. It is intended to echo the soul's origin in the chambers of memory. In terms of the rhythm, folk and other music with 6/8 time signatures are favorable because they produce the soul's distinct rhythm that reflects the three-quarter time of the heart.

The Waltz

3/4 time (***1***-2-3)
12/8 time (***1***-2-3-***4***-5-6-***7***-8-9-***10***-11-12)

www.SummitLighthouse.org/SA3 14

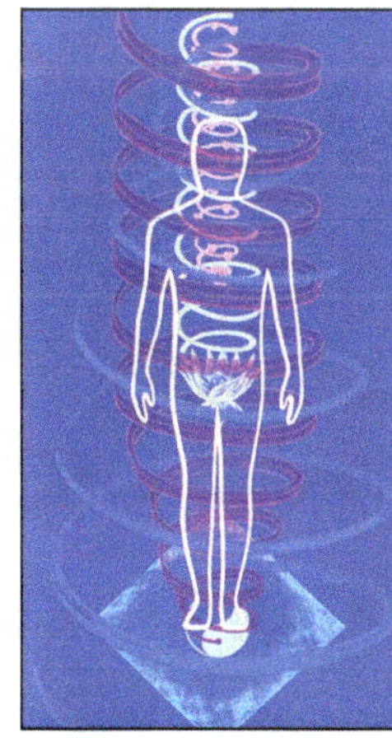

Waltz music uplifts the aura

Johann Strauss statue in Vienna, Austria

The waltz is one of the most beneficial types of music because its three-quarter time is the rhythm of the heartbeat. Waltz music therefore creates a sense of internal harmony because the ***1***-2-3 rhythm accents the flow of energy in the four lower bodies. This relationship between the rhythm of the waltz and that of the heart can open the door to cosmic consciousness. Lady Master Venus explained how this works:

> Right there within the heart chamber is the mighty manifestation of the alchemist's focus, the focus of the cosmic transformer. Moment by moment, then, the currents idle in the cosmic interval—the pause, the delicate pause in three-quarter time, after the first beat, before the second and the third.
>
> The accent on the first beat is the opportunity for the threefold flame to be expressed by the soul's attunement with the cosmic interval. Therefore, you count **one,** two, three; **one,** two, three. . . .
>
> Therefore, as you perform the ritual of the waltz or the invocation to the violet flame or the meditation upon the heart, remember that that rhythm is the means whereby every soul encased in Matter form can have a split-second experience of cosmic consciousness in the cosmic interval.[25]

The three-quarter time of the waltz also carries the rhythm of transmutation. Saint Germain introduced the waltz in the nineteenth century as a forerunner of the violet flame by inspiring its magnificent renditions upon Johann Strauss and Johann Strauss, Jr. People living in that era actually drew the violet flame into their midst through waltz music. When they danced and whirled to it they were participating in the ritual of speeding up the electrons around the core of the atom without ever realizing it. When singing or dancing to the waltz, a rising violet-flame spiral carves a pathway of light through one's subconscious. This action paves the way for the raising of the ascension coil up the spine to its culmination in the crown.

Saint Germain, who gave us the gift of the violet flame, also gave us an impetus to listen and dance to the waltz: "Whether you whistle the violet flame, sing it, perform it in a violet-flame orchestra, whatever it takes, understand that the power of the three-quarter time in the movement of the waltz creates a vortex of light that draws in all sons and daughters of God who are attuned to the true music of the spheres."[26]

25 *Pearls of Wisdom,* vol. 43, no. 53.
26 *Pearls of Wisdom,* vol. 40, no. 41.

The March

4/4 time (**1**-2-3-4)
2/4 time (**1**-2)

www.SummitLighthouse.org/SA3-15

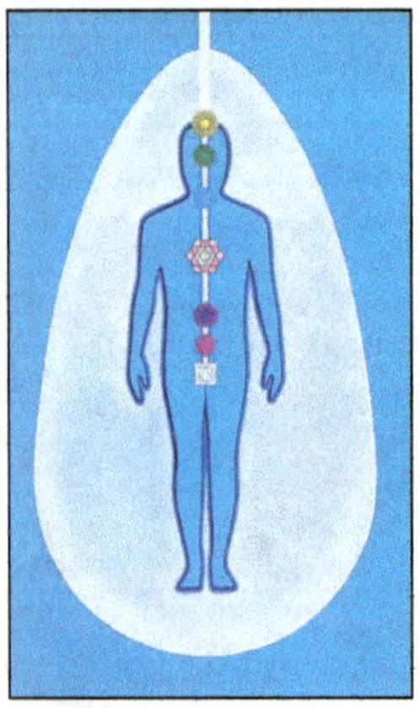

Music based on the 4/4 time signature is harmonious to human nature since it affects the base-of-the-spine chakra in an upbeat way. The 4/4 time is the beat of the Mother, the Kundalini force. In it, we can feel the release of Mother energy in a disciplined rhythmic cycle. Marching to this type of beat is excellent training for people of all ages because it regulates the sacred fire in the four lower bodies through physical action.

Music that is set to 2/4 time is similar to that written in 4/4 time, but it affects the seat-of-the-soul and third-eye chakras. Marches and other music with a steady 2/4 beat give us the vision of the soul through these chakras. This music is often described as being martial since it has historically been used by the military. In 1959 Kuthumi explained that it releases the energy of the I AM Presence:

> Now, martial-type music belongs primarily to the activities and beings of the first ray, although sometimes used by those who serve on the fourth and fifth rays—these three expressing a more dynamic type of service than the other four of the seven rays. Its use stirs up the living energies within the body, mind and soul of all who hear it and produces a great lift in consciousness. In military activities, one of its uses has been to draw more energy into the outer self by causing the "silver cord," from the heart of the I AM Presence into the physical heart, to expand. Thus do those greater currents of pure, scintillating life rush into the physical and then out into the four lower bodies. So, used before going into battle, martial music releases more energy to the soldier to use in conflict.[27]

Sound and color are related when it comes to music; both are ways to express vibration. Some people even see colors when sound is played.[28] Mark and Elizabeth Prophet explained that the color of martial music is blue. The blue ray does have a frequency and a physical sensation that impinges upon the eye as blue. But it also has a cosmic harmony and a rhythm that is the beat of marching, which is the beat of power. All music written in 4/4 or 2/4 is integrated with an aspect of the blue ray. In fact, all the rays have a special vibratory action upon the body. Mrs. Prophet said when we become sensitive to their vibration, we will know immediately which of the seven rays is flooding our being by its physical action upon us.

27 *Pearls of Wisdom*, vol. 2, no. 29.

28 This phenomenon is called "synesthesia."

Indian Ragas and Bhajans

5/4 time (**1**-2-3-4-5)
7/4 time (**1**-2-3-4-5-6-7)

As mentioned before, the music of India reflects the spiritual awareness we have inherited from Lemuria. Included in this music are sacred vocal chants called "bhajans"[29] and instrumental music called "ragas." Ragas have a traditional mode or melodic pattern. They express specific moods and are associated with precise times of the day. The Buddha Manjushri said the raga has the ability to penetrate to the heart of being:

> The ancient ones knew the science of music and they used music to penetrate the atom with the mind—penetrating the atom (long before its rediscovery in the West in recent history), penetrating the atom of being, penetrating the five secret rays. . . .
>
> If you would know the power of music whereby the soul follows sound to the heart of being, then study this form of music, the Indian raga. . . . For it does bring you into the encounter with the cosmic teacher. It does bring you into a polarity of the plus and the minus—you, the minus, negative, feminine polarity; the teacher, the plus, positive, masculine polarity. When you are in polarity, beloved, with such music, you enter into a compartment of being that truly is the heart and the goal of meditation.[30]

www.SummitLighthouse.org/SA3-16

A sitar

The music of India requires the listener to go within to the white-fire core of the chakras. It may use the beat of the Mother (4/4 time) like march music, or it may use the more unusual 5/4 or 7/4 time signatures. The sound of bhajans puts the soul in contact with the music of the spheres. The 5/4 rhythm stimulates the solar plexus, the place of devotion to God. The 7/4 accelerating rhythm of the bhajan raises the energies of the Divine Mother up through the seven chakras.

Music That Lowers Our Aspirations

When we listen to any music long enough, we become accustomed to it and begin to prefer it. Without being aware of it, we can therefore become habituated to unwholesome sounds that cause harm. Instead of uplifting our spirits, they actually stunt our spiritual growth by causing the sacred fire of the Kundalini to descend from the crown chakra to the lower desire centers, where it then seeks outward expression in negative choices like anger, sex, drugs and alcohol. Instead of being beautiful, the aura then becomes distorted and contorted, no longer an ovoid of light holding the light of pure chakras. When this music is used consistently, the aura turns into a receptacle of negative energy that carries the consciousness of death, instead of life, to oneself and others. It also perverts the light of the chakras. Rock, jazz and "soul music" are examples of such unwholesome music. They are described below; additional references are found in the chart on page 106, "Chakras, Rhythms, Instruments and Musical Expressions."[31]

29 Pronounced "bujuns."

30 *Pearls of Wisdom*, vol. 37, no. 21.

31 A complete explanation of the positive and negative effects of types of music by Elizabeth Clare Prophet is available on the DVD album, *The Power of Music: To Create or Destroy*, DVI13009.

Rock Music

Syncopated 4/4 time (1-**2**-3-**4**)

One of the most pervasive types of modern music is rock. In grocery and department stores, doctors' offices, the media and even some churches, we hear rock in one of its many forms—country rock, folk rock, Christian rock, hard rock, heavy metal, etc. Research, however, has shown that rock is one of the most harmful types of music that exist.

The rhythm of rock originated in the voodoo beat which the ascended masters say has clear connections to Satanism. Rock music uses a syncopated beat, which accentuates the secondary beat, which would normally be weak. The syncopated beat contradicts the natural rhythm of the heart. In fact, it creates a type of static electricity that alters the heart rate and causes it to lose its perfect rhythm. Research has found that rock music is also bad for digestion, raises the blood pressure and is harmful for those with hypertension.

Rock music also perverts the light of the throat chakra. Mark and Elizabeth Prophet said that it reverses the spin of the atom as well. The light that flows from the I AM Presence over the crystal cord to the four lower bodies is normally received by every atom in a clockwise spin, charging it with light from the Central Sun. Rock music, by its syncopated 4/4 beat, channels energy through the aura and chakras in a counterclockwise spin, turning the life force into a spiral contrary to life—a death spiral of the forces of darkness. Because of this action, the sound, vibration and energy of rock acting in the chakras contributes to the death of the soul, the mind, the consciousness and the cells of the body.

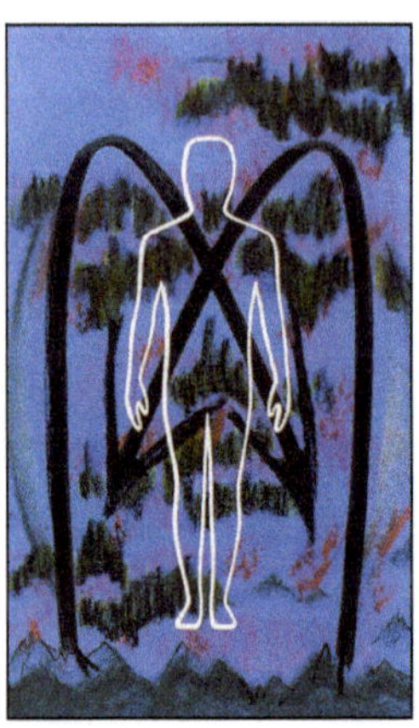

Many who listen to rock music say that it gives them energy. The ascended masters have explained that the energy they sense is deceptive. Listening or playing rock causes one's energy to descend from the crown chakra to the base chakra.[32] It goes down with a rush that causes a release of the light from the lower centers. This rush gives listeners a temporary thrill. But this blast of energy actually injures the chakras, tearing them as light is expelled. People experiencing rock in dance parties, such as raves and rock concerts, often begin to scream and have tremendous highs. At the moment it seems like the experience is positive, but in the long run the listener's divine energy is lost and squandered. Because of this thrill, rock music can actually become an addiction. People get addicted to the high of energy rushing out of the chakras the same way they get addicted to sugar, alcohol or nicotine. Fortunately, as with all addictions, we can always call to Archangel Michael to be delivered of the addiction to rock music.

When rock is played loudly, it is deafening not only to the outer ear but to the inner ear of the soul, destroying the hearing on the etheric as well as the physical plane. This is because the soul's hearing in the etheric octave can no longer be transmitted via

32 For more information on the science of energy flow, see chapter 4 in *The Spiritual Quest.*

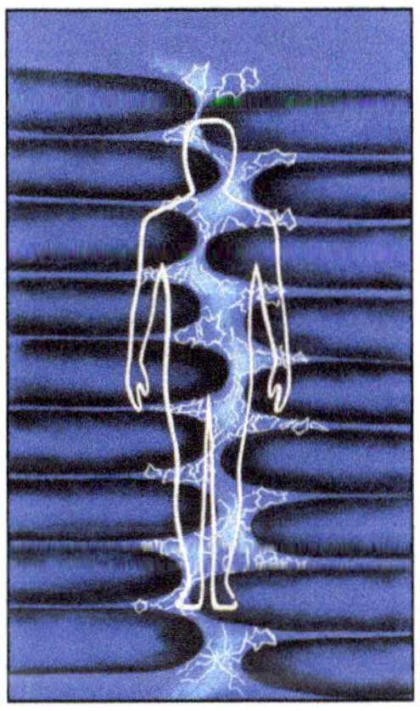

the soul faculties to the outer awareness. As a result, rock music actually drowns out the music of the spheres. Rock's negative effects on the aura can also clearly be seen, as in this illustration.

It's already been mentioned that rock music damages plants. David Tame tells a story that makes us think about the internal damage to humans that rock music might cause:

> Drs. Earl W. Flosdorf and Leslie A. Chambers found in a series of experiments that shrill sounds projected into a liquid media coagulated proteins. A recent teenage fad was that of taking soft eggs to rock concerts and placing them at the foot of the stage. Midway through the concert the eggs could be eaten hard-boiled as a result of the music. Amazingly, few rock fans wondered what that same music might do to their bodies.[33]

One example of how rock music can be harmful is shown in the case history of someone who had a medical relapse after attending a loud rock concert. A 40-year-old man who had had coronary artery bypass surgery was discharged from the hospital. About twelve days after the surgery, he had hardly any soreness from the incision wound in his chest. Twenty days after the surgery he felt well that day, took it easy all day and had no symptoms of pain, so he decided to attend a rock concert. He was careful not to get too close to others at the concert so they would not bump up against his chest. After listening for about one hour and being immersed in the vibrations of the intensely loud music, his chest began to feel really sore and he had to leave the concert early. The next day his sternum was quite painful and he went back to the doctor. His wound was tender to the touch, although it appeared to be healing normally. After a few days of rest the symptoms disappeared. The doctor reported that this was a case of severe chest pain that had been brought on by the intense vibrations and shaking produced by the extremely loud rock music.

The rock beat is often made even worse by unwholesome lyrics. Common rock themes have long been controversial because of their potential harm. Destructive themes such as drug and alcohol use, suicide, violence, demonology, sexual exploitation, racism and bigotry are common. Such music is questionable, especially for children and adolescents. One indication of what graphic rock music and lyrics can do occurred in 1969 at the Altamont festival, during a performance of the Rolling Stones. "Sympathy for the Devil" and other songs contributed to an agitated climate where an audience member with a weapon tried to reach the stage and was killed by a member of the Hells Angels motorcycle gang who had been hired as security guards.

The ascended masters and the messengers have been quite vocal on the subject of rock music's negative effects. Because the rock beat shatters the forcefield of atoms, they say, it can literally cause society to disintegrate. Archangel Gabriel vividly described it thus:

33 Tame, *The Secret Power of Music,* pp. 137–38.

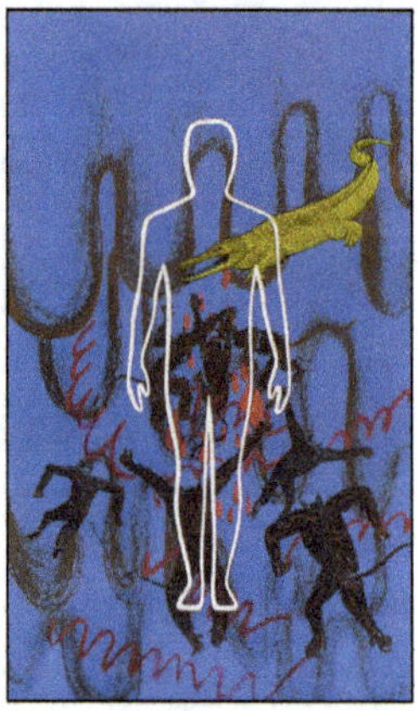

> The delicate rhythm of the divine Word is compromised in the noises, the sounds that come out of hell itself—made popular, called music, yet it is a creeping-and-crawling devouring of the soul. For sound itself is creation, and that which is the unformed cannot coalesce as an integral whole when bombarded by the "hard-rock" music, accompanied by images ungodly, chaotic. All this is nihilism, for it is nonintegration.[34]

Just as the ancients believed, such dissolution can ultimately bring about personal and planetary cataclysm. However, the correct use of the science of sound in music and in the science of Word is always available to restore planetary energy and exalt life.

Jazz

Jazz had its origin in blues melodies sung by African-American slaves. When it began in 1835 in New Orleans, jazz was initially accompanied by acts of voodoo. It later became accepted in public dance halls and saloons, and ultimately became woven into the fabric of American culture.

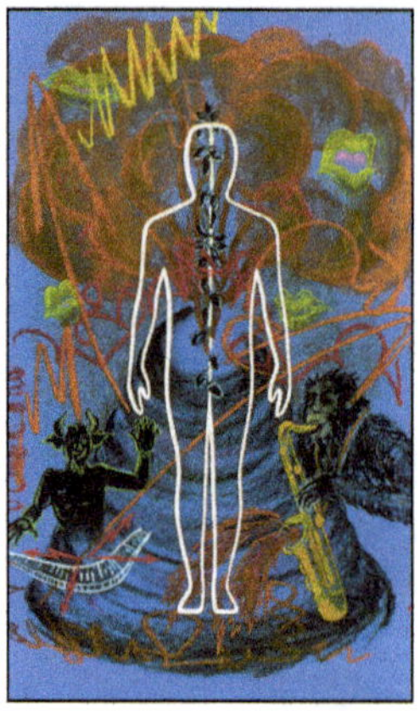

Like rock, jazz rhythms are harmful to the soul because they incorporate the voodoo beat, which in ancient times brought down two African golden-age civilizations. Jazz distorts the energies of the Father, Son and Holy Spirit through a lack of musical discipline. Its rhythm is chaotic—the antithesis of the rhythm of the Divine Mother. Researchers have found that jazz has little or no therapeutic value. Like all compositions featuring broken rhythms, dissonance and exaggerated tempo, jazz stimulates and irritates the chakras, stripping them of light. Because of its repeated rhythms it also has a hypnotic effect and like rock, affects the rate of the heartbeat in an adverse way.

Mrs. Prophet explained that upon one's first contact with jazz, the soul experiences it as violence. The unchanneled energies of jazz are destructive and frenzied, much like boxing which became popular in history at about the same time. One's senses are dulled and broken by its harsh rhythms and jagged energy. Jazz has a subtle but persistent influence on both the mind and the emotions that puts the individual out of contact with reality and prevents contact with the mind of God.

Jazz is the perversion of the crown chakra. It causes the light of the Father in the crown to descend through irregular rhythmic patterns to the lower chakras, where the energy becomes concentrated and seeks an outlet. Like rock music, it overemphasizes the sexual nature through a syncopated rhythm which has a tendency to make the nerves hyperexcited and to relax the power of self-control. Because of the rapid downward release of light in the chakras, jazz can also become an addiction. One has to keep hearing it in order to receive an additional stimulus once the energy of the chakras has been released.

Lord Shiva—a divine being who focuses the Holy Spirit aspect of the Hindu trinity Brahma, Vishnu and Shiva—made a strong statement about jazz. Shiva is

34 *Pearls of Wisdom*, vol. 30, no. 12.

known as Nataraja, the graceful King of Dancers. He said: "Beloved ones, there is nothing, and I say *nothing whatsoever* that is constructive in *any* form of jazz. And I say this unequivocally. And if you desire to have Shiva in your midst, you will hear the truth straight from that focus of the sacred fire which I AM."[35]

Lord Shiva

Soul Music

What today is sometimes called "soul music" has been explained by the ascended masters as actually being the opposite. Webster's dictionary defines "soul music" as "music that originated in African American gospel singing, is closely related to rhythm and blues, and is characterized by intensity of feeling and earthiness."[36] One example is "Respect" by Otis Redding.

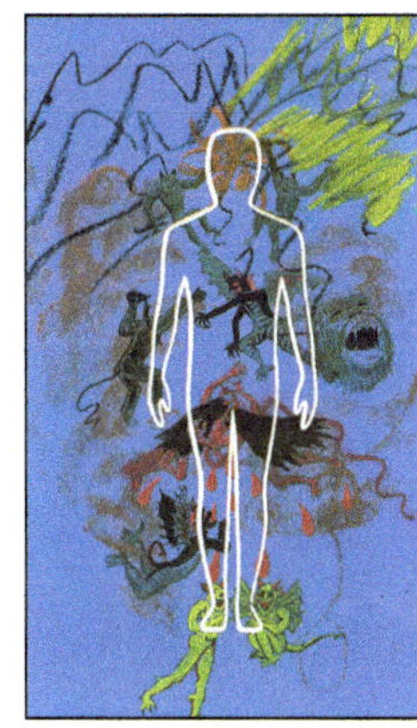

However, instead of calling souls to their homeland (as in folk ballads like "Greensleeves"), so-called soul music has a distinctly negative effect. As a perversion of the seat-of-the-soul chakra, it actually drowns the soul by causing an unwillingness to hear the longing for our true spiritual home because it is too painful. The false rhythm destroys the light of the Divine Mother and the soul senses so that one is no longer sensitive to the spiritual path and the call home toward God. The music causes self-destruction instead of raising individuals into the ascension. It brings the African people back to the level and era of their voodoo enslavement instead of impelling their souls forward into a golden-age civilization.

Musical Tips

We know that music can be both positive and negative in terms of its effects. The choice is ours as to which kinds of music we listen to. The ascended masters have provided many suggestions to help us raise our vibration through elevating music. The suggestions listed below can increase the light in our chakras and four lower bodies and propel us forward on the spiritual path.

1. **Fill your home with spiritual music.** Play any or all of the following types of music to uplift your consciousness and replace the attraction to negative types.
    - Christmas carols, no matter what time of year. They are one of the best ways to permeate the home with a sense of holiness. The Ascended Master El Morya has explained that playing carols throughout the year will attract the angels of the Christ Mass.
    - Beethoven's nine symphonies and his other works
    - Music by Dorothy Lee Fulton, Messenger of Music
    - Operas inspired by the ascended masters upon gifted composers, including:
        - Richard Wagner's opera *Parsifal,* which is the story of the quest for the Holy Grail

35 *Pearls of Wisdom,* vol. 21, no. 37.
36 *Merriam-Webster's Collegiate Dictionary,* 11th ed., s.v. "soul music."

    - Puccini's *Madama Butterfly,* which tells the story of two souls who symbolize twin flames
    - Wagner's opera *Lohengrin,* which illustrates the relationship of twin flames when one has ascended into Spirit and the other is still on earth

Lord Krishna

- Bhajans to Krishna or Shiva. They can help sustain and hold the balance for one's life, family, country and the planet. Because bhajans are written in Sanskrit, they also invoke violet flame, as do all the Buddhist mantras.
- The ascended masters' keynotes, which draw their presence into the environment. A number of keynotes are listed on page 100 in the chart, "Ascended Master Keynotes."
- Music for the seven rays, listed on page 123 in the chart, "Music on the Seven Rays."
- Classical music of the great composers. Ascended master favorites are listed on page 123 in "Favorite Musical Selections."
- Songs from The Summit Lighthouse, which enhance attunement with one's Higher Self and the ascended masters.[37]

2. **Go to the retreats of music while your body sleeps.** Among the most well-known of these is the Royal Teton Retreat, the principal retreat of the Great White Brotherhood in North America, congruent with the Teton Range near Jackson Hole, Wyoming. It features a music room with beautiful instruments that send out the music of the spheres. Le Chateau de Liberté in southern France, the retreat of Paul the Venetian, Chohan of the Third Ray, also has workshops for musicians. Ascended masters serving there introduce new musical techniques in an atmosphere permeated by the celestial sounds of piano, cello, organ, harp and the caroling of many choirs.

Teton Mountains

37 *Book of Hymns and Songs* (Gardiner, Mont.: Summit Publications, Inc., 2014).

INTRODUCING...

Cyclopea and Virginia

Cyclopea and Virginia are the Elohim of the fifth ray of music, truth, mathematics, healing, science, constancy and the desire to precipitate the abundance of God through the immaculate concept. Holding the focus for the All-Seeing Eye of God, these twin flames assist mankind and elemental life to bring the abundance of Spirit into physical form. Cyclopea's aura is green and reflects the prism of Christ consciousness, resembling the action of crystal. Virginia's aura is green tinged with white. Their retreat is in the etheric realm high in the Altai Mountains where Mongolia, China and Russia meet, near Tabun Bogdo.

Altai Mountains

Cyclopea is a member of the great Karmic Board where he represents the fourth ray of purity. He and Virginia are also known as the Elohim of Music, or the God and Goddess of Music. Through the music of the spheres, they govern the activities of speech, hearing and sight, focusing the rays of concentration and consecration to the evolutions in their care. They are cosmic patrons of music in charge of the release of the music of the spheres through the masculine and feminine rays of Alpha and Omega in the Great Central Sun. Cyclopea and Virginia also focus the action of the emerald ray and its precipitation flame from their etheric retreat.

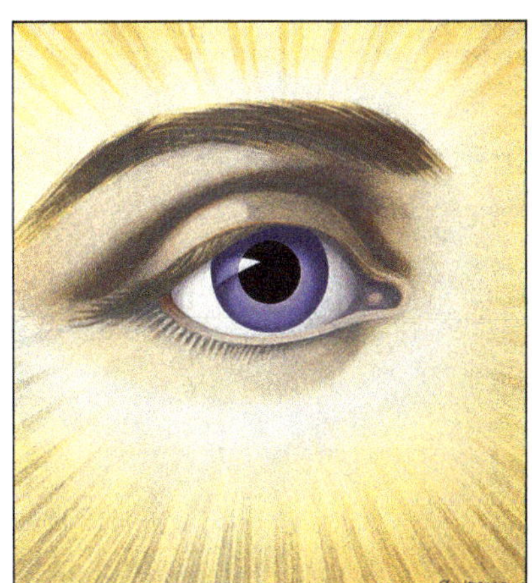

All-Seeing Eye

Cyclopea's cosmic consciousness ensouls the vision of the Creator, so he is the Elohim of Divine Vision as well. In this capacity, he is known as the All-Seeing Eye of God. He teaches mastery of the third eye and lends his momentum of vision for the freedom of lifewaves and planetary homes such as earth as well as countless others beyond our solar system and galaxy.

Cyclopea and Virginia radiate the truth of each one's original divine plan through a single green flame emitting the seven color rays of the Elohim. The All-Seeing Eye of God is a focus of purity released through the third-eye chakra that enables the individual to raise his divine energies up from the base of the spine to the crown, anchoring them in the third eye.

Cyclopea and Virginia guard the virgin consciousness of the Christ. During the solstice conclaves held at each half year in the Royal Teton Retreat, Cyclopea releases etheric balls of blue fire into the atmosphere of earth through the focus of the All-Seeing Eye at the north end of the central sanctuary. These balls, with their accompanying light rays, charge the earth with the action of the will of God and the purity of the divine conception of every man, woman and child on the planet. The action of the blue lightning cuts through dense effluvia and paves the way for the crystal flame of purity and the emerald ray to cleanse the four lower bodies of the lifestreams to whom the Elohim minister.

The Science of Vibration

For eons the sages of Hinduism have known that the science of sound holds the key to the mysteries of the universe, to the formation and sustaining of our world, and to the means of extricating ourselves from its bonds. They long ago perfected this science and provided us with the fruits of their higher perspective. Their belief includes the science of vibration as the causative agent behind all creation. Once we have an insight into how vibration shapes our world, we can appreciate how music relates to the science of the spoken Word. This study begins with an understanding of what is known as the "soundless sound."

The Soundless Sound

Indian metaphysics describes sound as the cause and not the effect of vibration. There can also be sound without vibration, although it takes a certain stretching of the mind to embrace the nature of this soundless sound. We learn from the Indian masters that sound not only manifests without vibration, but sound can occur without the usual mediums of conveyance such as air, water or other states of matter. This is the concept of potential sound, the driving energy and force behind all manifestation. It is considered an infinite, endless continuum—indivisible, unfragmented and potent—the most powerful Source of all.

The soundless sound is still primarily unrecognized by the relatively coarse instruments of modern science. It is the subtlest element, being finer than earth, air, fire, or water. Beyond the speed of light, it is all pervasive and the source of cohesion, electricity and magnetism. Reaching the sphere of this potential sound has been the goal of yogic practitioners, adepts and esoteric brotherhoods since time began because its exploration reveals the path to infinite Spirit.

The Vibratory Nature of Sound

The texts of the world's major religions say that creation began with an original sound or vibration. In the Vedas we read, "In the beginning was Brahman with whom was the Word, and the Word is Brahman."[38] Likewise, in Christianity the apostle John wrote, "In the beginning was the Word, and the Word was with God, and the Word

38 Sir John Woodroffe, *The Garland of Letters: Studies in the Mantra-Sastra* (Pondicherry, India: Ganesh and Co., n.d.), p. 4.

was God."[39] The first biblical book, Genesis, says that when God *spoke* the words "Let there be light,"[40] the process of creation began. The Word that was spoken was not just any word. It was the Word of God—a frequency released as the sacred word Aum at the origin of creation.

The cause of the primordial sound of cosmos was an oscillation, a back-and-forth pulsation of energy. The first sound was a pure tone. As more and more vibratory patterns were added, the resulting notes formed a chord. The world of phenomena is therefore a reflection of the infinite combinations of these sound patterns, which were all derived initially from the soundless sound of the Creator.

Scientists today realize that all matter is constantly in a state of vibration at the microcosmic level. Atoms are, in fact, only energy in an unceasing condition of oscillation. We can visualize the world of matter as a vast symphony of individual vibratory patterns, working together to compose the warp and woof of the universe. The elements and substances are all different because they are formed by a specific combination of vibrations. These vibrations, at a certain point, crystallize into form. They densify, coalescing into physical matter.

> *In the beginning was the Word.*
> *In the ending is the Word.*
> *And the Word went forth.*
> *Elohim sent forth the Word of the One*
> *And the universes were framed*
> *And Light came forth*
> *And Mater appeared.*[41]
>
> —ELOHIM CYCLOPEA

Human beings have a vast ability to produce all types of sounds and vibrations with our mouths. We can emit everything from an angry outburst to the shattering of a crystal goblet by a high-pitched voice. Decrees and mantras also produce a characteristic type of sound as well as their own unique results.

Dictations and Decrees Are Music

Dictations spoken by the messengers, Mark L. Prophet and Elizabeth Clare Prophet, are timeless messages and releases of light from the ascended masters. When played as recordings, they come to us as spoken words accompanied by the radiation of the master who is dictating. Cyclopea also said that in the etheric plane, music and dictations have a great deal in common: "on another track dictations are all music."[42]

Chants produced by the science of the spoken Word enjoy a similar comparison. Justinius, Captain of Seraphic Hosts, explained that the synchronized chants of the seraphim produce harmonies heard in heaven as harp music. A sequence of timed chants causes the release of light of their bands:

> I draw to you the understanding of the use of the science of the spoken Word by mighty seraphim who at times in their chants sound like aeolian harps as they give forth their invocations and affirmations in praise of the Deity.

39 John 1:1.

40 Genesis 1:3.

41 Cyclopea, *Keepers of the Flame Lesson 32* (Corwin Springs, Mont.: The Summit Lighthouse, 1999), p. 44.

42 *Pearls of Wisdom,* vol. 31, no. 43.

> Their timing is such that they may synchronize in four-four time the descent of lines of recitation that fall one after the other. . . .
>
> The light release does mount, as it were, the keys of the octaves, forming chords of light as the chanting does increase and resonate; and the echo across the inner sky does create a reverberation for alchemy, for the creation and the uncreation of worlds.[43]

Because of their vibratory nature, decrees and mantras produce results like those from highly beneficial music. When we listen to uplifting music, we are experiencing the science of the spoken Word in another form. Just as music releases the light of the various chakras for the balancing of our four lower bodies, decrees produce light in our spiritual centers, creating comparable results. Our chakras are the means by which the science of the spoken Word resonates into the earth body. God Surya, a cosmic being who is the hierarch of the God Star Sirius, explained that our decrees and mantras are one of the vibratory means by which the discord of rock music and noise are neutralized. Our decrees and mantras are therefore supremely important in maintaining harmony on the earth.

Aside from their vibratory action, decrees have a poetic rhythm. Elizabeth Prophet explained that the poetry of decrees is always accompanied by a divine melody, the music of the spheres. In fact, she said, at inner levels music accompanies all poetry and the spoken Word. This is because the angelic hosts cause the sacred Word to manifest simultaneously as both music and poetry. At times, decrees even resound like melodious tones. This most often occurs when they are given at a quick pace. After continuously reciting a decree, the person decreeing reaches a point where he transcends the individual words, and the decree or mantra begins to naturally accelerate. The words then blend into a continuous tone and the effect is one of harmonious sound.

This is especially true with the violet flame, which is also called the violet singing flame. When the violet flame passes through one's molecules and cells, it gives them a spin and they accelerate. They come into the rhythm of the Great Central Sun, the soul's Source, and begin to "sing" like the humming of the tone of a cosmos. In analogy, Elohim Arcturus and Victoria said that our chakras should "be the seven openings for the flame of violet fire to pass through" as we allow ourselves to become the musical instrument of Lord Krishna, Krishna's flute.[44] Mrs. Prophet explained that when the darkness in one's being is consumed by the violet flame, the perfect pitch of the person's individual keynote is released.

---

43 Justinius, *Keepers of the Flame Lesson 32* (Corwin Springs, Mont.: The Summit Lighthouse, 1999), p. 55.

44 *Pearls of Wisdom,* vol. 36, no. 30.

SPOKEN WORD PRACTICE: MANTRAS AND SONGS

Mantras and songs powerfully enhance the vibratory action of sound. The more devotionally they are given, the greater the power, since devotion always engages the heart. Try giving the mantra and song below several times to maximize the benefits.

www.SummitLighthouse.org/SA3-17

Mantra to Sarasvati

Sarasvati

To achieve harmony with the spoken Word, chant the mantra to Sarasvati. Sarasvati, the divine complement of Brahma in Hinduism, is associated with speech, poetry, music and culture. She is known as the Goddess of Learning and the Patroness of the Arts and Music. She is called the Flowing One, the source of creation by the Word.

Her sacred "seed syllable," or bija, is Aim (pronounced *Ah-eem*). A bija mantra encapsulates the essence of a cosmic being, a principle or a chakra. Sarasvati's mantra is *Om Aim Sarasvatye Namaha.*

OM AIM SARASVATYE NAMAHA

(Om Ah-eem Sah-rah-swaht-yay Nah-mah-hah)

Song to Mother Mary

The Hail Mary prayer, which was dictated by Mother Mary to Elizabeth Clare Prophet for the Aquarian age, can be spoken or sung. Giving it with deep devotion gently raises up the Mother light from the base-of-the-spine chakra to the crown. Sing it as often as you like when walking from here to there or whenever you want to be enfolded in Mother Mary's healing Presence.

Mother Mary

www.SummitLighthouse.org/SA3-18

Hail, Mary, full of grace.
The Lord is with thee.
Blessed art thou among women
And blessed is the fruit of thy womb, Jesus.

Holy Mary, Mother of God,
Pray for us, sons and daughters of God,
Now and at the hour of our victory
Over sin, disease and death.

For more music to attune your heart and soul, use the selections on the following charts. May you and your household be blessed with the sounds of this holy music.

MUSIC ON THE SEVEN RAYS

1st Ray, Throat — Brass

SIR EDWARD ELGAR: "Pomp and Circumstance," Military March, op. 39, no. 1 in D

JOHN PHILIP SOUSA: Marches

2nd Ray, Crown — Strings

GIACOMO PUCCINI: "Un Bel Di" ("One Fine Day") from *Madama Butterfly*

3rd Ray, Heart — Harp

FRANZ LEHÁR: "Thine Is My Heart Alone"

4th Ray, Base of the Spine — Drum

CHARLES-FRANÇOIS GOUNOD: "Apotheosis" from *Faust*

GUISEPPE VERDI: "Triumphal March" from *Aïda*

5th Ray, Third Eye — Piano

SERGEI RACHMANINOFF: Concerto no. 2 in C Minor

6th Ray, Solar Plexus — Organ

SIGMUND ROMBERG: "One Alone" from *The Desert Song*

7th Ray, Seat of the Soul — Woodwinds

JOHANN STRAUSS, JR.: "On the Beautiful Blue Danube"

FAVORITE MUSICAL SELECTIONS

ADOLPHE ADAM: "O Holy Night"

JOHANN S. BACH

- "Sheep May Safely Graze"
- "Jesu, Joy of Man's Desiring"
- "Sleepers Awake!"
- Magnificat in D Major
- Toccata and Fugue in D Minor
- Passacaglia and Fugue in C Minor
- Air from Suite no. 3 in D
- Mass in B Minor

BACH-GOUNOD: "Ave Maria"

LUDWIG VAN BEETHOVEN

- Symphonies nos. 1–9
- Piano Concerto no. 5 ("Emperor")

JOHANNES BRAHMS: "Lullaby"

ERNST EICHNER: Andante from Concerto in C Major for Harp and Orchestra

EDWARD ELGAR

- "Pomp and Circumstance," nos. 1 and 4
- Variations on an Original Theme ("Enigma"), op. 36, no. 9

STEPHEN FOSTER: "Beautiful Dreamer"

CÉSAR FRANCK

- Symphony in D Minor
- "Panis Angelicus"

GIOVANNI GABRIELI

- A Capella Mass
- Canzonas and Sonatas

CHARLES GOUNOD

- "Soldier's Chorus" from *Faust*
- St. Cecilia Mass

EDVARD GRIEG

- "In the Hall of the Mountain King" and "Morning Mood" from *Peer Gynt,* Suite no. 1, op. 46
- Concerto no. 1 in A Minor
- "The Last Spring" from *Two Elegiac Melodies*

GEORGE F. HANDEL

- Messiah
- "Largo" from *Xerxes*
- "Thanks Be to Thee"
- "See, the Conquering Hero Comes!" from *Judas Maccabaeus*

FRANZ LEHÁR: "Thine Is My Heart Alone" from *Land of Smiles*

FRANZ LISZT

- Liebestraum no. 1
- "Resurrected," "Easter Hymn," and "March of the Three Kings" from *Christus*
- Concert Etude no. 2 in F Minor
- "Benediction of God in Solitude"

EDWARD MACDOWELL: "To a Wild Rose"

GUSTAV MAHLER: Symphony no. 2 ("Resurrection Symphony")

ALBERT MALOTTE: "The Lord's Prayer"

PIETRO MASCAGNI: Intermezzo from *Cavalleria Rusticana*

JULES MASSENET: Meditation from *Thaïs*

FELIX MENDELSSOHN

- "Wedding March" from *Midsummer Night's Dream*
- "War March of the Priests"
- "On Wings of Song"

WOLFGANG A. MOZART

- Symphony no. 41 in C, K. 551 ("Jupiter")
- "Die Zauberflöte," Act 1
- "Eine Kleine Nachtmusik," K. 525: I Allegro

JOHANN PACHELBEL: Canon in D Major

GIOVANNI PALESTRINA

- Pope Marcellus Mass
- Missa Brevis

AMILCARE PONCHIELLI: "Dance of the Hours" from *La Gioconda*

GIACOMO PUCCINI

- "O Mio Babbino Caro" from *Gianni Schicchi*
- "Love Duet," "Humming Chorus" and "One Fine Day" from *Madama Butterfly*

SERGEI RACHMANINOFF

- Concerto no. 2 in C Minor
- Rhapsody on a Theme of Paganini, 18th variation
- Vocalise, op. 34, no. 14

NIKOLAI RIMSKY-KORSAKOV

- "Song of India"
- "Procession of the Nobles" from *Mlada*

SIGMUND ROMBERG

- "Golden Days of Youth"
- "One Alone" from *The Desert Song*

CAMILLE SAINT-SAËNS: "The Swan"

FRANZ P. SCHUBERT

- "Ave Maria"
- German Mass

JEAN SIBELIUS

- "Finlandia"
- Karelia Suite, op. 11; III Alla Marcia

BEDRICH SMETANA: "The Moldau" and "Vysehrad" from *Ma' Vlast* (My Fatherland)

JOHANN STRAUSS

- "Emperor Waltz"
- "Vienna Blood"
- "Blue Danube Waltz"
- "Tales from the Vienna Woods"

PETER I. TCHAIKOVSKY

- Piano Concerto no. 1 in B-flat Major
- String Quartet no. 1, op. 11; Andante Cantabile

RALPH VAUGHAN WILLIAMS

- "Lark Ascending"
- "Fantasia on a Theme by Thomas Tallis"
- "Five Variants on Dives and Lazarus"
- "Fantasia on Greensleeves"
- Mass in G Minor

GIUSEPPE F. VERDI: "Celeste Aïda" and "Triumphal March" from *Aïda*

ANTONIO VIVALDI: *The Four Seasons*

RICHARD WAGNER

- Preludes to Acts 1 and 3, and "Bridal Chorus" from *Lohengrin*
- Overture from *Rienzi*
- Prelude from *Die Meistersinger*
- Prelude to Act 1 and "Good Friday Spell" from *Parsifal*
- "Forest Murmurs" from *Siegfried*
- "Dawn and Siegfried's Rhine Journey" from *Götterdämmerung*
- Prelude from *Tristan and Isolde*
- "Magic Fire Music" and "Entry of the Gods into Valhalla" from *Das Rheingold*
- "Evening Star" and Overture from *Tannhäuser*

CHAPTER 5

The Power of Love in Action

The Love of Service

Who hasn't heard the adage, "It is more blessed to give than to receive"?[1] This simple statement is the foundation of the concept of service, which can be defined as "love in action."[2] As the Ascended Master Djwal Kul said, "Love is something that does not stand still but must be practiced. We can affirm that God is love; then we must turn around and be that love in action by being our brother's keeper."[3] Indeed, the ascended masters teach us that service to life is the practical outcome of a soul's commitment to the spiritual path.

The sixth ray encompasses a number of different aspects that all relate in one way or another to ministration to life. These include service, brotherhood, peace, justice and the energy of the resurrection.

The colors of this ray are purple and gold with flecks of ruby. Purple and gold are the main hues, interspersed with ruby particles that represent the intense love and desire to serve God and man. The chakra associated with the sixth ray is the solar plexus, the place of peace, intended to be a calm reflector of the boundless energies of peace that stream forth from the divine consciousness.

The sixth ray is a most practical, down-to-earth ray because it involves supporting and caring for other people. Good examples of individuals working on this ray are homemakers raising their families, employees in the social services, public servants in government, and lawyers and advocates who champion justice and the rights of the people. It is also the ray of ministers and missionaries who practice and preach the righteousness of God's law.

Until 1956 the chohan of the sixth ray was Jesus the Christ, a sixth-ray master *par exellence.* At that time, when Jesus assumed the higher office of World Teacher with his friend and brother Kuthumi, the chohanship went to Lady Master Nada. As the female chohan among the lords of the seven rays, Nada brings a softness and tenderness to the notion of service that inspires many to want to follow in her footsteps and minister daily to life in need.

1 Acts 20:35.
2 *Pearls of Wisdom,* vol. 32, no. 31.
3 *Pearls of Wisdom,* vol. 41, no. 23.

> *When I walk the earth strewing flowers along the pathways, in the valleys and the mountains. . . , I shall look for, and I shall expect to find, chelas glowing in the meditation of the blue sphere of goodwill, chelas glowing in the action of goodwill. I look for the eyes that sparkle, for hearts abounding in joyousness and love. I look for smiling, upturned faces waiting on the Presence all the day. I look for those who listen with intent to hear the word of goodwill and then run to do that word, to be that will, to prove the law as love in action, in service, and in service, and in service.*[4]
>
> —GAUTAMA BUDDHA

Qualities of the Sixth Ray

The sixth ray is a multifaceted flame with many qualities. Through it we learn how to care for all parts of life. We experience it as a sense of brotherhood when we selflessly give of our time, talents and energies to others. The sixth ray also brings the action of cosmic justice through the righteous judgment of all that is unreal, and it draws the quality of peace into our world as we learn to master our emotions. In addition, the sixth ray contains the remarkable power of resurrection, which can revitalize and heal our four lower bodies.

The way of the sixth ray has been demonstrated in great detail by the Ascended Master Jesus Christ, who embodied in Galilee 2,000 years ago to teach mankind how to love and care for one another. Throughout his ministry Jesus healed the sick, cast out demons from those who were suffering and performed many other miracles by the power of the Holy Spirit. In addition to caring for people's spiritual needs, he was deeply concerned with physical conditions afflicting many, such as disease, hunger and oppression. He preached the divine justice of God's laws and was finally crucified for his beliefs and actions after just three years of ministry. He was the sacrificial wayshower on the path of personal Christhood. Jesus' sixth-ray ministry can be aptly described by the statement: "Greater love hath no man than this, that a man lay down his life for his friends."[5]

Sixth-Ray Mottos

I serve.

I am my brother's keeper.

The servant is not greater than his lord.[6]

Service

A dictionary definition of the word *service* is "contribution to the welfare of others."[7] Nada defined it in a more complete and unique way: "The letters in the word *service* stand for sacred energy, the ray of victory in the consciousness of each energy spiral. Service is God's way of releasing his light from man to man. And as that release is given from hand to hand, from heart to heart, it does impart the sacred antahkarana, the web of life whereby brotherhood becomes a canopy of golden thread woven of love

4 *Pearls of Wisdom,* vol. 18, no. 28.

5 John 15:13.

6 Prophet and Prophet, *Lords of the Seven Rays,* p. 207.

7 *Merriam-Webster's Collegiate Dictionary,* 11th ed., s.v. "service."

and wisdom and power expressed—blessed between hearts serving hearts."[8]

Service to others comes naturally to many people. We serve our family members, support those who are less fortunate and make donations to good causes. Some people allocate a steady portion of their time to helping people, like the local food bank or hospital. Many professions are service-oriented. Employees of nonprofit organizations, firefighters, policemen, social workers and teachers, for example, all accept an often lower paycheck in return for the inner satisfaction of assisting people. Service to life has a payback all its own—it makes the giver feel good. An added benefit is it can also help us balance karma.

Genuine service contains the aspect of selfless giving, of being unattached and nonpossessive toward others. As we become immersed in the process of doing good, we tend to forget ourselves in joyful giving. Over time, we may come to understand it is our Higher Self who does the work through our hearts, heads and hands. Yet, it takes effort and application to truly become service in action. As the Ascended Master Cuzco said, "Love is an exercise, like a piano exercise, beloved. You must do your exercises of love daily. You must practice love, practice giving, practice receiving, practice doing acts of love, practice serving with Nada on the sixth ray."[9]

The unassuming person who quietly ministers to others can be an instrument of profound change. Consider for example, Mahatma Gandhi who devoted his life to reaching a noble goal. Through a lifelong practice of passive resistance to violence and to laws he felt were unjust, he inspired and successfully moved millions to the goal of independence for India. Gandhi was intensely practical while pursuing the highest ideals. He said, "Whenever you are in doubt or when the self becomes too much with you, try the following expedient: Recall the face of the poorest and most helpless man you have ever seen and ask yourself if the step you contemplate is going to be of any use to him."[10]

In the same way, Mother Teresa, founder of the Missionaries of Charity, dedicated her life to helping the sick, blind, disabled, aged and dying in India and later around the world. She also established schools and orphanages for the poor. Seeking no personal recognition, she accepted numerous awards, including the Nobel Peace Prize in 1979, on behalf of the needy. She then used the award money to fund her centers. Her life of ministration was rooted in the profound humility and active practice of divine love. The Catholic Church publicly recognized Mother Teresa's innate sainthood; in 2003, six years after her death, the Church proclaimed her beatification, and she was canonized in 2016.

Mark and Elizabeth Prophet with Mother Teresa, ca. 1970

8 Prophet and Prophet, *Lords of the Seven Rays*, p. 485.

9 *Pearls of Wisdom*, vol. 32, no. 46.

10 Richard Attenborough, comp., *The Words of Gandhi* (New York: Newmarket Press, 2000), p. 15.

> *Make us worthy, Lord, to serve our fellow-men through the world who live and die in poverty and hunger. Give them, through our hands, this day their daily bread, and by our understanding, love, peace and joy.*[11]
>
> —MOTHER TERESA

Jesus Christ is the ultimate example of selfless service because he gave his life to save others. He was the avatar of the Piscean age, bearing the world's karma for 2,000 years. He continues in this service until such time as mankind collectively have learned enough about the laws of karma to be able to transmute their own karmic creations. We can participate in bearing the same cross of our brothers' and sisters' karma by letting go of some of our own self-interests in order to help them. In so doing, we can walk the path Jesus demonstrated.

> *For I was an hungred, and ye gave me meat: I was thirsty, and ye gave me drink: I was a stranger, and ye took me in: Naked, and ye clothed me: I was sick, and ye visited me: I was in prison, and ye came unto me.*
>
> *Then shall the righteous answer him, saying, Lord, when saw we thee an hungred, and fed thee? or thirsty, and gave thee drink? When saw we thee a stranger, and took thee in? or naked, and clothed thee? Or when saw we thee sick, or in prison, and came unto thee?*
>
> *And the King shall answer and say unto them, Verily I say unto you, Inasmuch as ye have done it unto one of the least of these my brethren, ye have done it unto me.*[12]
>
> —JESUS CHRIST

An attitude of service can quickly be negated by selfishness and ego-centeredness. Ego-consciousness is the opposite of God-consciousness. Elizabeth Clare Prophet explained that the ego is a devouring cancer that lies at the root of all sorrow. Enlightened self-interest dictates that we break through this shell and serve others instead of dwelling in our own self-concern because our Higher Self cannot act through us as long as we are centered in the ego.

Brotherhood

Brotherhood, as the fruit of selfless service by many, is another sixth-ray quality. Amaryllis, Goddess of Spring, said, "You will find, in the surrender of the tiny self to the allness of God, a welling up of the feeling of universal brotherhood which is the hum of the universe: *Om mani padme hum!*"[13] When we selflessly give of ourselves, we open the door for God to give us more of his energy.

11 Desmond Doig, *Mother Teresa: Her People and Her Work* (London: Nachiketa Publications, 1976), p. 113.

12 Matthew 25:34–40.

13 *Pearls of Wisdom*, vol. 12, no. 19.

The masters have said the tenets of brotherhood can be clearly demonstrated by following the golden rule and treating others the way we would like to be treated. This approach to life allows each person to develop his inner Christ flame and become one with his inherent divinity.

> The cellular structure of brotherhood is like a DNA chain, each link carrying his flame, doing his part, sharing the beauties of God reflected in his energy pool, enhancing the mission of every other monad.
>
> Thus, brotherhood creates a chain reaction of joy—waves of light rippling through the interconnecting antahkarana of souls wedded to a common purpose and fulfilling that purpose by the geometric law.
>
> Wherever souls are evolving toward oneness, there is brotherhood in action—an instinctive rapport of heart-flames intertwined, braiding energies in a common bond and a common strength, dancing around the maypole of the white-fire core.
>
> Without brotherhood, this golden chain mail of strength born of union cannot be forged. Without brotherhood, sunbeams do not merge. Without brotherhood, there is no contact between souls; hence the cosmic flow is absent. Without brotherhood, love is unexpressed; and without brotherhood, structures that would carry the triune energies of Father, Son and Holy Spirit disintegrate.[14] —*Mark and Elizabeth Prophet*

The antithesis of brotherhood is war, which, aside from battles on the world scene, can show up in the form of the warring in our own souls or between people in general—even among those who profess to strive for the same goals and who yet find fault with one another. It helps to remember that progress is best made by seeking peaceful resolution to all problems in our personal, social and professional relationships. The way to do this, according to the Goddess of Liberty, is to always overlook trivial things in our dealings with others. Just as we ourselves are not perfect, other people also fall short of the mark. We therefore should give to them the same love, grace and mercy that we expect to receive from others. The Goddess of Liberty said that if we do this, the Brotherhood of Light will be able to unite us as never before.

Judgment and Justice

Righteous judgment is a different action of the sixth ray. Divine justice fulfills the law of karma, which can be expressed in everyday language as "what goes around comes around." Cosmic law requires that we repay every erg of energy we have ever expressed in a negative way. The sixth ray involves understanding and upholding this action of cosmic justice. We can do this as we practice thoughts, words and deeds of *righteousness,* meaning "the right use of God's laws."[15] In so doing, we balance the negative karma we have incurred in this and previous lives. We can also exercise righteous

14 Mark L. Prophet and Elizabeth Clare Prophet, *Foundations of the Path* (Corwin Springs, Mont.: Summit University Press, 1999), p. 11.

15 *Pearls of Wisdom,* vol. 29, no. 26.

judgment through the science of the spoken Word, giving decrees and mantras specifically for this purpose.

> *I lead in the way of righteousness, in the midst of the paths of judgment: that I may cause those that love me to inherit substance; and I will fill their treasures.*
>
> —PROVERBS 8:20

Honorable lawyers, attorneys and judges (professions that serve on the sixth ray) uphold this aspect of righteous judgment. Lady Master Nada said that human laws are meant to reflect cosmic law and to provide "justice, equality of opportunity, and an equal standard"[16] for all. But laws and regulations do not always mirror this divine intent and we sometimes encounter situations and circumstances where we can see that justice is not being served. That's where students of the light can move into action. Whenever we see unjust situations and take action to correct them, we are exercising the judgment and justice aspect of the sixth ray.

One way to put this quality into practice is by defending and helping the poor, the helpless or the homeless. By calling to the hosts of heaven and taking appropriate practical steps—such as speaking to those in charge or writing letters to public officials—we can help those at risk of falling between the cracks of a system that may not always have their best interest at heart. When we do this, we receive ample help from our own Holy Christ Self and the ascended masters.

The opposite of divine judgment is unrighteous or false judgment. Poor use of this energy shows up as criticism, condemnation and judgment of others. Arising from the ego and the pride of the lower self, it is actually an action of judgment without mercy. In Judaism, the Kabbalah teaches that judgment must be tempered by mercy and love in order to function properly. In fact, some kabbalists consider judgment that is untempered by mercy to be the root of evil. Without the balance of love, justice becomes destructive. We can understand how this works by noticing what happens when a seeming injustice enters our lives. We do not usually feel loving or merciful toward the source. Instead, our reaction may be somewhat angry or vindictive, which can perpetuate the karmic cycle through its own negativity. In these kinds of situations we should strive to forgive the wrongdoer and the injustice itself. "We receive forgiveness in like measure as we forgive others. This is a universal truth."[17]

Resurrection

The sixth ray has another important aspect: that of the resurrection, sometimes called the "resurrection flame." The resurrection flame is an acceleration of the threefold flame in the heart. When the threefold flame is balanced, the plumes of love, wisdom and power begin to rotate like a pinwheel, throwing off density and negative karma. The colors then begin to converge into the white light in a whirling spiral, causing the pink, blue and yellow plumes to blend as a single flame with a rainbow iridescence. This resurrection "coil" takes on the appearance of beautiful mother-of-pearl, spinning and radiating a milky-colored light with a hint of pink, gold and blue.

16 *Pearls of Wisdom,* vol. 27, no. 34.

17 Elizabeth Clare Prophet, *Forgiveness* (Gardiner, Mont.: Summit University Press, 2012), p. 83.

The flame of resurrection conveys a vibrant energy that has the power to infuse everything with healing and new life, restoring vigor and joy. When called forth through the science of the spoken Word, it can change a person from being spiritually asleep to being alert by awakening the soul to her divine nature. It can gradually open the chakras so that they receive more spiritual energy as well. The main function of the resurrection flame is to propel the soul to become one with the Eternal.

Mark Prophet once compared the effect of the resurrection flame on the soul to a dog's joy after swimming. He said the soul feels like a little puppy dog who goes down into a stream on a real hot day and then swims out a little way and dips his head under water. Then he comes up, jumps outs and shakes himself all over. Mark said the soul feels like that after being bathed with the resurrection flame. It feels like tingling and shaking all over with joy.

The resurrection flame can revitalize the body in the same way it transforms the soul. When we invoke it through decrees and mantras, the flame begins to work inside the physical cells, starting with the cell center and expanding outward until it infuses every part of the body, mind and emotions. Some have found that they feel the effects of aging and disease reverse. Others are freed from limiting concepts about themselves and are filled with the impetus and ability to do the things they have always wanted to do.

Mr. Prophet vividly described how he felt after invoking the resurrection flame. Several things occurred. He was generally physically stronger, and if he was fatigued mentally, his mind came into clearer focus. He noticed he had a sense of well-being and felt more at home in the universe. He also felt a sense of immortality.

By giving resurrection decrees you can call for the light of the resurrection to restore strength in yourself, your community, your nation and the environment. You can also visualize it bringing healing, renewal and rebirth to your four lower bodies and hastening your soul's reunion with the Divine.

The antithesis of this flame is seen in the human ego, which thwarts the resurrection of the true Self. As the point of pride within every individual, the ego stands in the way of the soul's resurrection in Christ. It has been called by many names: the enemy within, the not-self, the unreal self, the shadow self, and the inner adversary. The ascended masters refer to it as the dweller-on-the-threshold because it stands at the threshold of initiation, preventing the soul from taking her tests and moving higher on the spiritual path. Anyone who has not balanced 100 percent of his karma has a dweller-on-the-threshold. The dweller can be consumed by the violet flame and specific decrees to Archangel Michael and other ascended beings to bind this human substance.[18]

18 The decree, "I Cast Out the Dweller-on-the-Threshold," was released for this purpose. It is printed in *Prayers, Meditations and Dynamic Decrees*, p. 241, no. 20.09.

One evening an old Cherokee told his grandson about a battle that goes on inside people. He said: "My son, the battle is between two wolves. One is Evil. It is anger, envy, sorrow, regret, greed, arrogance, self-pity, guilt, resentment, inferiority, lies, false pride, superiority, and ego. The other is Good. It is joy, peace, love, hope, serenity, humility, kindness, benevolence, empathy, generosity, truth, compassion and faith."

The grandson thought about it for a minute and then asked his grandfather, "Which wolf wins?"

The old Cherokee simply replied, "The one you feed."

—*Native American Cherokee Story*

EXERCISE: INVOKE THE LIGHT OF THE RESURRECTION

Jesus Christ demonstrated the ultimate victory over the human ego and human condition when he used the resurrection flame to rise from the dead after being crucified and laid in the tomb. One of the most powerful mantras used by Jesus during his Palestinian mission and during his initiation in the tomb was, "I AM the resurrection and the life."[19] In this affirmation we acknowledge that God within us is the resurrection and the life. This mantra can be used to rejuvenate any area of body, mind or soul. It can also be given for imperfect conditions or situations such as pollution or natural disasters.

The exercises below can bring the benefits of the resurrection flame into your four lower bodies, your organs and the earth. Feel free to do them separately or all together. After doing one or more of them, conclude with the following brief ritual:

- Breathe deeply and relax. Then intone the *Aum.*
- Thank God for the energy and joy you have received.
- Record your experiences in your journal.

Exercise 1: The Four Lower Bodies

- Stand up. Visualize your spine as a thermometer, with the base-of-the-spine chakra as the bulb at the base of the thermometer. See the energy of the base as a radiant mother-of-pearl flame tinged with pink and gold, with an occasional flash of blue at its core.
- Visualize pulling up the energy of the resurrection flame from beneath your feet and then rising up your spine, all the way up to the crown chakra. See the energy radiating out from your spine through your four lower bodies.
- Now stretch your arms upward, alternating them as you reach for the sky and stand on tiptoes.
- While stretching, give the following mantra nine times with all your heart:

19 John 11:25.

I AM the resurrection and the life
of every cell and atom of my four lower bodies
now made manifest! (9x)

Exercise 2: The Organs

- Visualize the resurrection flame saturating a particular organ or area in your body that could benefit from its rejuvenating energy. You may want to use an exact anatomical image to help with your visualization.
- Give the following mantra nine times, inserting the name of the body area in the blank:

I AM the resurrection and the life
of every cell and atom of my ____________
now made manifest! (9x)

Exercise 3: The Earth

- See the resurrection flame as shafts of light radiating out from your heart, enfolding the earth in a spiral of living flame, healing it all the way to its very core.
- Give the following mantra nine times:

I AM the resurrection and the life
of the earth now made manifest! (9x)

Mastering the Solar-Plexus Chakra

The sixth ray is focused in the solar-plexus chakra, or "plexus of the sun," located between the seat-of-the-soul chakra and the heart. Like the sixth ray, its colors are purple and gold with flecks of ruby. It has ten petals and is anchored in the etheric body in the area of the navel. In Hinduism the solar plexus is called the *manipura* chakra.

The solar plexus is the place where we attain control over the emotions. *Emotion*

can be defined as energy in *motion* (e-motion). We can recognize many emotions in ourselves, both positive and negative. Positive examples are love, hope, faith, enthusiasm and loyalty. Some negative emotions are fear, jealousy, hatred, revenge, greed and anger.

We know that negative emotions that are not under our conscious control often cause various forms of problems, distress and disease. For example, people can be so motivated by greed or a desire for escape from daily life that they sink all of their money into gambling or drugs and wreck their lives. Even positive emotions can be destructive if overdone. For instance, it is possible to love someone else so much that we constantly overlook their faults and thereby keep them from learning from their shortcomings, or to believe we can be cured by faith and forego appropriate medical care.

Emotional control can be accomplished through self-discipline in the solar-plexus chakra. When we develop equilibrium in this energy center, we eventually take dominion over our desires.

Assessing Your Solar-Plexus Chakra Mastery

The following exercise can help you assess and determine how to strengthen your solar-plexus chakra. It is based on four key areas that develop and maintain the positive qualities of this ray:

1. Using your emotions to produce peace
2. Striving for balance in realizing your desires
3. Keeping your desires in line with your goals in life
4. Setting aside your own desires when necessary to support and serve others

SELF-ASSESSMENT: YOUR SOLAR-PLEXUS CHAKRA

1. On a scale of 1 to 5, where 1 is "never true of me" and 5 is "always true of me," please rate the following statements based on your current perceptions.

1 Never true of me
2 Rarely true of me
3 Sometimes true of me
4 Often true of me
5 Always true of me

a) I use my emotions to produce peace.	1	2	3	4	5
1. I often catch myself before I get angry and channel my energies in a more positive direction.					
2. I am able to remain peaceful and centered in the midst of turmoil.					
3. If I get angry I act quickly to apologize and/or reestablish the peace.					
4. My emotions do not frequently range over wide extremes.					

b) **I strive for balance in realizing my desires.**	1	2	3	4	5
1. The attention I give to food, drink and exercise is balanced—not too much and not too little.					
2. I can let go of some of my own desires in order to work in partnership with others.					
3. I can be nonattached to my desires—not overly concerned, worried or distraught about their outcomes.					
4. I use moderation when pursuing my desires and passions.					

c) **My desires are in line with my goals in life.**	1	2	3	4	5
1. I know what I need to fulfill my goals in life, and my desires contribute to reaching those goals.					
2. I am satisfied with the life my desires have created for me.					
3. I feel I am in tune with God's desires for my life.					
4. I can distinguish between the desires others have for me and the desires God has for me.					

d) **I set aside my own desires when necessary to support and serve others.**	1	2	3	4	5
1. I am sensitive to and can easily recognize the needs of others.					
2. It gives me joy to respond to other people's needs.					
3. When I realize I've been selfish, I can forgive myself and quickly look for new opportunities to reach out to others.					
4. I am able to set healthy boundaries when it comes to responding to other people's needs. I love to serve but I know when to say no in order to protect my own health and effective functioning.					

2. After completing the assessment, add up your score in each one of the four sections and divide it by the number of statements in that section to get an average.

3. Use the following action plan to formulate a personal strategy that will enhance your performance in every area where your average score was "3" or below.

Solar-Plexus Chakra Action Plan

a) I use my emotions to produce peace.

I resolve to improve in this area by doing the following: ____________________

____

____

____

b) I strive for balance in realizing my desires.
I resolve to improve in this area by doing the following: ______________________
____
____
____

c) My desires are in line with my goals in life.
I resolve to improve in this area by doing the following: ______________________
____
____
____

d) I set aside my own desires when necessary to support and serve others.
I resolve to improve in this area by doing the following: ______________________
____
____
____

4. Put your action plan into practice for three months. Then take the assessment again and note the positive changes in your journal.

Balancing Solar-Plexus Energies

A sense of emotional balance helps us move through life with a minimum of sorrow. Gautama Buddha, who was a shining example of equanimity, taught that every time we desire something and don't get it, we suffer. In his meditations under the Bo tree he concluded that life is suffering and that the root of suffering is desire. In 1988, as an ascended master, he explained what we are up against when it comes to our emotions:

> Blessed ones, there is an emotional rut! You must beware of it! It is the pitfall whereby the soul may fall into the desire body, into the same old trap again and again. Understanding the sine wave of your emotions and your feelings on a cyclic basis day by day according to the cycles of the moon, according to the movements of such as the planet Mars and others, where you have not that Christ-dominion in you, you are subject, as are all of the members of the race of *Homo sapiens*, beloved, to astrology, you are subject to the tides of the sea, to the lunar influences and to the planetary bodies that represent the lower order of evolution.[20]

On the spiritual path, we often seek to clarify these desires. We can recognize in ourselves longings that do not contribute to our progress and consciously replace them with higher, or divine, desires. Examples of these loftier desires include wanting to help others, striving to practice harmlessness towards life and longing for union with the Divine. One way to replace lower desires with higher ones is to take specific action.

20 *Pearls of Wisdom*, vol. 31, no. 84.

For example, if we often observe ourselves wanting to have what belongs to someone else, we can cultivate the habit of helping those who are less fortunate. In this way the unhealthy desire is replaced with a benevolent action. After helping people for a while, we find that the covetous nature lessens and ultimately will disappear.

Lady Master Nada explained how correct desire creates a magnet that can propel us forward to greater self-mastery:

> Right desire magnifies the right answer and the right solution to life's problems. And wrong desire makes the whole world come tumbling down the vortex that goes down, down, down and does not allow the soul to ascend.
>
> Thus the path of right desire will lead to your magnetizing more of the Holy Spirit. And the more of the Holy Spirit you have, the more right desire you have—and so it goes. And you will find that the mastery of the solar plexus will make that center a sun of light.[21]

Sustaining Peace in Our Lives

During times of stress you may have noticed agitation in your solar-plexus chakra. For instance, your stomach may have become upset when you were nervous or anxious, which illustrates a loss of control over solar-plexus energies. Both our conscious and unconscious desires are fulfilled through the solar plexus, so it is wise to gain control over these longings instead of letting them rule us. This chakra is then free to emanate peace, the vibration of the solar plexus when it is in harmony with life.

Through the solar plexus we are destined to realize the Christ consciousness that Jesus demonstrated as the Prince of Peace. The Buddhas are noted for their mastery of the emotions as well. You may notice in looking at pictures and statues of Buddhas in meditation that they often have their hands in their lap or at the place of the solar plexus. This is because the Buddha, or the enlightened one, brings peace.

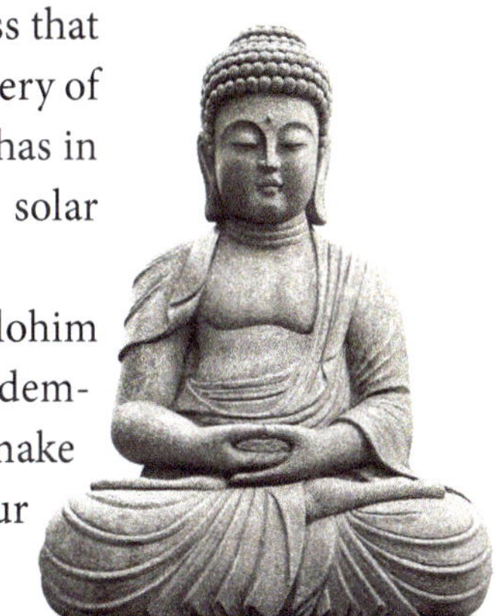

The vibration of peace also carries a guardian action that supports life. Elohim Peace said that the ascended masters can entrust us with more light when we demonstrate the ability to uphold harmony and peace in our lives. If we desire to make progress on the spiritual path it becomes important to maintain serenity in our everyday affairs. The masters can then release more light into our chakras for good. Elohim Peace said:

> I come to tell you that where there is not God-harmony there cannot be God-peace. Thus harmony is the other side of peace and peace the other side of harmony. . . .
>
> When you achieve the balance of harmony, beloved, then you can hold the greatest light. . . . When you find that equilibrium at each level of your being, beloved, and become alchemists of your own temple, you shall see how much more of God you can hold within those vessels of chakras, organs and all the components of being. . . .

21 *Pearls of Wisdom,* vol. 26, no. 51.

> Where there is the warring in the members, where there is the teetering and tottering of the imbalance from day to day between the emotions and the thoughts, where there is not strength and fire raised up. . . , how can we add unto you increments of fire when the fire would only make matters worse?[22]

Tips for Keeping the Peace

Over the years the ascended masters have given us many suggestions to help us sustain a sense of peace. Elohim Peace and his divine complement, Aloha, gave us the following tips. You may find them helpful whenever your inner equilibrium threatens to become upset.

1. **Make the best of things.** When working with others, make the best of each situation. Peace and Aloha said, "We cannot guarantee anywhere perfect people, perfect parents, perfect teachers, perfect administrators, perfect children, perfect classmates. Do not lament another's shortcomings but by the flame of Peace supply the difference! *Give* of your heart and *see* how the blossoms of peace spring forth in the hearts of those who may not be serving you as well as you think they ought to be serving you. Turn around and serve the Christ in them and see how positively they will respond."[23]

2. **Resolve issues day by day.** "Seek daily resolution. Put everything into the violet flame! . . . Each one of you must examine the rightness of your heart daily to be certain that you have not left frayed edges in any relationship, that you have not abruptly parted from someone without resolution, that you have not left any matter hanging, such as a simple disagreement or discourtesy."[24]

3. **Practice humility.** "To receive the power of Peace . . . be humble before your God. Don't be a know-it-all but come to a lawful reverence for those things that ought to be revered. Have a sense of holiness in the presence of one another's Christ Self and a sense of the holiness of the flame that burns in the heart of the one that sits next to you, before you, behind you."[25]

4. **Eliminate chatter.** "Take a vow of silence from senseless chattering, if you will. . . . Let there be fasting from vain and unseemly conversation, for therein you unhinge the four lower bodies and allow yourself to expend precious light that is for the holding of balance and harmony."[26]

5. **Meditate on the Great Sun Disc.** In 1965 the Elohim Peace provided instructions on how to maintain peace using an energy shield called the Great Sun Disc. The Great Sun Disc is a mighty spiritual armor you can place over your solar plexus

---

22 *Pearls of Wisdom,* vol. 34, no. 48.
23 *Pearls of Wisdom,* vol. 32, no. 14.
24 *Pearls of Wisdom,* vol. 36, no. 21.
25 Ibid.
26 *Pearls of Wisdom,* vol. 31, no. 45.

to instantaneously deflect all discord directed at you and keep you centered in the flame of peace. Elohim Peace explained:

> I would like you to learn how to magnify the power of that disc of light so that you are not so vulnerable to the onslaughts of others. . . . When peace has gone, *everything* has gone and there is nothing left. And only when you come to a point where once again, through the power of interior equilibrium, you have found your balance does the power of peace begin to flow and do you start again to build those wondrous castles in the air—castles of hope—that may well materialize into the blessings you seek *because* you have kept the peace.[27]

The meditation below invokes the Great Sun Disc. It can be helpful in sustaining peace in your solar-plexus chakra and for protecting your internal harmony.

MEDITATION: THE GREAT SUN DISC

1. Center in your heart and breathe deeply several times until you feel calm and centered.
2. Chant the bija syllable for the solar plexus nine times:

   HRIM
   (pronounced *Hreem*)

3. Place your left hand over your solar plexus at the navel, and your right hand on top of the left.
4. Visualize over your solar plexus a large round golden shield reflecting the dazzling, blinding light of the sun in all directions.
5. Give the following decree:

   In the name of my mighty I AM Presence, I call to the Elohim of Peace to release into my world the action of the Great Sun Disc to sustain peace in my world.

   O disc of light from heaven's height,
   Descend with all your perfection!
   Make my aura bright with freedom's light
   And the masters' love and protection! (3x or 9x)

6. Intone the *Aum* to seal your meditation.

27 See *Prayers, Meditations and Dynamic Decrees*, pp. 6–7, no. 0.02.

> *For every individual upon earth who is right with God and right with the hierarchy of God whom he has sent, there shall be added ten thousand angels unto the bands of the legions of the sixth ray of the Lord Jesus Christ ministering to the peoples of planet Earth.*
>
> *Think of it and rejoice! . . . Realize, then, beloved, just how great a multiplication factor ten thousand angels can be in advancing the cause of Peace on earth!*[28]
>
> —PEACE AND ALOHA

Increasing the Action of the Sixth Ray

We can enhance the action of the sixth ray in our lives by taking advantage of special opportunities to absorb the cosmic emanations of peace, brotherhood, judgment, resurrection and service. On Thursday, when this ray is amplified on earth, we can more readily assimilate its qualities by meditating on them or giving sixth-ray decrees. We can also wear purple and gold or use these colors in our environment. Kuthumi gave a glowing description of the action of these sacred energies:

> The purple and gold (the sixth ray) are the vestments that imbue man with the desire for cosmic service, emblems symbolical of the priesthood of true believers. The purple speaks of the illumed fire of the soul. This fire must assist every part of life to find reunion with its Source and with the golden law that God has dispensed to men. It is the ministration of the Christ to his disciples, of the servant who is greatest. This twofold action of God's body (purple) and his essence (gold) bathes the earth on Thursday.[29]

The sixth ray also contains flecks of ruby but since ruby is a minor color, it is not usually worn to attract the sixth-ray qualities.

Harmonize with Organ Music

The sixth ray can also be enhanced with organ music, which most effectively stimulates the solar-plexus chakra. The tremendous power of that instrument expands our desiring to be one with God, so playing, meditating upon or singing with uplifting organ music can inspire a longing for oneness with Spirit and motivate people to achieve that goal.

Elizabeth Clare Prophet once asked her students, "What is the perfect instrument that the Ascended Master Kuthumi wants us to be like?" The answer was the organ, the instrument played by Kuthumi in his etheric retreat at Shigatse in Tibet to woo the souls of those who made their transition into higher octaves of light. By playing upon the organ, Kuthumi releases the harmony of healing for all mankind. He wants us to become an organ on which the ascended masters can play, "the perfect instrument through which the Divine One may play those exquisite harmonies of healing light and

28 Peace and Aloha, "The Path of True Love."

29 Prophet and Prophet, *The Science of the Spoken Word,* p. 67.

comforting tone, revealing to all, through a more perfect example, the efficacy of heaven's grace."[30]

Make Use of Crystals

Another way to amplify the energies of the sixth ray is by wearing and using the proper crystals to focus its light. When crystals are treated as sacred objects, they become holy by absorbing our spiritual energy. The gemstones topaz, ruby, alexandrite, and diamond with pearl focus the qualities of the sixth ray.

- Pink and yellow topaz help develop the wisdom of the heart as well as the crown.
- According to Hinduism, the ruby can strengthen the heart and increase blood circulation. It can also enhance courage and lift sadness and sensuality. Be cautious about wearing the ruby, however. Its energy is so strong that when one is not fully centered in the heart, the stone can amplify anti-love emotions like irritation or anger.
- Alexandrite is a rare green gemstone that turns a violet-red color in the presence of natural or artificial light.
- Diamond with pearl increases one's ability to calm the emotions.

Nada, Chohan of the Sixth Ray

Ascended Lady Master Nada

Nada is an ascended lady master with great attainment on both the third and the sixth rays. This chohan teaches us the unfolding of the rose of the heart. She has graciously promised to tutor us in the practice of love as a necessary step on the path of ministration and service, saying: "I AM Nada, servant of God, your friend and sister. Call upon me and I shall increase love in your life, love that will surely give you the victory you desire in the Holy Spirit."[31]

Nada was once a priestess in the Temple of Love on Atlantis where she practiced the healing arts. She was also a lawyer on Atlantis where she defended the poor and oppressed, as she also did in other embodiments. Through her roles in defending the innocent and righteously judging the guilty, she learned that love is always the salvation of a living heart.

As Chohan of the Sixth Ray, Nada helps teachers and healers, psychologists and attorneys, and those who serve in all branches of the human and health services. You will also find her at the sides of business men and women as well as skilled and unskilled workers, farmers and ranchers. She heartily assists defenders of freedom and revolutionaries of love in every field. Nada aids ministers, missionaries and public

30 Jesus and Kuthumi, *Corona Class Lessons* (Livingston, Mont.: Summit University Press, 1986), pp. 10–11.

31 *Pearls of Wisdom*, vol. 38, no. 5.

servants as well—all who are involved in serving the needs of others. "It does not matter what your training and what your position," she says. "It is not in what you do with your hands, it is in what you do with your heart that counts."[32]

Nada is deeply involved in working with families, being concerned that incoming souls receive the necessary spiritual, practical and academic education. She draws a protective circle of love around homes of light where parents set the example of high standards and right action and children are tutored in the laws of disciplined love. She says: "Let us teach our children the reality of love. Let us realize that love, as the intense white fire of God, is that quality which molds and perfects and elevates and disciplines. It is a love that loves so much that it does not fear to chastise, to bring into alignment—but always *by love.*"[33]

Nada and her legions of angels take special care of children and youth who offer their prayers to them. The angelic hosts are waiting to hear their prayers and those of their families so that they may intercede for them whenever possible.

Nada spoke about the burdens of crime and drugs upon our children, remarking that the solution to these problems lies in the establishment of an environment full of love:

> The love that must be instilled, beginning with yourself, is a love so tangible for God in the person of one another, for God in the person of his saints, his angels, the masters, nature, and the simplicity of life itself, that in the presence of such love the abrogation of the laws of God is altogether unthinkable. . . .
>
> I believe that this love instilled within the child must also be a sense of self-worth. For if the child is taught only to love those things outside of himself, he is also taught to have a dependency on something that is at a distance. And therefore, the attention is taken away from the self as an individual, the self as worthy, as accountable, as having ability and integrity.[34]

How Nada Kept the Flame of Life for Her Family

Nada's focus on the family had its roots in ages past. In her final incarnation 2,700 years ago, she was the youngest of a large family of exceptionally gifted children. When Nada was still at a very early age the archeia of the third ray, Charity, appeared to her. Charity taught Nada to expand her threefold flame in order to help quicken the chakras of her brothers and sisters so that they might be inspired to bless people and enrich the culture through their artistic talents. Her brothers and sisters became famous while Nada herself remained anonymous. She tells her story in the book, *Lords of the Seven Rays:*

> As I was embodied in a large family of many brothers and sisters of great talent, I saw how each one in pursuing his career needed love and ministration

32 Prophet and Prophet, *The Masters and Their Retreats,* p. 239.

33 Prophet and Prophet, *Lords of the Seven Rays,* p. 46.

34 *Pearls of Wisdom,* vol. 25, no. 62.

> and the keeping of the flame of the sacred fire in order to be successful.
>
> And thus, although the choice was given to me to pursue my own career, unbeknownst to my brothers and sisters I quietly kept the flame in deep meditation and prayer as well as outer helpfulness. . . .
>
> I can assure you that at the conclusion of my incarnation when I saw the victory of each one of my brothers and sisters, the fullness of my joy was in a heart of love expanded, keeping the flame—keeping the flame and knowing that I was needed, that I was essential to their victory. . . .
>
> It seemed to the world, and perhaps even to my own, that I had not accomplished much. But I took my leave into the higher octaves thoroughly understanding the meaning of the self-mastery of the pink flame. Thus it was from the point of the third ray that I entered into the heart of Christ and saw the application [on the sixth ray] as ministration and service.[35]

In working with the Ascended Lady Master Nada we strive to perfect the heart through the path of service. Some of this work can be done during the hours of sleep while studying in her etheric retreat.

Nada's Etheric Retreat

Nada has an etheric temple of healing over New Bedford, Massachusetts, where some who work in the many medical schools and facilities in New England are trained at inner levels. The Rose Temple, as it is called, is designed after the pattern of a rose with each room being one petal. This retreat is the etheric replica of the Temple of Love on Atlantis where Nada once served as a priestess. In the center of the temple, a healing flame of divine love is tended by brothers and sisters of the third ray for the healing of earth's evolutions by love.

Jesus has a magnificent retreat over Israel and Saudi Arabia that Nada also uses to instruct those who study at the universities of the Spirit.[36] Here one can find a vast library of the wisdom teachings set forth by great religious teachers, including some treatises not published since earth's early golden ages. Like many others, Nada received her training in the retreat directly from the sacred heart of Jesus.

Saudia Arabia and Red Sea

In this retreat Nada gives instruction in emotional self-mastery and in quieting the excessive passions of the desire body. She stresses the path of devotion, or *bhakti yoga,* to help students develop a love-tie to their Holy Christ Selves. Those who study with her also learn a sense of community that comes from caring for each other and for everyone on earth. Nada is always concerned with teaching, disciplining and showing the way of ministration and service to life. It is her daily desire to comfort, love and buoy students up in the power and presence of the aura of the Christ.

35 Prophet and Prophet, *Lords of the Seven Rays,* pp. 205–6.

36 For more information, see chapter 3 in *Meeting the Masters.*

You can work with Nada in Jesus' retreat over Saudi Arabia during the appropriate fourteen-day cycle of the universities of the Spirit.[37] By studying with her in her retreat and asking her to help you solve problems related to the sixth ray, you can become more attuned with her heart and become a better ministering servant to all those in your care.

Keys to Working with Nada

Nada has given us many keys to bringing her presence into our lives, several of which are listed below. Practicing them can help us become more like her and assist us in mastering the sixth ray.

1. **Pray to Nada.** A simple call for help with your family or the people you serve can bring Nada immediately to your side. You can say, "Nada, please help me deal with my daughter's temper tantrums!" To bring the quality of service into your life in a greater way, you might pray: "Beloved Nada, open my heart! Help me to minister to life. Help me to reach out to the homeless, the poor and the children. Increase my heart of love through service. O Nada, teach me the way of selflessness and ministering love, for only then can I be love in action!"

2. **Command peace to enter your world.** Whenever you feel discord, command your four lower bodies to be still and to stop saying, "Give me this. Give me that. I want this. I want that." Direct the peace-commanding presence of your Holy Christ Self to still the elements of your lower self by giving the following mantra three or more times:

   In the name of Jesus Christ,
   Peace, be still! Peace, be still!
   Peace, be still and know that I AM God![38]

3. **Be grateful for gifts both great and small.** Nada remarked that gratitude can prevent selfishness. She explained: "And do you know what I deem to be the greatest flaunting of the law of love, beloved? It is ingratitude itself, ingratitude for the simple things of life as well as for the great things that are beyond man's ability to make happen. Ingratitude, it seems to me, must be the ultimate selfishness—always wanting more yet not appreciating the vibration of love that intensifies in your hearts as I come, or the vibration of Kuan Yin or of the Lord Christ, who will follow."[39]

4. **Screen out harmful images and music.** Impure pictures and sound can block our gifts of spiritual visualization and imagination. They can also hinder the manifestation of the inner patterns of the soul. Nada noted: "You would be surprised how long it takes you to remove the patterns of motion pictures and the

37 Ibid.

38 This mantra is printed in *Prayers, Meditations and Dynamic Decrees,* p. 245, no. 20.11.

39 *Pearls of Wisdom,* vol. 36, no. 25.

amplification of modern so-called music. This is because the heavy emotions and the misqualified energy of the lower chakras projected through modern movies and music affect the emotional body and the soul with an intensity that is severe. And the younger your children are when you allow them to watch violence on TV and in the movies, the more damage that is done—for life."[40]

5. **Make time for stillness.** Sometimes we become burdened by worldly distractions and noise that hinder our spiritual pursuits. It then becomes important to withdraw to a quiet place:

> When there is an agitation of the nervous system and the chakras through the five senses—overpowering noise, overpowering sound of many kinds, a supersaturation of the four lower bodies with the tastes of this world, with its vibrations, with that entering in to the orifices of being of all of the disturbing conditions—then you are not clear to *hear* and see the message of your own Christ Self, whose messenger in reality you are!
>
> Thus you go to the mountains, you go within, you go beyond the stars in meditation to come away from the bombardment of the senses in the physical octave of this world."[41]

6. **Love yourself.** According to Nada, "One must love oneself not only as the handiwork of God but as one's own handiwork. And if you do not love what you see or what you have made of yourself, you know that love is the power to consume all that is unreal." She added, "Personally I like people who get along well with themselves, who are happy with themselves, are self-entertained, can laugh at themselves and their own mistakes and even at their own jokes. I like people who don't take themselves so seriously and thus dive into a spiral of self-condemnation when they make an error on the way."[42]

7. **Give "The Keeper's Daily Prayer."** Just as Nada kept the flame of life for her brothers and sisters in her final embodiment, we can fan the threefold flame on the altar of our own hearts by reciting "The Keeper's Daily Prayer," which she dictated for that purpose. The prayer is nondenominational and unrelated to any human institution or to a particular faith. In giving it, we link up with the network of Keepers of the Flame, members of a worldwide spiritual fraternity sponsored by Saint Germain who have committed to keeping the flame of life.[43]

---

40 Ibid.

41 Nada, "El Morya's Plan for Prayer Vigils for the Nations."

42 Nada, "Message of the Chohan of the Sixth Ray: A Path of Love."

43 For those aspiring to serve with members of the cosmic hierarchy, the Keepers of the Flame Fraternity provides the counterpart here below to the Brotherhood above. Keepers of the Flame pledge their support to the Ascended Master Saint Germain, the hierarch of the Aquarian age, to assist him in the publication and distribution of the teachings of the ascended masters. As Keepers of the Flame give their support to Saint Germain, he in turn releases instruction in cosmic law leading to self-mastery through monthly Keepers of the Flame lessons and spiritual sponsorship at inner levels. For more information, call 1-800-245-5445.

www.SummitLighthouse.org/
SA3-19

THE KEEPER'S DAILY PRAYER

A flame is active—
A flame is vital—
A flame is eternal.

I AM a God flame of radiant love
From the very heart of God
In the Great Central Sun,
Descending from the master of life!
I AM charged now
With beloved Helios and Vesta's
Supreme God consciousness
And solar awareness.

Pilgrim upon earth,
I AM walking daily the way
Of the ascended masters' victory
That leads to my eternal freedom
By the power of the sacred fire
This day and always,
Continually made manifest
In my thoughts, feelings, and immediate awareness,
Transcending and transmuting
All the elements of earth
Within my four lower bodies
And freeing me by the power of the sacred fire
From those misqualified foci of energy within my being.

I AM set free right now from all that binds
By and through the currents of the divine flame
Of the sacred fire itself,
Whose ascending action makes me
God in manifestation,
God in action,
God by direction and
God in consciousness!

I AM an active flame!
I AM a vital flame!
I AM an eternal flame!
I AM an expanding fire spark
From the Great Central Sun

Drawing to me now every ray
Of divine energy which I need
And which can never be requalified by the human
And flooding me with the light
And God-illumination of a thousand suns
To take dominion and rule supreme forever
Everywhere I AM!

Where I AM, there God is also.
Unseparated forever I remain,
Increasing my light
By the smile of his radiance,
The fullness of his love,
The omniscience of his wisdom,
And the power of his life eternal,
Which automatically raises me
On ascension's wings of victory
That shall return me to the heart of God
From whence in truth
I AM come to do God's will
And manifest abundant life to all![44]

Blessed ones, it is my prayer that you shall find in the path of the sixth ray the key to love and to the mystery of love whereby the necessary acceleration of light to win . . . may be yours, not merely by grace or gift but by a certain attainment measure for measure. Thus, in dignity and in the honor of love, in integrity and wisdom walk the path all the way home to your perfect love.

I AM Nada where I stand. I AM always love as the sixth ray in action. . . . I AM with you always as you perfect the true science of love.[45]

—NADA

44 This decree is printed in *Prayers, Meditations and Dynamic Decrees*, p. 24, no. 1.00.
45 *Pearls of Wisdom*, vol. 32, no. 51.

Magda, Twin Flame of Jesus

The Ascended Lady Master Magda is the twin flame of Jesus Christ,[46] serving with him and Mary, his Mother, from the Temple of the Resurrection Flame. Her devotion to the Christ through the centuries, particularly to Jesus, has enabled her to build a great momentum of his healing power. She holds high the flame of hope to all who desire to overcome the temptations of the world.

Magda was embodied as Mary Magdalene, out of whom Jesus cast seven demons. Her victory attests to the fact that all who truly desire to be free are indeed worthy of the great master's love. We may invoke in his name the power of God to expel the unclean spirits that have gained entrée into the temple of our being. Mary Magdalene was also the first of Jesus' disciples to see him in his resurrected body after his crucifixion.

Magda's final embodiment was as the evangelist Aimee Semple McPherson (1890–1944). Aimee's life story shows that she spent her whole life intensely serving God, enthusiastically preaching Jesus' message of healing and salvation worldwide. Thousands flocked to her revival meetings where they were caught up in the rapture of her soaring devotion. In 1919, prior to a sermon in Baltimore, Maryland, Jesus spoke to her about her ministry: "When you lay your hands on them, I will lay my hands on yours. And all the time you are standing there, I will be standing right back of you. And when you speak the Word, I will send the power of the Holy Ghost. You are simply the mouthpiece of the telephone. You are the key on the typewriter. You are only a mouth through which the Holy Ghost can speak."[47]

Aimee was greatly persecuted and stood alone through great challenges, but during her entire ministry she lived in anticipation of the day Jesus would come to receive her as his waiting bride. Although she made her ascension at the conclusion of this lifetime, she still had karma to balance. On November 22, 1990, Jesus announced in a dictation that Magda had finally balanced 100 percent of her karma, over forty-five years after her transition. Beloved Magda later spoke in a dictation about this and

46 For an introduction to the Ascended Master Jesus Christ, see chapter 1 in *Meeting the Masters.*

47 *Pearls of Wisdom,* vol. 28, no. 37.

of her life as Aimee, giving testimony to the advantages of invoking the violet flame. She made the point that it takes much longer to balance one's karma in heaven without having used the violet flame while on earth.[48]

We can call and sing to Magda to help us on our spiritual quest. Since she has lived on earth, she knows of the *via dolorosa,* the sorrowful way. She has walked by our side for many centuries. Now she says that she is just a little bit ahead of us on the path of life. Magda's charity is truly boundless!

Aimee Semple McPherson

48 *Pearls of Wisdom,* vol. 40, no. 36.

Spiraling Upward

Have you ever pledged or vowed to do something for yourself or others? The first day of each new year brings this opportunity through the making of New Year's resolutions. On that day, we can pledge to change our habits or behaviors to increase our quality of life. Our commitments may fade with the passing of time, but if we sustain them we invariably see improvement and find ourselves happier as a result. The ascended masters encourage us to make pledges and vows, and to prepare well for them so we can keep our promises over the course of time.

Making Pledges and Vows

According to the dictionary, a pledge is "a binding promise or agreement to do or forbear."[49] A vow involves a bit more of a commitment; it is "a solemn promise or assertion; *specif*: one by which a person binds himself to an act, service, or condition."[50] The ascended masters speak of pledges and vows in the context of rendering service to the Brotherhood of Light. They are the means by which we can bind ourselves more closely to the masters and to our Holy Christ Self by promising to do good deeds, serve a worthy cause, or give certain decrees or rituals. Sustaining our promises allows the desired results to precipitate through the flow of energy that returns to us from our Higher Self. The vow helps us make good on our promises.

Sometimes people make vows before they are born. Mrs. Prophet tells the story of how she remembered making an inner vow to Saint Germain before coming into her final embodiment. At the age of eighteen she saw his picture in a book and then recalled standing before him and making the vow to take up the torch of freedom and serve him. A few years later, Saint Germain contacted her through the Ascended Master El Morya and saw to it that she was trained as a messenger. The teachings you are reading were released through her as the result of that vow and that training.

On January 1, 1987, Saint Germain spoke about the meaning of the vow:

> A vow, beloved, is the victory of the oneness of the Word. A vow is more than a promise. It is more than a human word or a human contract. A vow is the pledging of one's life and being and soul to a mission or to a cause. . . .

---

49 *Merriam-Webster's Collegiate Dictionary,* 11th ed., s.v. "pledge."

50 Ibid., s.v. "vow."

> Thus, beloved, we come to understand what is the principle of a holy vow. It is a commitment to serve in a holy order as a brother or a sister, to espouse certain virtues such as poverty, chastity, obedience. A vow is an entering into God, and it is God entering into oneself. A vow is a promise that one does not break, for one understands one has made this vow directly to his heart and in so doing has evoked from the heart of God a commensurate measure of support, even privilege, even rank in the spiritual hierarchy of the planet. In order to make a vow, one must have had the maturity of thinking through a lifetime and the meaning thereof and whether or not one is willing to give an entire lifetime to such a cause.[51]

In the same dictation, Saint Germain speaks of breaking the vow. While breaking it is always a risk, it is also true that when one makes a vow, it draws all of a cosmos to itself in order to fulfill it. At the same time it repels all contrary to it. This cosmic action allows us to more readily keep our spiritual commitments. Breaking our vows can also be avoided by being realistic about what we seek to undertake. For instance, it is better to forego a vow if we think it will just be broken. Instead, we can pray for assistance in developing the first-ray qualities that will help us keep it. Then, after being strengthened in resolve and willpower, our pledge will be easier to keep.

If we do take a vow and break it, however, it is not the end of the world. Elizabeth Clare Prophet explained that everyone has a learning period on the spiritual path, and we need to be patient with ourselves. No human being is perfect and we should not condemn ourselves if we make a mistake. Mistakes can be forgiven. We go to the altar and ask for forgiveness, confess our wrongdoing in writing and burn the letter, or confess it in our heart. Then we give calls to the violet flame, Elohim Astrea and Archangel Michael to reestablish our internal harmony. We can also assign ourselves some type of service or penance such as doing good deeds for our family, church or community, which provides the inner sense that we have balanced any burden we placed upon life through making the mistake.

The Bodhisattva Vows of Kuan Yin

Buddhism teaches that every bodhisattva[52]—or Buddha-to-be—makes a vow at the beginning of his career. The vow is taken so the bodhisattva can strengthen his resolve and keep himself from giving up his intended goal. One well-known bodhisattva is Kuan Yin, the Bodhisattva of Compassion. Kuan Yin ascended thousands of years ago and took a bodhisattva vow to serve the planet until all earth's evolutions are free. From her etheric retreat, the Temple of Mercy, over Peking, China, Kuan Yin ministers to the souls of humanity, teaching them to balance their karma and fulfill their divine plan by serving life and applying the violet flame.

---

51 *Pearls of Wisdom,* vol. 30, no. 2.

52 *Bodhisattva* means "a being of bodhi, or enlightenment," who is destined to become a Buddha but has foregone the bliss of nirvana with a vow to save all children of God.

We can follow in Kuan Yin's steps on the bodhisattva path by giving her Ten Vows.[53] Mrs. Prophet said that the Ten Vows of Kuan Yin are a part of our spiritual path. They affirm our desire to be, to do and to transcend the matrix of the lesser self. Kuan Yin's vows express our highest hopes and the best of our striving. They are also for the raising of the sacred fire on the spinal altar. In giving Kuan Yin's vows, we can magnetize her aura and her mighty manifestation around us to hold the balance for those things we are asking her to precipitate in our lives. The exercise below gives us an opportunity to apply one of her vows as an example.

The first vow of Kuan Yin, which involves overcoming the poison of ignorance, is "I desire, I vow, to quickly know the entire dharma." The "dharma" is the body of the Law, your causal body or body of First Cause. So when you give this mantra, you are saying "I desire to know my causal body, my I AM Presence, to walk in the living presence of my Dharmakaya."[54] To know the entire dharma also means to embody the teachings, doing what is required to fulfill our lives through the work of our hearts, heads and hands. One way to do this is to get up fifteen minutes early, read the teachings of the ascended masters, contemplate them and meditate on them throughout the day.

Buddhist teaching emphasizes the importance of renewing one's vows each day. Before doing so, the disciple confesses his transgressions before the Buddhas, repenting of all sins he has ever committed in the past. Mrs. Prophet said if we daily confess our wrongs and renew our vows before we go to sleep, the vow will be like an arrow whereby the soul can go out of the body into higher octaves. You can practice the following exercise before retiring or at any convenient time to help you achieve this goal.

SPOKEN WORD PRACTICE: RECITING A BODHISATTVA VOW

1. Sit upright in a chair, or in a full- or half-lotus position.
2. Center in your heart and breathe deeply until you are calm and serene.
3. Focus on an image of Kuan Yin, establishing a connection to her in your heart.
4. Bow physically or mentally to Kuan Yin's Presence.
5. Give the following prayer to dissolve error, the cause of suffering:

In the name of Kuan Yin, let this vow transmute the cause and core of all suffering, and dissolve all my errors from the recent or distant past: [*state past errors or mistakes you have made* **].**

I am grateful for your intercession, beloved Kuan Yin. I accept this done according to God's will. Amen.

53 The "Ten Vows of Kuan Yin" are printed in the *Book of Hymns and Songs*, p. 670.

54 *Dharmakaya* is the Buddhist term for the I AM Presence and causal body.

6. Give the following vow of Kuan Yin 33 times:

   I desire/I vow to quickly know the entire dharma!

7. Chant the *Aum* to conclude your session.
8. Give thanks to the Goddess of Mercy, Kuan Yin, for her presence in your life.

SPOKEN WORD PRACTICE: DECREE "TO THE SPIRIT OF THE RESURRECTION FLAME"

Another valuable way to assimilate the qualities conveyed by the purple and gold ray is by giving decrees to the resurrection flame. Try giving the short decree below to experience the rejuvenating action it brings.

TO THE SPIRIT OF THE RESURRECTION FLAME

In the name of Almighty God, I call to the angels of initiation that are with me to convey into the world of form the beauty of holiness, the love of God, the power of brotherhood, and the sustainment of the torch of freedom.

O Spirit of the Resurrection flame in these thy children:
O Spirit of the Resurrection, consecrate their lives anew!
O Spirit of the Resurrection, make them many, not few!
O Spirit of the Resurrection, love them free!
O Spirit of the Resurrection, expand, expand in thee!

Peace to the world,
Peace I give.
Peace to the world,
By Peace I live.
Peace to the world—
And Freedom, too,
For the many, and not the few.[55]

55 This decree is printed in *Prayers, Meditations and Dynamic Decrees*, p. 408, no. 60.02A.

CHAPTER 6

Exploring Elemental Life

The Beings of the Four Elements

Have you ever thought you caught a glimpse of a shadowed figure darting out from the bushes or a silvery form moving upon a lake? Have you seen fantastic shapes in the clouds or wondered why the flames in a fire suddenly dart up for no apparent reason? The elementals—or nature spirits—may have been responsible for these unusual experiences. Most people can't see them, but some can. Elementals are the life and breath of planet Earth, delivering the manifold gifts of Mother Nature to all.

> *When I consider thy heavens, the work of thy fingers, the moon and the stars, which thou hast ordained; What is man, that thou art mindful of him? and the son of man, that thou visitest him? For thou hast made him a little lower than the angels, and hast crowned him with glory and honour. Thou madest him to have dominion over the works of thy hands; thou hast put all things under his feet: All sheep and oxen, yea, and the beasts of the field; the fowl of the air, and the fish of the sea, and whatsoever passeth through the paths of the seas.*
>
> —PSALMS 8:3–9

The Elemental Kingdom

What exactly are elementals? In a nutshell, they are spiritual beings who tend the natural processes of the planet. They go about their lives primarily invisible to us, living where the etheric meets the physical in a dimension outside the spectrum of human eyesight.

The earth has four lower bodies just as we do. The body of fire in the planet's core distributes divine energy throughout the globe. The air bears the prana of the Holy Spirit to every part of life. The water nourishes and cleanses all of nature, and the earth body is the physical chalice of Spirit. Earth's bodies are as necessary to life as our own.

What elementals do for earth's lower bodies they also do for ours—cleanse, purify, uplift, balance and maintain the four elements of being. Our etheric body is composed of spiritual fire, our mental body works in the realm of the air, our emotional body is of the water element, and our physical body is composed of earth's substance. The cosmic hierarch of the air element, Aries, said that we can recognize each of these elements in our physical body if we think of it as a sponge. The body is filled with the substance of water and earth; it is charged with the spiritual fire that beats the heart, and it is permeated with holy air. The commingling of these four elements provides the balanced action of life.

> *The tending of the four lower bodies in man is like the tending of planet Earth. The tending of planet Earth, beloved, is just as important. As you know, the earth body consists of spheres within spheres, the four major lower bodies of the planet. The sickness of the planet is reflected in the sickness of the people.*[1]
>
> —THE UNASCENDED MASTER BABAJI

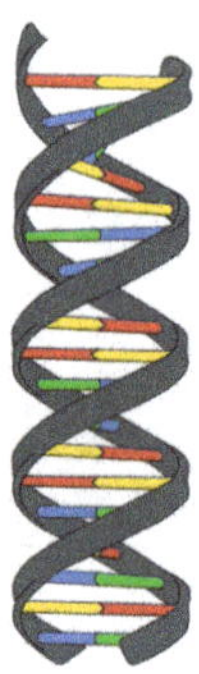

Elementals are integral to all creation because they are charged with building, repairing and maintaining the earth. They begin their service by proving their ability to sustain simple and then more complex patterns in nature. For instance, first a drop of rain, then a blade of grass, a forget-me-not or a rose, then a mighty oak until finally, a great redwood.

Elementals sustain nature by memorizing the very complex DNA formulas that set the pattern for life in plants, animals and human beings. The elementals hold in their consciousness the formulas of nature so they can bring into existence every manifestation of life on the planet.

There are three kingdoms of servants in cosmic hierarchy, each serving as one aspect of the threefold flame. Elemental life falls into the first kingdom of Elohim, which represents the blue plume of power. The Sons and Daughters of God are the second kingdom, representing the wisdom aspect which is reflected in the color yellow. Human beings, ascended masters and cosmic beings are all part of this kingdom. Finally, the third kingdom on the pink flame of divine love consists of the Angelic Evolution which includes all the angels and archangels serving mankind.[2]

The Elohim are the highest beings in this order of hierarchy. They are the builders of form, the Seven Spirits of God who responded when God gave forth the fiat, "Let there be light; and there was light."[3] When God directed the formation of the cosmos in the physical plane, it was the Elohim who brought forth the creation. Under the Elohim serve the directors of the elements who in turn are in charge of the gnomes, sylphs, undines and salamanders—the elemental beings who take care of the four elements of the nature kingdom. The hierarchs of the four elements are pledged to sustain the balance of life on Terra, in nature and in mankind. Their armies of elementals occupy a most important position as they heed each beck and call of God and man.

1 *Pearls of Wisdom,* vol. 47, no. 5.

2 For more information on the three kingdoms, see chapter 1 in *Meeting the Masters.*

3 Genesis 1:3.

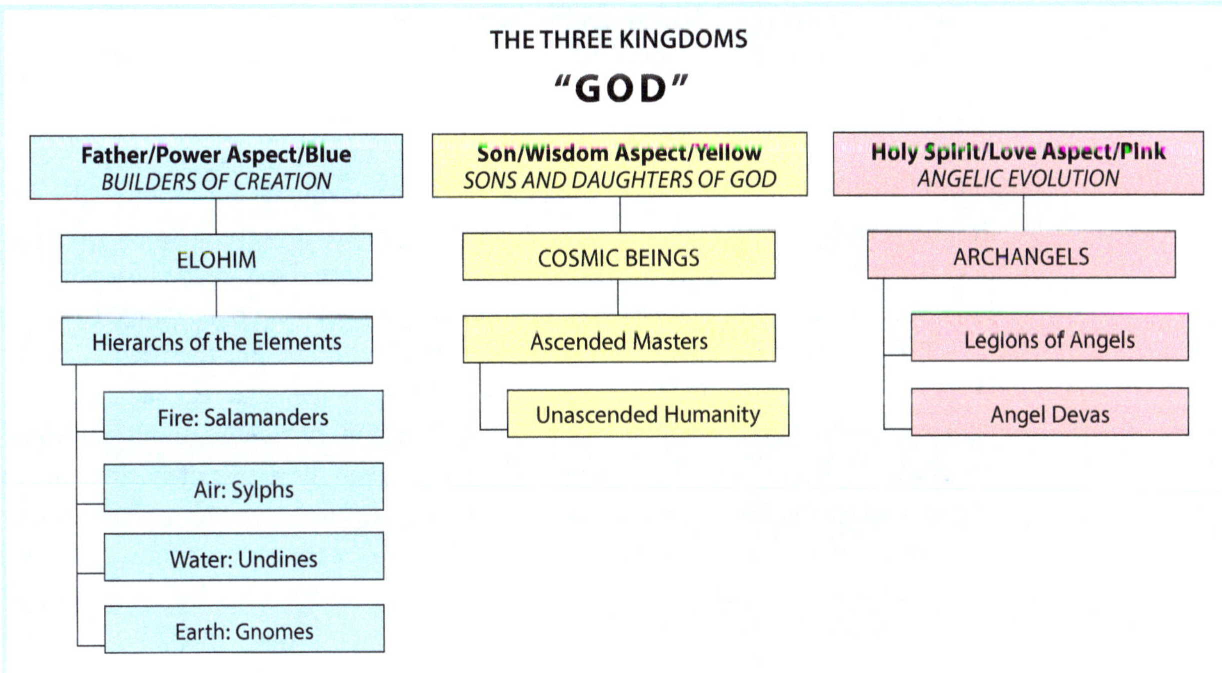

Four Types of Elementals

Nature spirits of the four elements work with the physical and spiritual elements of fire, air, water and earth. Elementals of the fire element are called salamanders. Those involved with the air are the sylphs. Water elementals are called undines, whereas those tending the earth body are known as the gnomes. These mighty beings of light range in size from an inch to the size of a large mountain range.

As in all systems of cosmic hierarchy the elementals serve under mighty spiritual beings, twin flames who direct the cosmic forces of the elements under their command. These hierarchs, their elementals and the corresponding elements are shown in the following chart.

THE ELEMENTS, ELEMENTAL HIERARCHS AND ELEMENTALS

ELEMENT	ELEMENTAL HIERARCHS	ELEMENTALS
Fire	Oromasis and Diana	Salamanders
Air	Aries and Thor	Sylphs
Water	Neptune and Luara	Undines
Earth	Virgo and Pelleur	Gnomes

Oromasis and Diana, Hierarchs of the Fire Element

Oromasis and Diana are the directors of the fire element and are in charge of the salamanders, the elemental beings of fire. Fire is a symbol of the Holy Ghost and the Spirit of God. It is also a symbol of regeneration because fire consumes that which is old and outworn. Yet spiritual fire can burn without consuming. For instance, the biblical book of Daniel tells how three Hebrew children were thrown into a fiery furnace but were not destroyed. And Moses, a past embodiment of the Ascended Master Lord Ling, spoke to an angel in a bush that burned with fire but was not consumed.

Prince Oromasis and Princess Diana, as they are addressed by their retinue, work closely with the etheric, or fire, body of man, assisting to open and regulate the flow of light through the seven chakras. Together with the legions of blue-lightning and white-fire angels in their command, they intensify and quicken the action of spiritual fire in answer to our calls. Using their momentum of the sacred fire, they help purify our four lower bodies and free our physical form from the densities of impure foods, drugs and other harmful substances.

Mark Prophet once saw Oromasis and described him as having a wonderful beauty. He said that Oromasis didn't look a day over twenty-two and that his gorgeous face shone like the sun. He was surrounded by expansive concentric rings of light that gave him a magnificent appearance. Mark said that if Oromasis walked through a room he would consume on the instant any negative quality. Stale odors and energies would be vaporized immediately.

Oromasis and Diana have asked us to invoke the violet flame to bring forth the "rainbow fire"—the fire of the salamanders—to transmute and erase the burdens upon elemental life. The rainbow fire is a spiritual fire that ascends in rainbow colors, passing through the elementals and through our bodies as well as the bodies of those in our care. To take advantage of this dispensation simply give violet-flame decrees and make the following call after the preamble or as a fiat by itself:

In the name of my mighty I AM Presence, I call for the rainbow fire from the heart of beloved Prince Oromasis and Diana to burn out of my four lower bodies and the planet all that is not of the light!

The Fiery Salamanders

The salamanders in the command of Oromasis and Diana are fiery beings whose auras ripple with the rainbow rays of the causal body. Composed of liquid fire that reflects the consciousness of those they serve, their appearance is constantly changing as their chameleon-like nature instantly reflects the prism of the Christ consciousness playing upon their form.

Their job is crucial because in addition to sustaining physical fire, they serve at the atomic level of all organic and inorganic life to infuse the molecules of matter with the spiritual fires of creation. The salamanders imbue the entire world with the energies of Spirit necessary to sustain life on earth. Capable of wielding both the most intense fires of the physical atom and the purifying flame of Spirit, they control the spiritual-material interchange of light within the nucleus of every atom. Whether in electricity, firelight or the flame of a candle, the salamanders are agents for the transfer of the fires of the subtle world for mankind's daily use. Without the spark of life sustained by the salamanders, life and matter begin to decay, corrode and disintegrate.

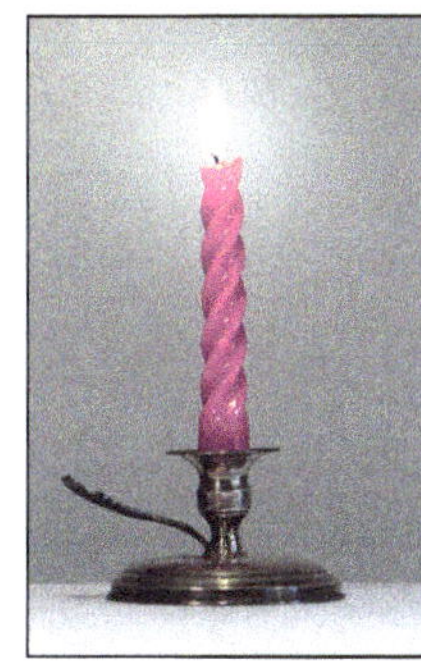

These dazzling beings are actually mirrors of the Great Central Sun Magnet,[4] the blazing sun-fire that is the spiritual center of cosmos. They are mighty instruments at the disposal of every ascended and cosmic being. Powerful in their outreach and service to life, the salamanders carry rods of white lightning as scepters of authority to hold the balance of the fire element in the world of form. They also work with the seraphim of God who are angels of fire.

Light a candle now as you read this book to bring the fiery salamanders into your environment.

Oromasis and Diana have suggested the burning of a candle when giving decrees in order to take advantage of the presence of physical fire. Even a single votive is a magnet of the fiery salamanders, who can use the action of the sacred fire to purify personal and world conditions.

Salamanders are not confined to any dimension since they are of the realm of Spirit. Magnificent fiery salamanders can be fifteen, twenty, thirty and fifty feet high with some one hundred feet tall, focusing the rainbow rays of God in solemn reverence for the flame of life. With the flicker of a flame, they may reduce their size to an inch in height. Beings of tremendous power in the service of those who love the Christ—where they love to be—there is nothing they cannot do to uplift the standards of the race.

4 The Great Central Sun Magnet is a center of flaming love-purity within the Hub (the Great Central Sun). It is the focus of the Holy Spirit of God and the source of energy for the flame of life wherever it manifests.

Aries and Thor, Hierarchs of the Air Element

Aries and Thor oversee the trackless realms of the air. As directors of the air element, they teach mankind the mastery of the mental body as well. They control the activities of illumination that proceed from the mind of Christ such as inspiration, and they guide the in-breathing and out-breathing of respiration as the breath of the Holy Spirit. In essence, they oversee the purification of the air element, the atmosphere and the mental belt of the planet. Aries and Thor described this work:

> Aside from our daily rituals of . . . purifying and washing the atmosphere of a planet and a people and aerating the mind and heart and every cell of life with esters of sunshine carried on the winds, we who so love the light of life that is borne to earth's children molecule by molecule within the air itself are committed to be the bearers of that prana of the Holy Spirit that is the very life breath of the soul.[5]

As an aspect of the air element, the Holy Spirit rides on the physical breath and comes with the wind. So by getting plenty of fresh air and exercise we allow its pure energy to flow through our cells and molecules. Elohim Cyclopea and Virginia said we should take moments in our day to breathe the sacred fire breath, to venture outside and take in the wind, the sun and the elements and blend ourselves with the universal Holy Spirit of God. Doing this reacquaints us with our reason for being. God Tabor gave a similar instruction: "I say walk upon the hillsides and in the forests. Walk in nature and among the flowers, and make nature your dearest friend. For in the blending of the energies of mankind and elemental life there is to be found the key to the golden age."[6]

Below is an exercise to help you experience the benefits of such a healthy approach to life. It contains two parts: walking and sitting. If doing both is not possible, pick just one.

EXERCISE: NATURE BREAK

1. Take a walk outside.
2. Breathe deeply, allow your breathing to become slower and more regular as you walk.
3. Notice the surrounding air. Is it hot or cold, moist or dry? Take note of the air's movement. Is the wind blowing or is it still? Feel the sensation of air on your skin.
4. When you are ready, sit down in a peaceful place, in the sun if possible.

5 *Pearls of Wisdom*, vol. 23, no. 16.

6 *Pearls of Wisdom*, vol. 16, no. 40.

5. Deepen your breathing, allowing your breath to bring you into a state of relaxation or meditation.

6. Count your breaths (1-2-3-4) as you inhale and exhale. Do this for several minutes.

7. Seal this exercise by chanting the *Aum*. Thank the elementals for the bounties of nature they have provided for you.

The Graceful Sylphs

Under Aries and Thor serve the mighty sylphs who control the four winds, the air currents, the atmosphere, the clouds, air pressure and the purification of the air. Since all elementals are essentially mimics, the sylphs create patterns in the clouds based on the designs they perceive in the physical, astral, mental and etheric planes of the earth. When we see images of angels in the clouds, we know they are nigh at hand for the sylphs have seen them and have formed the clouds after their image and likeness. Similarly, the beasts of prey and monsters that loom as dark clouds are actions of the sylphs rendering mankind's discord which agitates elemental life and prevents them from functioning according to the law of harmony. Thus, the signs of the times can be read in the activities of elemental life who faithfully record the mandates of angels and men upon the face of nature.

The sylphs carry the Holy Spirit throughout the air element. As the "great transmitters of the currents of the Holy Spirit from heaven to earth," they are "giant transformers, conductors of the currents of the mind of God unto the mind of man."[7] The sylphs wash and purify the atmosphere and aerate every cell of life.

Aries and Thor said the sylphs possess the power to charge the atmosphere where true worship is being conducted with a greater luminescence of Christ-intelligence. They can charge the holy breath by entering the atmosphere in such places with an intense radiation of light. The worshippers therefore inhale air purer than elsewhere upon the planet. The ionization of the air and all the various functions taking place can produce miracles by proper attunement and understanding in working with the sylphs of the air.

The sylphs can instantly expand from being the size of a thumb to fill a large portion of the sky. They are beings of grace who can move through the atmosphere like ballerinas, lovely without compare. Sylphs are so attractive that many of the more attuned artists of the world have used their faces to illustrate greeting cards and books of fairy stories for young children. Some who have seen them have mistaken them for angels. Mark Prophet described them as being incredibly lovely with pure, beautiful faces and golden hair, able to bend their thin, shapely bodies into different shapes as they glide through the air.

7 *Pearls of Wisdom*, vol. 23, no. 16.

Neptune and Luara, Hierarchs of the Water Element

Neptune and Luara are the hierarchs of the water element on this planet. These mighty beings command the undines, the elementals of the water element. Together they govern the tides of the seas and the waters, precipitation over the landed areas and purification of water wherever it is found, even in the body of man. Neptune and Luara teach mankind the mastery of the emotional body and the water element in the physical and etheric bodies. This includes the balancing of the threefold flame.

Statue of Neptune, Bologna, Italy

Neptune carries a trident as a symbol of the threefold flame and his authority over the action of the Christ consciousness governing the water element. Luara, his divine complement and the feminine representative of the water element, teaches us the mastery of the emotional body and the dominion over the emotional energies of the moon. Kuthumi speaks of their service: "Neptune is the king of the deep, and his consort, Luara, is mother of tides, governing cycles of fertility and the water element as it affects the emotional body (known as the water, feeling or desire body) and the communications of mankind's joy, grief, guilt, anger and love through the astral plane."[8]

The Elegant Undines

The undines live wherever water is found, sometimes appearing in the form of a mermaid. They intensify the purity and flow of God's light in the waters, following the example of Neptune and Luara. As more than two-thirds of the surface of the earth is covered with water, the undines are kept very busy.

The undines are charged with keeping the waters of the earth—the oceans, rivers, lakes and seas—pure for the sustenance of life. All the waters are important, but Neptune and Luara said the seas have special significance in relationship to humanity:

> The seven seas are man's desiring for wholeness in the seven planes of being. They represent the seven colors, tones and vibrations of the seven days of creation. . . . The seas and the bodies of water that dot the earth with jewels of glacial blue, aquamarine and gorgeous sapphire hues actually exist in seven layered planes corresponding to the seven bodies of man.
>
> Elemental beings of light and angel ministrants provide the focus for the interchange of these "seven seas" with the sacred fire of the seven vehicles of man's consciousness. Most people in your octave observe only the physical body of man and therefore they likewise observe only the physical body of the sea.[9]

Human beings can go for about a month without food, but only for a few days without water. Since water is so vital for life on earth, it is important that we pray for

8 The astral plane is the frequency of time and space immediately above physical matter, which is the repository of mankind's thoughts and feelings, conscious and unconscious. Though it was originally intended to reflect pure thoughts and emotions, the astral plane has been polluted by mental and emotional negativity, multiplied many times over by cycles of repetition.

9 Prophet and Prophet, *The Masters and Their Retreats,* p. 244.

the undines and tell them how grateful we are for their magnificent work—and encourage them to keep on keeping on. By making the proper calls and invoking the violet flame for them, we can help restore the health of the oceans as well as unbalanced river and lake ecosystems and reverse the damage of forests caused by acid rain. All of earth's bodies of water can benefit from a call like this:

> **In the name I AM THAT I AM, I call to Saint Germain and your legions of violet-flame angels to transmute all contaminants and debris polluting the waters of planet Earth. Let earth's drinking water be purified and abundantly available for all. Restore Spirit's fire to the oceans and seas and lighten the weight borne by the undines. Protect the precious whales so they can continue to transmit cosmic light and cosmic rays to all life. According to God's will, let it be done. Amen.**

Virgo and Pelleur, Hierarchs of the Earth Element

Virgo and Pelleur, directors of the earth element, are known as the Earth Father and the Earth Mother. Virgo is also sometimes known as Prosperina. These mighty beings teach mankind the mastery of their physical bodies and of the earth element. Ruling from the sun of even pressure in the center of the earth,[10] these cosmic beings direct the rays of their causal body through the earth element. During the first three golden ages the earth was transparent, pure as crystal with rainbow hues. But after the descent of mankind's consciousness into duality, it took on the dense substance of man's consciousness, as did the water and the air.

This karmic density has now reached great proportions which the elemental servants of earth, the gnomes, are working hard to transmute. Virgo and Pelleur explained that "there are billions upon billions of gnomes tending the cycles of earth in the four seasons, purging the planet of poisons and pollutants so dangerous to the physical bodies of man, animal and plant life."[11] Saint Germain said that the amount of violet flame invoked by the evolutions of earth has, unfortunately, not been sufficient to completely transmute the karma the elementals are trying to balance. When individuals do not invoke its light, then Nature must enact the transmutation. Nature's way of transmuting burdens of world karma too hard to bear is cataclysm. Virgo and Pelleur therefore spoke with great concern about the need to invoke more violet flame to prevent earth changes:

> In past ages when the discord, death and disease self-created by mankind have reached proportions greater than that which the elementals could bear, Nature herself has convulsed as it did when elemental life unleashed the fountains of the deep, causing the great deluge that resulted in the sinking of the continent of Atlantis and the flood of Noah. . . .

---

10 The sun of even pressure is the white-fire core of the earth, the forcefield in Spirit and Matter for all energy distribution of the planet; the interaction of Spirit-Matter in the nucleus of the earth.

11 Prophet and Prophet, *The Masters and Their Retreats,* p. 383.

> Unless there is great intensification of the saturation of the earth body with the violet flame…, there will be in this decade major planetary upheavals, changes in weather conditions and earthquakes that result in great loss of life as well as permanent changes in the geographical surface of the earth.[12]

A brief but effective way to transmute more of earth's karma is to recite this violet-flame mantra while visualizing the earth enfolded in violet flame. Giving it many times causes the mantra to accelerate and increases the action.

Earth is a planet of violet fire;
earth is the purity God desires!

The Mighty Gnomes

The gnomes who maintain the earth kingdom are loyal servants of Virgo and Pelleur. Kuthumi said, "the gnomes, although scarce recognized by the average Westerner—yet made known to the Irish as the 'little people,' or as mischievous fairies called leprechauns—do exist and impart to the mineral kingdom a wonderful quality of spiritual radiance which passes through the consciousness of the elemental's own being directly from the sun parents of this system, Helios and Vesta. The gnomes are charged with the responsibility of administering the divine pattern for each rock, precious stone, and element of mineral life."[13] Virgo and Pelleur also described the gnomes and their work:

> The beings you call gnomes, whose image has been dwarfed in the story of *Snow White and the Seven Dwarfs* and other fairy tales, actually range in size from three-inch-high elves playing in the grasses, to the three-foot dwarfs,

12 Ibid.
13 Jesus and Kuthumi, *Corona Class Lessons,* pp. 375–76.

> all the way to the hierarchies of the mountains who attend the Great Hall of the Mountain King and Queen glimpsed by Grieg and portrayed in his musical tribute to the special gnomes of Norway and the Norsemen.
>
> There are giants in the elemental kingdom of the earth. These are powerful beings who wield the fire of atom and molecule and hold the balance for the continents through cataclysm, flood and fire. . . .
>
> The mighty gnomes, gentle and merciful, are the archetype in nature of the ox who treadeth out the corn, the great burdenbearer of mankind's karma. Self-sacrificing, they even deny their own evolutionary fulfillment in order that man, as the highest manifestation of God, might continue to have the opportunity to prove the law of grace and enter into the rite of spring in the true spirit of the resurrection flame.[14]

Courtesy of sculptor Kathleen Wilkins

The gnomes, as well as all other elementals, depend upon humans who have a threefold flame to support them in their work. They need our heartfelt calls in order to effectively consume the karmic dross of the planet. They will also join with us in giving decrees if we invite them. But because they are servants of the sons and daughters of God, they require our patronage. Pelleur explained: "Until the gnomes and the elementals have been endowed with a threefold flame by their Lord and Saviour Jesus Christ, they must make the call under the sponsorship and mantle of your individual Christhood, your individual threefold flame. Therefore, it is as much a benefit to the gnome for you to receive him or her as it is for the gnome to receive you. It is a mutual pact, if you will."[15]

The Body Elemental

A description of elementals would not be complete without acknowledging the elemental that serves our physical form. What is a body elemental? It is the playmate that children often see and that their parents come to accept as part of children's make-believe world. When we first took physical embodiment we were assigned a caretaker, a gardener, so to speak, known as the body elemental—a little being who has been with us and has taken care of our physical form throughout every single embodiment since we began the long trek of evolution.

Unlike other elementals, the body elemental enjoys a continuous existence throughout a person's embodiments. Created simultaneously with the physical body of man, he becomes a part of the evolving soul consciousness as it gains experience in the physical plane. Between the soul's embodiments the body elemental identifies with the etheric body and is prepared with the soul for the next incarnation. Recharged by the Christ Self for the service ahead, this dear friend assumes the form of the sometimes changing polarity—masculine or feminine—of the body the soul will inhabit. When the time comes, the body elemental lowers into physical form the divine pattern and etheric blueprint of the incarnating soul under the direction of the Holy Christ

14 Prophet and Prophet, *The Masters and Their Retreats,* p. 384.

15 Ibid., pp. 384–85.

Self and the I AM Presence. He remains as an unseen bodyguard and personal physician throughout one's life.

The body elemental gains immortality only when the soul earns her ascension. Having no further need for a physical body, the soul no longer requires the services of the body elemental, who is likewise freed from the rounds of re-embodiment. Having increased his mastery through service, the body elemental may be retained by the ascended master as an immortal aid. Ascended twin flames, each possessing such a friend, make a spiritual foursome. The immortal bond between the master and his elemental helper is one without parallel in the human scene.

The source of energy that the body elemental uses to tend the physical body is the individual's own heart flame and the light emanations of the chakras. If these centers—which distribute energy from the heart to the four lower bodies—are clouded with negative energy, the body elemental is slowed down in his efforts to bring about physical perfection. The more light the person anchors in his body temple, the more light the body elemental can use to perfect the physical form.

Innocent and childlike yet masterful and intelligent, the body elemental stands approximately three feet tall and is almost an exact replica of his master. He dresses according to the mold of his master's consciousness, donning the garb most resembling either the individual's current predominant quality or an outstanding trait from a past life. This little elemental is, as are all elementals, a servant of man—and a mimic. He takes on our faults and our ideas. If we are determined to be beautiful and abundant, then the body elemental has this sense and he brings about the perfection of the body. If we feel sickly, if we have concepts of chronic conditions, the body elemental begins to bear the weight of that consciousness and may even begin to stoop over. Some body elementals are hunchbacks because they're so weighted down by people's fears about their bodies.

Often we set our own limitations in regard to our bodies. We decide we must have so many hours of sleep and can eat only certain foods; we can only do a specific type of work or we will catch a cold if we are in a draft. These concepts can become accepted by our subconscious mind and affect us more than we may realize. They may even be carried out by our body elemental who thinks he is obeying our wishes. All of our thoughts and feelings are electronically transferred to our body elemental and he immediately brings them about within our cells. Thus, we often make ourselves ill by first making our body elemental ill. We train this little servant of ours to think negatively and to feel negative. While our fears and doubts can completely paralyze the body elemental, a positive attitude toward life releases him to establish good health, well-being and abundance.

We can help our body elemental help us by giving violet-flame decrees to purify our four lower bodies and cells. We can also give healing decrees. Oromasis and Diana recommended the following call:

By the authority of my I AM Presence and Holy Christ Self I call for the freeing of my body elemental from the desires of the mass consciousness and the indoctrination of the dark ones. Cut free my body elemental to do his/her work in my temple!

The Lives of Nature Spirits

Nature spirits have their own characteristics and ways of life. In many respects they are like man and imitate him, although over the centuries humans have also picked up some of their habits. Mark Prophet could see elementals and knew of their role in the nature kingdom. He was especially interested to see the pirouettes and various acrobatic maneuvers of the fairies. He said they reminded him of the finest ballet dancers such as Pavlova and Nureyev. Mark was also delighted to learn that mankind, through some form of spiritual alchemy, has picked up many of these most gracious and graceful movements of the elementals. We find some of them reflected in the "Water Music" of Handel and in the musical scores of various composers such as Grieg's "Hall of the Mountain King."

As beautiful as they are, the lifespan of these servants of nature is finite. Many elementals live hundreds and thousands of years while others have lifetimes of shorter duration. Mr. Prophet said that the elementals are not old until they are around nine hundred years of age. They sometimes have white beards, as depicted in Walt Disney's *Snow White and the Seven Dwarfs.*

Elementals are not immortal because they were created like all growing things, such as the roses and the falling leaves. Unlike plants, however, elementals have consciousness, and when they finally do die they cease to exist. Elementals marry and have children while on earth. Their existence continues only through their offspring, and they continue to have young ones up to a certain age. Within their families they have strong ties and make realistic commitments. Since death is permanent among elementals, they wail and cry when a loved one passes. The original sorrow at funerals by mankind was more or less borrowed from these lamentations of the elementals. Man developed the consciousness of weeping, crying and lamenting at funerals because the elementals did so.

Because their lifespan is limited, elementals can become immortal only by crossing into one of the other two kingdoms. They can go into the human kingdom and ascend or jump from the human to the angelic kingdom and rise through the angelic hierarchy. They can even become an archangel. Archangel Michael did this. At one time he was an elemental charged with keeping the responsibilities of life in a simple field. But he bridged the gap, passed through the human kingdom and then graduated to the angelic kingdom. He attained greater and greater mastery there and finally became an archangel.

Sometimes we meet people who are embodied elementals. There is usually a very distinct appearance about these individuals. For example, we may notice in them a similarity to the elementals in their faces and features, bone structure or body shape.

More frequently, elementals evolve through the animal kingdom, accelerating in their service to man through highly intelligent species such as elephants, whales, porpoises, dogs, horses, etc. Of course, elementals also evolve within their own kingdom. After passing many tests of endurance, an elemental and his feminine complement might evolve upward in the scheme of cosmic hierarchy to become the overseers of an entire regiment or possibly the directors of all of the elementals serving under one element. They can even advance upward through the ranks to become an Elohim.

Working with the Elementals

Elemental life salutes the divinity of our I AM Presence and Christ Self, looking for leadership and for example. Oromasis and Diana said that as we give ourselves in the service of nature, all of nature will come and serve us. Wherever we go and wherever we walk thousands of elementals will follow after us, singing and anchoring the light of the violet flame to make our burdens light. The elementals will go before us and give life a sense of joy, compassion and the bliss of divine experience.

Elizabeth Clare Prophet gave some excellent instruction about working with the nature spirits. She said it is our duty to command the elementals. When you begin teaching them, you can call to any of the elementals—the undines, sylphs, fiery salamanders or gnomes—and tell them just what you expect them to do on a given day. They are devoted and loving and are just waiting for you to give them their orders. As eager pupils, they will carry out your directives. It is also helpful to call to the hierarchs of the elementals who can direct them for the greatest possible benefit.

The elementals simply await your word for the clearing of the waters of the earth and for taking charge of all nuclear energies being used on the planet and everything destructively used by man against man. The fiery salamanders and all of the beings of the elements can be sent on a mission of light to clear the cities, to rescue all lightbearers and those on earth who are persecuted for their love of God. You can send forth elementals to gather around souls of light and draw them into the teachings of the ascended masters. You can also ask them to do the following:

- Restore balance to the ecosystem, clean up pollution and bring the right weather.
- Heal yourself and others. (All elemental life knows how to heal.)
- Stop or mitigate war. (The sylphs can protect all forces of the air and, together with the fiery salamanders, can stay the destructive forces of modern technology such as laser beams and nuclear weapons.)
- Help children behave and do well in school.
- Help you do your job, housework or other tasks.

- Create joy in your environment.
- Help you remember or find things you forgot.

Your imagination is the only limit to asking elementals for assistance. One longtime student of the ascended masters calls on them to help her move large items:

> I often find myself moving things that are too big or heavy to carry. So I always ask the elementals to help. Once, though, they nearly toppled a mattress I was moving by too much pushing. Then I learned that I should call to their hierarchs first, because the elementals do need supervision. That worked much better! The job always gets done perfectly now. The elementals are also very helpful for fastening jewelry and working with tiny objects. I recommend them to everyone!

Mrs. Prophet said that if you start calling on the elementals you can develop a loyal following all over the planet. Millions will come in your service and will report back that they have accomplished what you have asked. When you deal with elementals, they come trooping like armies in vast numbers, she said. So what you instruct them to do is immediately duplicated in millions of them. And you can see the immediate effect in the skies, in vegetation and in climactic conditions.

Not only can we command the elementals at large, we each have our own little troop just waiting for our instruction. On July 8, 1990, Diana announced:

> I have brought with me today representatives of the four kingdoms. To each one of you is given a troop of elementals, some from each of the kingdoms. They will stay with you and obey your command that is heart-centered in the diamond heart of Mary and Morya. And they will remain as long as you tend them and nurture them, include them in your calls and give them assignments only in keeping with the will of God—so long as you do not abuse them but invoke them for many, many purposes in your life, not excluding the healing of the four lower bodies or the tending to practical matters.... Thus, they are children. And you may consider that you have adopted a little tribe today numbering twelve.[16]

Elizabeth Clare Prophet was adept at commanding elemental life, having had many embodiments of momentum in directing nature spirits. She told the story of how, on March 28, 1979, she gave the salamanders, undines, gnomes and sylphs directions to heal and cool the nuclear reactor core meltdown that occurred at the Three Mile Island nuclear power plant near Middletown, Pennsylvania. The tale shows how adept elementals can be.

After receiving their orders, they performed their assignment with absolute perfection, containing the radiation and saving the surrounding environment. When they had completed their mission, they reported back to Mrs. Prophet, giving a blow by

16 *Pearls of Wisdom,* vol. 33, no. 32.

blow account of what they had done. The reports of the successful results didn't come over the news until quite a few hours later. The result of their work was then stated on The Nuclear Regulatory Commission fact sheet for that accident: "Although TMI-2 suffered a severe core meltdown, the most dangerous kind of nuclear power accident, consequences outside the plant were minimal. Unlike the Chernobyl and Fukushima accidents, TMI-2's containment building remained intact and held almost all of the accident's radioactive material."[17]

Mark Prophet also had a number of personal experiences with commanding elementals, like this one when a storm was averted by the science of the spoken Word:

> I remember driving an automobile near the city of Chicago, Illinois. And as we arrived in the vicinity of Chicago, the entire area was black with storm clouds. It was an absolute scene of terror, because in these storm clouds were cyclones and tornadoes. So when we perceived the ominous and threatening danger to the city, our entire group in the car immediately went into action contacting the sylphs of the air.
>
> Prior to our beginning, the storms and the winds began to howl. They howled something terrible, and they sobbed as a child would sob—you could hear it in the wind. We gave our decrees and we sang to the elementals and we called for the dissolving of the storm, and it was all done exactly as we called it forth. The storm clouds disappeared, and the city was saved from terrible destruction by calls to the elementals.[18]

Mrs. Prophet said the science of commanding elemental life, like everything else, takes practice. You must give a certain portion of your time—even ten minutes a day—to working with them. It's like feeding the birds; they get to know you're going to be there every day and they come back wanting to be fed. She also said you have to give elemental life the love of your heart, and they have to trust you. They see through you just like children see through you. They know your ulterior motives and whether they are manipulative or pure.

Elementals can be tremendously helpful in so many ways. Just as when using the science of the spoken Word for any purpose, however, one should observe the following protocol to avoid making negative karma when commanding them to perform certain tasks:

1. Give your calls in the name of your I AM Presence and Holy Christ Self.
2. Ask the elementals to only do helpful things for you, for others and for the planet.
3. Always ask that your requests be adjusted according to God's will.

---

17 U.S. Nuclear Regulatory Commission. 2013. "Backgrounder on the Three Mile Island Accident." http://www.nrc.gov/reading-rm/doc-collections/fact-sheets/3mile-isle.html.

18 Prophet and Prophet, *The Masters and their Retreats*, pp. 84–85.

Elemental Immortality

For many years, the cosmic hierarchy has wanted to convey elemental immortality upon the elemental kingdom, but it hasn't yet been done. Mark Prophet said the plan to bestow immortality upon elementals is a type of pact between the elementals and the angels because some of the angels were once elementals. Prayer is one way to help grant them this freedom. The Ascended Master Fun Wey said we must make calls every day to strip them from the fear and doubt they have carried for centuries. Our prayers can hasten the day of their freedom and help them shed the overlay of human creation that burdens them, which they are most willing to do.

Ultimately, the freedom of elementals depends upon humanity. Elementals hold out hope of immortality through mankind who have a threefold flame and who they serve and look to for guidance, training and assistance. Lord Maitreya explained this dependency:

> Elementals also receive the initiation of the Cosmic Christ. But the initiation of elemental life can only come to a certain level; and then all of nature, the entire evolution of the nature spirits, must wait upon the coming of the Christ in mankind. For mankind are intended to bear the scepter of the authority of the Christ mind, while elemental builders of form are servants of God and man in nature. The servant is not greater than his lord, and therefore the servant waits for his lord to pass the initiations that will move all of life higher in the spiral of being.[19]

Dispensations for the Elemental Kingdom

All of elemental life has the momentum of the resurrection flame that is in our threefold flame, and they have the awareness of the goal of life, the ascension. As steps toward the goal of immortality, the ascended masters have given several dispensations or grants of light on behalf of the elemental kingdom.

- In his March 29, 1964, dictation, Jesus Christ announced that the elementals "are endowed with my momentum of the flame of resurrection this day, that from this day forward the elementals shall never again have the sense of death." Later, El Morya explained that this gift did not make the elementals immortal, but "the elementals—feeling now a lesser measure of humanity's discordant vibrations—will be able to express more God-happiness, which, it is our hope, will in turn be communicated to mankind."[20]

- On April 6, 1977, Gautama Buddha sent forth the momentum and consciousness of the threefold flame that all elemental life might come before that flame and receive the calling to become sons and daughters of God.

19 *Pearls of Wisdom,* vol. 27, no. 53.

20 Mark L. Prophet and Elizabeth Clare Prophet, *The Path of the Higher Self* (Corwin Springs, Mont.: Summit University Press, 2003), p. 390.

- On that same day, the hierarchs of the fire element, Oromasis and Diana, transferred to elemental life the action of the threefold flame for a period of one minute. This dispensation was given so that they could have a foretaste of the flame of immortal life that will one day be their own in the process of evolution and to give them hope for their immortal reunion with God.
- In a dictation delivered on June 30, 1988, Elohim Heros and Amora promised the elementals that they could earn a threefold flame by assisting the sons and daughters of God. Heros and Amora said: "Those whom you, elementals, therefore serve who do attain the ascension, they shall in turn endow you with a threefold flame.... The hour draws nigh when those to whom you have given so much may turn and give to you what they have long desired to give."[21]

By honoring these dispensations and following the instructions the masters have given, we can help elemental life to maintain balance in the earth, to evolve and to ultimately attain their immortality.

Liberating Imprisoned Elementals

One valuable reason to assist the elementals is that some of them have been imprisoned in forms that are not their original design, such as the bodies of certain animals. Long ago, scientists on Mu and Atlantis began to use the knowledge they had acquired over the forces of nature to imprison life rather than to set God's creation free. In order to control the beings of earth, air, fire, and water, they locked the elementals in etheric patterns using advanced methods of magnetism and mind control. These patterns, which resembled animals, were actually electronic forcefields, which the scientists superimposed upon the elementals for a dual purpose—to limit their expression of the Holy Spirit and to manipulate their energies, thereby directing the functions of nature to their own ends.

Eventually the energies used to sustain these patterns densified around the elementals as physical forms. In this way millions of imprisoned elementals became subject to the laws governing the evolution of animal life.

However, not all animals are imprisoned elementals. Many are part of what is known as group souls and simply evolve with the animal group. Whereas each human being has an individual soul, animals have what is called a group soul, an energy forcefield that focuses their group awareness of life. Each of the species is a unit of evolution within the animal kingdom; the combined awareness of these components makes up the total animal consciousness on the planetary body. It is the group soul that produces the herd instinct—the gregariousness of cattle, the formations of birds in flight or the movements of schools of fish—and the migratory patterns of many of the species.

Elementals that have been evolving for thousands of years through the group soul

21 *Pearls of Wisdom,* vol. 31, no. 60.

of animals have come to identify with their animal bodies and animal consciousness just as our souls have come to identify with our human form and consciousness. The elemental that is tied to the body of a horse, cow, goat, dog or cat thinks that he is that animal. He has lost his awareness of himself both as an elemental and as an elemental inhabiting an animal body. This factor affects his fate. When the animal dies, the elemental remains tied to the matrix of the animal kingdom. He will have to re-embody within that kingdom again until a son or daughter of God makes the call for his liberation and breaks the matrix of the animal form in which he was imprisoned.

The domestic animal who exhibits more than ordinary talent and devotion is no doubt an imprisoned elemental who readily takes his place as a member of the family. These pets are worthy of being called the friends of man. Mrs. Prophet once told a story about one such pet—her dog, Job. She said that he wanted to talk so bad he couldn't stand it. She explained that the only difference between herself and Job was that she had the gift of speech and he did not. Job had to rely on her to talk and to create for him.

Mrs. Prophet and her dog, Job.

How do we go about freeing our animal friends from their limited forms? The primary way is for man to raise his own consciousness to the level of the Christ. Then the elementals will identify with the Christ in man rather than with the human consciousness, which binds the elemental to the group soul of the species.

We can also help liberate them by performing various types of service on their behalf, such as working at an animal shelter. And we can give prayers, calls and decrees for the elementals, especially the violet flame, to cut them free. This can be especially helpful for a beloved pet who you believe is an elemental when it dies. Pray for its liberation as your parting gift.

A Magnificent Mountain Being

Some of mankind's usually unseen helpers are large and towering beings.

Many years ago, my mother and I were driving from Kansas City to Colorado Springs. Western Kansas is pretty flat, you know, and I was so excited to see mountains in the far distance after so many miles of straight, flat driving. In my excitement, I started shouting greetings to the "gods of the mountains." I kept this up for miles, much to my mother's annoyance.

Finally, we got close enough to see Pike's Peak pretty clearly. Suddenly, I saw what looked like a huge being standing up over the peak! I thought I must be hallucinating. But just then, my mother calmly said, "Now you've done it. You've waked him up."[22]

22 Elizabeth Clare Prophet, *Is Mother Nature Mad? How to Work with Nature Spirits to Mitigate Natural Disasters* (Gardiner, Mont.: Summit University Press, 1998), anonymous witness, p. 125.

EXERCISE: ELEMENTAL EXPERIMENT

1. Take a close look at your own pet(s) or those at a local animal shelter.
2. Notice if there are any extraordinary qualities such as talent, intelligence, empathy, obedience, friendliness or ability to perform.
3. Give 5–15 minutes of violet-flame calls daily for one month to cut free the elemental embodied in the animal. Visualize him enfolded in violet flame. A great mantra to give is **"My [*type of pet*] is a [*type of pet*] of violet fire; my [*type of pet*] is the purity God desires!"**

4. After a month, look closely again at the animal to see if there is any difference in behavior or mannerisms. You can even ask how it feels after all that violet flame. You might be surprised at the answer! Take note of any unusual responses or intuitions and write them in your journal.

In addition to being imprisoned in animal forms, elementals can be controlled and manipulated through subtle energy patterns by black magicians. This practice can have tremendously negative results. One example can be seen in the life of the great Buddhist saint Milarepa, who lived in the eleventh and twelfth centuries. Milarepa used black magic to imprison elementals early in his life in order to wreak vengeance on his wicked relatives. During his cousin's wedding feast he brought down the home of his uncle by sorcery, causing the death of all the guests. Then when the villagers tried to avenge this slaughter, he manipulated the elementals to create hailstorms and destroy their crops. This evil command of elemental life incurred great karma, which Milarepa had to undo in the service of his master, Marpa the Translator, when he later became a spiritual student. After studying with Marpa, undoing the threads of manipulation of elemental life and passing many initiations, Milarepa finally reached the supreme goal of enlightenment.

Unfortunately, practitioners of black magic still manipulate energy to control elementals, both at physical and astral levels through hexes and spells. Oromasis and Diana said mankind has, as a result, "come to fear the nature spirits and to attribute to them mischievous and even malevolent designs."[23] The clear prescription for freeing the elementals in such cases is wielding the sword of the Spirit through the science of the spoken Word. Decrees to Archangel Michael and Elohim Astrea, covered in chapter 2, are effective in releasing elementals from hexes. Calls inserted after the preamble of the decrees, such as the following, are especially valuable:

23 Prophet and Prophet, *The Masters and Their Retreats,* p. 257.

In the name of my mighty I AM Presence and Holy Christ Self, I call to the Great Divine Director for the arresting of the spirals of the creation of grotesque forms of animal life and hexes that have imprisoned the fiery elementals, the sylphs, the undines and the gnomes in those forms in which they have been forced to evolve for tens of thousands and hundreds of thousands of years. On their behalf, I call forth the energies of blue lightning to focus the will of God that will cancel out and arrest the spirals of the misuse of the sacred fire.

Freeing Elementals from Earth's Karma

In addition to imprisonment of nature spirits, the increase of mankind's karmic weight upon the earth has resulted in a significant burden for elemental life. The beings of the elements have the power and the know-how to take care of earth, but they need our calls. Otherwise, natural disaster is the only choice they have to throw off excess karmic weight. Hurricanes, tornadoes, fires, floods, mudslides, drought, earthquakes and unseasonable weather are a few examples of the elementals' efforts to rid themselves of humanity's discord.

By intensifying the wind, rain, hail, waves or a fire, elemental beings hold in their hands the fate of thousands of souls. When a flood occurs or a volcano erupts, the elementals are implementing the return of mankind's karma. This happens simply because they themselves either don't have the capacity or they are not allowed by the Lords of Karma to create the balancing action necessary to sustain conditions in the climate and in the elements of earth that create the best environment for the life of the children of God on earth.

Visualization of violet flame to mitigate a hurricane.

Mankind has a tremendous influence on elemental life—for good or for ill. The elementals are very easily influenced, more easily so than a child. For example, wrong thought and feeling poured out in a small town day after day by a husband and a wife fighting could result in a tornado hitting that town.

> *The elementals and their hierarchs have reached their limit. They cannot and will not bear the sins of the world any longer. We call upon you to pray for them, for when they can no longer do their jobs, you can anticipate planetary cataclysm. It is in your best interest, then, to remember the elementals, to walk and talk with them, to call to their four hierarchs and to encourage them, to give them hope and stand by them. Otherwise you will see them giving up one by one. . . .*
>
> *What would happen if all the earth should become a place where the beings of the elements have gone on strike, saying: "We can no longer deal with the mountains of karma and polluted substance that mankind is dumping in the waters, in the earth, in the air!" Is it not true that you rely on the elementals to purify and make available to you the water, the air, the fire, even the fire of the sun that you need?*[24]
>
> —LANELLO

24 *Pearls of Wisdom,* vol. 40, no. 52.

A tornado can be generated by the thoughts and feelings of the people in that town if the elementals pick it up. Mark Prophet explained how the sylphs create this phenomenon by whirling extremely fast in the air to get rid of the discord, sometimes developing winds of a hundred and fifty miles an hour. This is also the force behind the hurricane.

Oromasis and Diana said that without the assistance of elemental life there can be no salvation for earth, so mankind must first give assistance to these beings of light. Although people consider themselves to be independent, all that it requires are a few elementals who fail to hold the balance in the climate and the earth elements, and suddenly there is a drought and the crops fail or there is a fire and homes are destroyed. Giving our energy through decrees to the elementals can solve the questions of weather, climate and pollution.

In a 1977 dictation by Oromasis and Diana, millions and millions of elementals gathered to petition those present to tell others about elemental life and to teach mankind how to call—in the name of Jesus the Christ, in the name of the Christ Self and I AM Presence—to release the energies necessary to help these guardian spirits protect life. Oromasis and Diana said the earth is the responsibility of all its inhabitants even as our body temple is our personal responsibility. The pollution of the earth, as impure substance adding layer upon layer to the earth's crust and the center, has resulted in the same condition existing in the body temple of many human beings—blockage of the flow of light. To correct this situation, the earth must be cleansed by the sacred fire and the fiery salamanders in response to our decrees and invocations.

Earth could be very different if the elementals were not bowed down with pollution and the weight of mankind's karma. Mark Prophet painted this scene for us in a picturesque way:

> If we had followed the divine plan, we would be able to see and be friends with the nature spirits. We would not have to deal with lesser or greater storms. No rain would fall, but dew would appear from the air to water our crops. The air would be saturated with moisture in just the right amounts everywhere on earth. The deserts would bloom as the rose, and there would be no excess moisture and no lack of it. It would be just right for every climate.
>
> You would have the most beautiful weather, and you would have the most beautiful flowers all over the world. You would have plenty of food, and you would find that people would not be killing animals to live. There would be abundant fruit. Many of the fruits that would manifest are not even on the planet now. . . . We would have communion with the elementals, showing them how to step up into a higher manifestation. And we would be receiving our instructions from angels.[25]

The elementals have helped us for so very long. Now it is our turn to help them. We have the violet flame and the power of the Holy Spirit to do it. Celeste, devic angel of the ascended hosts, pleaded for mankind to recognize the tremendous assistance

25 Prophet and Prophet, *The Masters and Their Retreats,* pp. 107–8.

these evolutions give unto humanity. She said the nature spirits need our love and constancy just as much as we need theirs. Celeste also invited us to release our love and gratitude to them as well as to the Elohim and archangels and to join her in calling for the flame of freedom from the heart of Saint Germain to infuse every elemental being on earth with the permanence of victory from the heart of Jesus the Christ. You can do this with the following prayer:

Visualization of violet flame surrounding a gnome.

> **I am calling for the freedom and victory of the fiery elementals, the salamanders; of the elementals of the waters, the undines; of the earth elementals, the gnomes; and of the beings of the air, the sylphs. And I call to beloved Mother Virgo and to beloved Pelleur for their enfolding love to blaze forth now from the heart of the earth and to cut all elemental life free! I accept this now in the name of beloved Saint Germain and in the name of my own mighty God Presence. It is done.**[26]

In addition to giving the calls and prayers listed earlier in this chapter, we can work with the elementals in a number of ways. Below are a few of them.

Tips for Working with Elementals

1. **Verbally thank the elementals for their beautiful creations.** Whenever you see a marvelous flower, river or other natural wonder, admire the elementals' work and give them your thanks.

2. **Give your love to the elementals.** God Tabor once asked: "Have you thought upon the concept of hugging a tree, of pouring forth the love of your heart to a tree and feeling the love return in the immense cycles of the building of the tower unto the skies, the mighty pines of life? How often do you pour forth your love to the birds of the air? And do they come and eat from your hands?"[27] You can give your love to the elementals in any of these ways, or by singing "Love to the Elementals." Children especially like this song. If you prefer, you can recite it instead.

LOVE TO THE ELEMENTALS

We love you, we love you, we love you
Our dear elementals, we do
All beings of air, fire, and water
And beings of earth, we love you.

I AM Presence, free all elementals
The great, the small
I AM Presence, through them
Give protection to all!

www.SummitLighthouse.org/SA3-20

26 Ibid., p. 72.
27 God Tabor, "The Earth Declares the Glory of the Lord."

3. **Teach the elementals to decree and sing with you.** Ask your own little troop of twelve elementals and millions of other nature spirits to gather with you as you invoke the science of the spoken Word, teaching them as you would a child. They are just waiting for your invitation!

4. **Develop a special whistle or a special song to call the elementals.** Oromasis and Diana said elementals behave many times just like the dogs, cats, horses or other animals we can summon. If we teach the elementals a signal we want them to recognize, they will come when we need them, especially during times of distress.

5. **Hang beautiful pictures of nature in your environment.** In 1983 Gautama Buddha said, "The vision of the elementals can affect world conditions. . . . And if you will place upon your walls and in your homes pictures of majestic beauty and of light and scenes of paradise, you will find that elementals will gather to meditate upon these focuses of light and will go forth to out-picture peace and the purification of the elements—of the seas and the earth and the air. And with some cooperation of hearts of light, there will be a cleaning up of the environment and of pollution."[28]

6. **Ask Elohim Cyclopea to give to every elemental the divine image and divine vision of the golden age.** Then they can hold the matrix for perfect form on earth. You can also ask for Mother Earth to be sealed in the emerald matrix, the image of the Christ for each of her four lower bodies, as well as the healing thoughtform.

7. **Guard your thoughts and feelings.** Negative energies create karma the elementals must bear. For example, thorns were caused by mankind's sharp thoughts of hatred and darkness toward one another. So it is best to keep the mind and emotions simple and sweet, like garlands of flowers.

8. **Call to Hercules in times of cataclysm.** Hercules has told us that in many cases, because of his office among the seven Elohim, he is the only representative of the Godhead who can stand between mankind and their returning karma. He said in 1974, "Wherever there is cataclysm, flood or fire or storm or drought, I ask you to call unto me, that I may intercede with the great power that God has given me. . . . Call on the name of Hercules, day and night."[29]

> *Let gratitude flow from human hearts to the eternal God for the wonder of the elementals' bountiful service, without which the fruit of the earth could never come forth and garland the world with that mystic splendor of cosmic dew upon the grass.*[30]
>
> —AMARYLLIS, GODDESS OF SPRING

---

28 *Pearls of Wisdom*, vol. 26, no. 39.
29 Prophet and Prophet, *The Masters and Their Retreats*, p. 127.
30 Ibid., p. 23.

Fun Wey

The Ascended Master Fun Wey serves under Eriel at this master's retreat in Arizona. Eriel rescued Fun Wey when his life was threatened as an infant in a Chinese family. Fun Wey attained his ascension from Eriel's retreat after giving enthusiastic and illumined obedience to the master.

Fun Wey began his evolution as an elemental and mastered certain disciplines. He was then transferred to the human kingdom, where he was given a threefold flame and the opportunity to earn his immortality. Fun Wey described in detail how he earned his threefold flame: As he consecrated himself to delight in God's law, beloved Eriel summoned him to his focus and gave him the training that would enable him to acquire the holy flame of life. Fun Wey then gave great devotion to obedience, chastity and divine love, and Eriel imparted to him the basic precepts of the Law.

The fire of Fun Wey's heart was of such enthusiasm that to do God's will was his greatest privilege and joy. He pursued it during the hours of the day when his fellows were having fun chasing the pleasures of the fields and the grasses. As he built up a reservoir of light and spiritual energy, the Holy Spirit himself bestowed upon him the spark of light. After receiving the threefold flame, Fun Wey realized his identity had become permanent. He then leaped into great joy and praise of God for a period of ninety days as he realized he would never again have to recognize even in his fellow brethren the reality of death.

Fun Wey teaches the "fun way" to the ascension. He says, "The fun way of living is the God way of living. It is the abundant life for which the Christ came into manifestation in ye all." According to him, the delight of God's Presence is the pinnacle of fun in the highest sense: "Precious friends of light, it was because I found the fun way to the ascension that the Father gave me this name, and so I come today to bring to you the knowledge and understanding of the meditations of my heart as I saw truly that the way back home was the way of delight in God's law."[31] Fun Wey experienced that delight long ago serving with his friends—the gnomes of the earth, the fiery salamanders, the sylphs of the air and the undines of the sea. With his elemental cohorts, he felt the carefree love that is the essence of the Holy Spirit.

Statue of a laughing buddha

As an ascended master serving on the third and sixth rays, Fun Wey continues to work with the elemental beings. It is his great desire to see all elemental life receive that

31 Fun Wey, April 23, 1967.

spark of immortality each of us has the great privilege and honor of bearing. Elizabeth Clare Prophet said children love Fun Wey, as do the elementals and angels. To all he radiates the qualities of joy and the desire to serve. One may draw in this radiation through the melody of "In a Country Garden." The best way to meet Fun Wey is to ask Archangel Michael to take you to Eriel's retreat over Arizona while your body sleeps and ask to be introduced to the Ascended Master Fun Wey.

Arizona desert landscape

INTRODUCING...

God Tabor

The Ascended Master God Tabor, the "God of the Mountains," governs the mountain ranges of North and Central America, working closely with the God of Gold. God Tabor is eight feet tall and his fragrance is the essence of pine. His majesty, beauty, intensity of light and perfection are almost terrifying, but he is extremely gentle and shows tremendous motherly love. His limitless power can be released like a flash of lightning to perform an act of necessary service.

Tabor has two retreats in North America's Rocky Mountains through which is released the action of the will of God in North and Central America. This discharge gives a special protective action to the emerging Christ consciousness in the sons of God, the youth and the elemental kingdom. One of Tabor's retreats is located in the Front Range of the Rocky Mountains above Colorado Springs. As a focus of God's will, it forms an arch of blue flame with the Temple of Good Will in Darjeeling, India. This retreat is described as having jeweled walls lined with crystal. It also contains a fountain of light emanating the rainbow action of the sacred fire. Waves of rainbow colors illumine the retreat, which is a perpetual focus of the seven rays of the hierarchy.

Colorado Springs, Colorado landscape

Mark Prophet told a wonderful story about God Tabor. In July 1960, Mark held his first major conference in New York City in the sanctuary of a lovely old mansion. It had a large fireplace containing the faded, dry bough of a pine tree left from Christmas some months before. During the conference El Morya delivered an address through Mark in which he said that God Tabor was with him on the platform and Tabor was prepared to perform a service for the entire earth. At that moment, Lord Tabor commanded every pine tree upon earth to exude an intensified fragrance that would saturate the earth with a purifying action. He charged the pine trees with a special quality of spirituality to penetrate and purify the intellect of mankind. As a result, Tabor said, many would find their intellect expanding tremendously. Mark wondered how this dispensation would manifest physically. After the service, the answer appeared. Suddenly a woman screamed, "It's happening! It's happening!" Lo and behold, in the fireplace the dead pine branch cut the year before was pouring out sap and the odor of pine was filling the room.

God Tabor is one of the masters who works closely with elemental life. He therefore recommends we draw apart into the world's quiet places to commune with the power derived from our eternal Source. He said, "Sometimes it is nice to go into the forests and the mountains throughout the world to see the scenery. As you do this, always remember the four kingdoms of elemental beings and consider what you can and shall do with them and for them."[32] Tabor is especially concerned with the levels of pollution—in the earth and in the bodies of her people—that burden the elementals. He has given us a prescription for the victory of these beloved nature spirits: "The joy of elemental life is to serve you. . . . And your joy must be to serve with them, to command the life-essence of the Christ to flow to the elementals, to infuse them with rejoicing and newness of being and fire and the spirit to bring the earth into a golden age!"[33]

Pine trees and forest land at the Inner Retreat

32 *Pearls of Wisdom,* vol. 41, no. 46.

33 Prophet and Prophet, *The Masters and their Retreats,* p. 82.

Set the Elementals Free

Making calls for the elementals brings them, us and the earth great joy. Plus, it answers the requests of the masters to free these gracious servants from all conditions that keep them from effectively doing their jobs. We can help the elementals in myriad ways through the science of the spoken Word, including giving the short calls described earlier in this chapter. We can also give regular decrees with formal preambles, since the phrase "elemental life—fire, air, water and earth" is included in the preamble to all decrees. When we give these decrees, we are therefore establishing a heart tie with the servants of nature. The elementals then, in response to the impulses of our heart flame, go forth to accomplish what the decrees ask them to do.

In addition, a few special decrees have been dictated specifically for the elementals to foster the process of healing and protection. Experiment by practicing those below.

SPOKEN WORD PRACTICE: "I GO FORTH TO HEAL MILLIONS OF ELEMENTALS IN THE EARTH"

In 1990, Oromasis and Diana dictated a decree to heal the elementals. In their dictation they proposed we be methodical and consciously plan to give this decree five to fifteen minutes a day. You can jump-start this process by giving it now. The title is spoken as the first line of the decree.

IN THE NAME OF MY MIGHTY I AM PRESENCE, I GO FORTH TO HEAL MILLIONS OF ELEMENTALS IN THE EARTH

Beloved mighty I AM Presence, in the name of my Holy Christ Self and by the love, wisdom and power of my threefold flame, I call forth the action of transmutation by the fire of my being, multiplied by the violet flame, multiplied by the fire of the Great Central Sun and the Great Central Sun Magnet. I call forth this action on behalf of all elemental life, including my body elemental and the body elementals of all souls evolving on planet Earth.

I call for that portion of the flame I invoke and all that I AM to go forth now to heal millions upon millions of elementals in the earth! This I decree in the

name of my own Christhood, in the name of my own becoming the ascended master who I shall be and who I am already, for the *seed* is within itself and the *seed* of my mighty I AM Presence is with me in my heart! And therefore I dedicate those percentages allowed me by the Lords of Karma of the fire of my lifestream to the liberation of all elemental life.

This I do in the name of the Father and of the Son and of the Holy Spirit and of the universal Divine Mother. And I accept it done this hour in full power by the blessing of the Lords of Karma, Amen.[34]

Another decree for elemental life is "Set the Elementals Free." It is given in a steady march tempo just like the marches of John Philip Sousa. The rhythm itself contains great power because it has the ability to uplift people's spirits. For example, have you ever gone to a parade feeling down in the dumps, only to experience a sense of revival in the instruments and the beat of the music that makes your tired heart beat like that of a six-year-old? The rejuvenation continues even after you go home because of the beat of the music. If used correctly, its rhythm will expand in positive energy waves all over the planet.

The rhythm present in decrees creates a beat and a step-up that works like a merry-go-round. As this merry-go-round whirls faster and faster, the little "passengers" of human discord—our wayward thoughts and feelings riding on the outer circuit—have to get off. And so at times we let the decree naturally speed up in order to step-up the tempo of our own electrons.

SPOKEN WORD PRACTICE: "SET THE ELEMENTALS FREE"

Mark Prophet instructed us to use a specific visualization while giving this particular decree. He said to imagine a violet egg with one elemental being in it. This single being symbolizes every elemental in the world. Then we see the violet energy of freedom of that flame penetrating the egg, taking from the elemental all feelings of despair. Give each of the endings after reciting the body of the decree or just pick the endings most appealing to you. Then give ending no. 9 once before reciting the closing.

In the body of the decree, you can also say, **"All body elementals, make and keep them free"** where it says **"Every elemental, set and keep them free."** Inserting the body elemental in this decree is a part of healing.

34 This decree is printed in *Prayers, Meditations and Dynamic Decrees,* p. 98, no. 7.07B.

SET THE ELEMENTALS FREE

www.SummitLighthouse.org/SA3-21

In the name and by the power of the beloved mighty victorious Presence of God, I AM in me, my very own beloved Holy Christ Self, Holy Christ Selves of all mankind, beloved Guru Ma and Lanello, the entire Spirit of the Great White Brotherhood and the World Mother, elemental life—fire, air, water, and earth!

I call to the heart of beloved Helios and Vesta, the beloved Maha Chohan, and the flame of cosmic comfort from the Great Central Sun; to beloved Virgo and Pelleur, beloved Aries and Thor, beloved Oromasis and Diana, beloved Neptune and Luara, the seven mighty Elohim, the seven beloved archangels, and the seven beloved chohans of the rays; to beloved Archangel Zadkiel, beloved Saint Germain, beloved mighty Arcturus, and their legions of violet-flame angels to answer this our call infinitely, presently, and forever for the precious elemental beings of earth, air, fire, and water:

Seal, seal, seal in an ovoid bright
Of the violet fire's clear light
Every elemental, set and keep them free
From all human discord instantly.

1. Beloved I AM (3x)
2. By Christ-command (3x)
3. By God's blue ray (3x)
4. By God's violet ray (3x)
5. By God's love ray (3x)
6. By Hercules' might (3x)
7. By Jesus' light (3x)
8. By Michael's sword (3x)
9. It's done today, it's done to stay,
   it's done God's way

And in full faith I consciously accept this manifest, manifest, manifest! (3x) right here and now with full power, eternally sustained, all-powerfully active, ever expanding and world enfolding until all are wholly ascended in the light and free!

Beloved I AM! Beloved I AM! Beloved I AM! [35]

35 This decree is printed in *Prayers, Meditations and Dynamic Decrees*, p. 97, no. 7.07.

CHAPTER 7

The Gift of Divine Freedom

Soul Liberation

The seventh, or violet, ray of divine freedom holds a special place among the seven rainbow rays because during the next 2,000 years—the age of Aquarius—it is being amplified on earth for all souls evolving here. We are in the early stages of this new era and are beginning to feel the winds of Aquarius sweeping away the remnants of the age of Pisces.[1]

Four thousand years ago, the age of Aries brought us the image of God as Father. The age of Pisces gave us the understanding of God as the Son, exemplified by Jesus, the hierarch and sponsor of that age. Aquarius brings us the awareness of God as the Holy Spirit and as the Divine Mother. During this cycle, the opportunity is given to mankind to apply the laws of freedom and justice, the science of precipitation and transmutation, and rituals of invocation to the Creator that can bring in an age of enlightenment and peace such as the world has never known.

The Ascended Master Saint Germain is the hierarch of the Aquarian age. He is also the chohan of the seventh ray who teaches us the path of soul liberation. By following his wisdom and using his gift of the violet flame, we can purify and raise our consciousness to fully embrace this new age of freedom and responsibility.

The seventh ray, a deep violet in color, is the ray of freedom fighters in all walks of life who strive to break the shackles of what holds back the evolution of the soul. Traditionally it is the realm of adepts and alchemists who have learned to transcend the human limitations and change the base elements of the lower self into the brilliant gold of the Christ mind. It also has the qualities of mercy and forgiveness—which have the ultimate power to free the soul.

The chakra associated with this ray is the six-petaled seat-of-the-soul chakra, the soul's native home in the body as well as the platform from which she undertakes the challenging journey to the heart of being.

Qualities of the Seventh Ray

The uplifting energies of the seventh ray are meant to inspire and enfire the soul on her road to ultimate freedom and victory. The underlying question she is destined to answer is, "To be or not to be."[2] The free-will decision to unite with Spirit (or not) is

1 The Aquarian age is the 2,150-year cycle following the age of Pisces, which was marked by the birth of Jesus Christ.

2 Shakespeare, *Hamlet,* act 3, sc. 1, lines 55–87.

hers and hers alone. Saint Germain said, "That choice to be free, beloved, is the mark of the man, the woman and the child of the Aquarian age."[3]

> *Therefore, let the violet flame—the action of Omri-Tas, the action of the seventh ray—saturate planet Earth so that you will not need to enter over and over and over again those levels of consciousness that by this time you should have put behind you.*[4]
>
> —ARCHANGEL URIEL AND AURORA

As the soul earnestly walks the spiritual path, invoking the violet flame of the seventh ray, the soul is gradually cleansed, purified and granted a mercy and forgiveness that can be extended to all life. The violet flame is truly a magnificent key to the alchemical transformation and transcendence of the soul from her earthly state into divine Reality. The following qualities are inherent in the seventh ray, and they can be amplified most especially by the violet flame.

Freedom

Freedom is a foremost quality of the violet ray, also known as the freedom flame. The drive for freedom is familiar to all. It is innate in the child's efforts to learn to walk, talk and do things for himself. It is also strong in the hearts of people to live their lives freely as they choose. The cry for soul freedom is, in fact, paramount today because the Aquarian age is the age of freedom.

Freedom is also inextricably tied to our divine endowment of free will and the very urge of the soul to ascend. The soul needs to be free to re-create herself in the divine image and blueprint she was given at the moment of her birth in cosmos and be free to reach her spiritual goals. Soul freedom is also essential to the cosmic scheme, as Elohim Arcturus and Victoria explained:

> If all of your willing, your wisdom and your love, your purity in the Law and your science and your devotion in religion do not culminate in freedom in the religions of the world and in the governments of the nations, then the planet and the evolution has lost its cosmic purpose. Without cosmic purpose, where, then, is the opportunity for self-mastery? Where is life, where is freedom, where is the soul?[5]

These Elohim of the seventh ray instructed those who sincerely love freedom to "enter the path of initiation . . . and establish freedom within themselves."[6] The following steps explain how this can be done.

1. First, define the enemy within yourself. "See the enemy as sloth, self-indulgence, self-centeredness, pride and ambition and all of the sins that have been clearly outlined by the great avatars of the ages."

2. Second, "summon the forces of light of your own Christ-potential and the energies that God has vested in you, and . . . swiftly put down the enemy of freedom

---

3 *Pearls of Wisdom,* vol. 46, no. 36.
4 *Pearls of Wisdom,* vol. 41, no. 4.
5 *Pearls of Wisdom,* vol. 44, no. 37.
6 Ibid.

and thereby define your wholeness . . . as an individuality and as an identity in God."

3. Next, examine your nation and "define the enemy within. . . . You will see the consequences in government, in education, in the economy, in the law, in the people themselves, and you will begin to invoke the light of the Elohim to conqer that enemy within. And by the power of the spoken Word, you *will* conquer that enemy."

4. Finally, examine the earth and ask, "What is the enemy of world freedom?" Then move forward from that vantage point.

This cosmic perspective helps us focus on what freedom means not only to ourselves but to the entire planet. Moreover, it outlines what is really involved in establishing the golden age of freedom and enlightenment that Aquarius is intended to be.

Justice

Justice is an outstanding quality of the seventh ray as well as of the sixth ray. Portia, the Goddess of Justice and beloved twin flame of Saint Germain, said, "justice is the highest quality in the universe, the balance of all life and the absolutely accurate assessment of right, of wrong. . . . Justice is to speak the word of truth, to have compassion for those who have broken the law and yet to compel them to come up higher and to embrace the path of chelaship, of true divine justice."[7] So this quality involves more than just judgement. Our Father-God, Alpha, explained: "I desire that each and every one of you should realize that God-justice is the power for the righting of all wrong. It is the wisdom for the righting of all wrong. It is the love for the righting of all wrong."[8] True justice therefore depends upon the power, wisdom and love of the threefold flame.

As different as this conception may seem, Portia explained "the key to divine justice is in the realization that all life is one."[9] Her words are a reminder that we are all born of the Spirit with the potential to become one with the Divine. We are God in manifestation in the physical world, and as such we have spiritual authority for the victory, justice and freedom of earth.

Injustice does not originate in God; human beings initiate injustices, so they themselves must stop them. With this in mind, it can be helpful to understand that divine justice is first and foremost "an inner humility whereby outer action for God is emboldened."[10] Such action is the result of acknowledging that God really exists inside of us. With that knowledge, we can live our lives and act "with the true sense of justice and honor and integrity that flow from the fount of our heart's unending love for that God who is where we are."[11]

---

7 *Pearls of Wisdom,* vol. 46, no. 37.
8 *Pearls of Wisdom,* vol. 30, no. 38.
9 *Pearls of Wisdom,* vol. 19, no. 23.
10 *Pearls of Wisdom,* vol. 23, no. 50.
11 Ibid.

This concept empowers us to embrace the golden rule,[12] which the ascended masters have affirmed as the standard of justice. Doing unto others as we would have them do unto us means dealing fairly with one another and the world in business dealings, and giving every part of life the benefit of the doubt, a just sense of co-measurement with the Creator. It means holding the immaculate concept or divine ideal for everyone we meet, always giving more than is required and working harder than our job's compensation demands.

Sometimes it is helpful to examine the concept of "injustice" in order to get a better perspective on the quality of justice. In looking around at people and situations, injustices do seem to exist everywhere. Some people are born with riches or good looks while others have deformities or are impoverished, for instance. One teaching from the masters about such disparities is that injustice, persecution and condemnation may come to those on the path of chelaship as part of their spiritual initiations. The biblical story of Job is a good example. Job was an upright, good servant of God whom Satan wanted to test. He wanted Job to curse the name of God in the midst of a great tribulation. All sorts of terrible things came upon Job but he refused to curse the Almighty. In the end, everything Job had lost was restored to him many times over.

Gautama Buddha offered another explanation—that justice and injustice rely upon an energy equation: "Every act of misqualified energy is an act of injustice; every right qualification of energy is an act of God-justice."[13] In this sense, the laws of karma and reincarnation make sense out of seeming disparities. Through freewill choices, we have used the light of the universe from the time of our first embodiment to create the current circumstances of our lives. Situations in the present reflect past actions coming full circle through the cycles of karma and reincarnation to balance the negative energies and amplify the good deeds we have sown.

Padma Sambhava taught how understanding these laws of karma enables one to truly be at peace in any circumstance and say, "I know not what is the karma of the players in this drama. I know only that God is just and that there is no injustice anywhere in the universe. And yet justice is meted out in justice's time."[14] This is the resolution to which each person on the spiritual path must come. When questioning something beyond our control that seems unjust, we simply have to be at peace and remember the teaching: "Vengeance is mine; I will repay, saith the Lord."[15] We can also find comfort in the masters' explanation that sometimes justice is meted out only through the violet flame as mercy's resolution. In fact, the world's victims of injustice may have no recourse other than the violet flame they invoke or that others call forth on their behalf.

---

12 See Matthew 7:12, "Therefore all things whatsoever ye would that men should do to you, do ye even so to them."

13 *Pearls of Wisdom,* vol. 26, no. 39.

14 *Pearls of Wisdom,* vol. 38, no. 36.

15 Romans 12:19.

Although we know justice comes in her own time, whenever we observe something we feel is unjust we can give the following prayer from Portia. It is adjusted to the divine will, so if our observation is incorrect, the call will only extend grace into the situation.

Beloved I AM Presence, beloved Lords of Karma, I desire this day, by the authority of the Christ within me, to register a complaint, to call to the attention of the hosts of heaven this injustice which I have witnessed and I have perceived. [*Here describe the injustice and name the persons, indicating the time and place of the event.*]

And in the name of Almighty God, I withdraw all of God's energy from that injustice and I command that that spiral of injustice be arrested now.

I ask the Lords of Karma to diligently consider the righting of all wrong, the balancing of God-justice in the lives of all individuals concerned; and I ask my call to be adjusted according to the will of God and that it be implemented according to that will.[16]

> *It is always best when engaging in justice to have the companion of justice, which is compassion. Compassion, beloved, may go only as low as the level of the heart. Where justice becomes injustice is where acts and states of consciousness fall below the level of the heart.*[17]
>
> —ASCENDED LADY MASTER PORTIA

Mercy

Kuan Yin

Mercy has been defined as "compassion or forbearance shown especially to an offender or to one subject to one's power; a blessing that is an act of divine favor or compassion."[18] It is a seventh-ray quality God grants to souls of light as a major key to soul freedom. Mercy's flame is the violet-pink flame of transmutation that forgives, forgets and erases all that never should have been. When invoked, it has the capacity to forgive a portion of an individual's karma by transmuting the records standing in the way of the soul's reunion with the Divine.

The masters say the merciful heart is the heart of God, so this quality is definitely worth attaining. The Ascended Lady Master Kuan Yin, the Goddess of Mercy, said it brings power through the surrender of the lesser self. "Mercy is a power of endowment. For to give mercy endows you with power—the power of complete soul liberation whereby you let go and the temptation toward resentment or revenge or envy or covetousness is utterly consumed by your love for mercy itself."[19]

Many confuse this attribute with sympathy, but mercy actually produces

16 *Pearls of Wisdom*, vol. 46, no. 37.

17 Ibid.

18 *Merriam-Webster's Collegiate Dictionary*, 11th ed., s.v. "mercy."

19 *Pearls of Wisdom*, vol. 35, no. 16.

reconciliation of the soul with her divine plan. The ascended masters teach that mercy is not a state of human consciousness but rather a state of the Christ mind, of the Holy Spirit and of God's heart, and we manifest it according to our capacity to contain and sustain that Divine Presence. In order to receive mercy, cosmic law requires that we repent of wrong actions and be willing to do penance. The violet flame is a wonderful agent for this atonement.

Divine mercy has both a personal and an impersonal action. Its impersonal action shines its light rays upon the just and the unjust. The personal action of mercy involves meditating upon the Christ mind and making a decision whether to utterly forgive someone or require recompense. It is a choice whether to lean in favor of mercy or justice; it therefore involves the exercise of right judgment. We must be careful not to judge in the sense of condemnation or when it is not within our domain or the reach of our understanding. We can pray for understanding, transmutation, divine mercy and justice, and then turn the matter over to God so the person for whom we are praying receives the perfect answer for how his soul can be reconciled with her divine blueprint.

At times we may witness an action of judgment falling upon those who do evil; for example, when a criminal is apprehended and brought to justice. When this happens, Kuan Yin explained, "mercy becomes the presence of the judgment of nonmercy."[20] When mercy descends as judgment, those who are making karma are stopped in their tracks. It causes them to stop making karma, to pause and perhaps to be confined. In the case of children who have done something wrong, this might be a simple "time out" where they sit and think about what they did. For adults, it could result in being incarcerated for years or a lifetime of rethinking the actions they once took. Mercy gives the person the opportunity to reconsider, to change his ways and to bend the knee by following the voice of the Christ in himself and others.

Forgiveness

Forgiveness is another indispensable violet-ray quality, as it paves the way for the righting of every wrong. The law of forgiveness is a cosmic principle; as one forgives others, so he will be forgiven. Jesus expressed it by saying, "Forgive us our debts, as we forgive our debtors."[21] The rule of thumb he gave is to forgive seventy times seven, an incredible extension of the heart showing how vital forgiveness is. Everyone needs to be forgiven because all have made mistakes, done or said things they wish they hadn't, and thought things they wish they hadn't thought. Sometimes people also need forgiveness for things they failed to say or do that could have helped another person.

Forgiving mistakes applies to grievous offenses as well as minor ones. No matter how serious the infraction, we need to extend forgiveness, remembering that we are not forgiving the deed but forgiving the soul, the pure part of the person that never

20 *Pearls of Wisdom,* vol. 26, no. 54.

21 Matthew 6:12.

intended to err. We know each individual has a not-self or shadow self, the dweller-on-the-threshold. This is the part of each of us that does, as Saint Paul said, what we "would not do."[22] Forgiving the soul of the wrongdoer enables the person to move on.

Though it is important to forgive others, it is equally important to forgive ourselves. Elizabeth Clare Prophet said the first initiation required on the spiritual path is to exercise the flame of forgiveness by invoking it, and entering into our own Christ consciousness and pardoning ourselves so we are free of self-condemnation and guilt. Most souls of light are their own worst critics and in this harshness they are not quick to extend the same grace of forgiveness to themselves that they give to others. To accelerate on the path, a person must be willing to forgive, to receive forgiveness, and to put all sins into the violet flame of the Holy Spirit.

As we open up our hearts and send forgiveness, forgiveness is returned to us and greater peace and harmony are established in our lives. In the process we can receive more abundant grace by extending forgiveness into all circumstances unknown to the outer mind such as things done to us that we have no awareness of, or errors we don't know we have committed. Perhaps we are carrying burdens because of an interaction we had with someone a thousand or ten thousand years ago. Since the veil of forgetfulness about previous lifetimes descends as we come into embodiment, it is certainly the better part of wisdom to send forgiveness into all situations we cannot remember but that need resolution.

Elohim Peace and Aloha said forgiveness is the key to the golden age of Aquarius, and they instructed us to forgive and ask to be forgiven even when we think we are not in the wrong. We do this because we desire to live by the divine code of forgiveness. When we ask to be pardoned, we are giving others the opportunity to sincerely do the same, which raises the consciousness of everyone involved.

When we or anyone else makes a mistake, the masters have outlined an easy three-step process to follow. The first step is to ask for forgiveness from God and from any other person(s) involved. The second is to put on our tube of light,[23] and the third is to call to Archangel Michael to seal the tube of light in his blue-flame protection.

MEDITATION: A RITUAL OF FORGIVENESS

This ritual is based on the process above. Although it can be used for known errors, it is designed to cover a broad scope. You will need some paper and a pen or pencil as well as a safe place to burn a letter to God.

You can also use portions of the ritual without writing and burning the letter, naming those things you would like God to forgive and then giving the prayer in step 9. This is especially helpful to cleanse your consciousness right before you go to bed.

22 See Romans 7:19: "For the good that I would I do not: but the evil which I would not, that I do."

23 For more information on the tube of light, see chapter 4 in *The Spiritual Quest.*

1. Find a quiet place where you will not be disturbed. You may want to play some soft meditation music in the background.
2. Sit up straight and place your feet flat on the floor to allow light to flow freely up and down your spine.
3. In the name of your I AM Presence, ask the angels to protect and seal you and the forcefield of your meditation during this ritual.
4. Close your eyes and focus your awareness in your heart, letting go of all distracting thoughts and feelings.
5. See a doorway in front of you guarded on both sides by flaming white seraphim. Open the door and enter the secret chamber of your heart. Visualize there an altar on which burns your threefold flame. Kneel in reverence to your heart flame.
6. Take several minutes to commune with your Holy Christ Self within your heart.
7. Open your eyes and give the following prayer:

    In the name of my Holy Christ Self and I AM Presence, I call to my Father-Mother God for forgiveness for every error I have ever made. I call to the angels of record to bring forth all the scrolls of my lifestream that the Law will allow in this hour. I ask to be given the records of my errors whose time is come to be transmuted in the sacred fire, that I may place them on paper to be put into the physical flame. I ask not to be given the record of a burden too great for me to bear. I also pray for forgiveness for any records unknown to my outer mind and ask that they be put into the violet flame. I trust in the mercy of your heart, O God, and I accept the information given to me. I also send forgiveness to all who have ever wronged me. I accept it done in accordance with thy holy will.

8. Now write a letter addressed to God, putting down everything that comes to your mind.
9. When you have finished writing, hold the letter to your heart and give the following prayer slowly and deliberately. Concentrate on the meaning of the words and see the violet light of forgiveness flowing into your consciousness and through your four lower bodies.

    God has washed me clean.
    God has baptized me with his light.
    The Holy Spirit has come into my room.
    And I have received the forgiveness of God.
    And therefore in that forgiveness of my Lord and Saviour,
    Jesus Christ, I will go forward this day!
    I will not remember the sin of another.
    I will not remember my own sin, save as a reminder that I shall not sin again.
    And I will not hold against anyone anything he has done to me in our entire existence.
    And I pray that those against whom I have sinned will not hold my sins against me.[24]

24 *Pearls of Wisdom*, vol. 36, no. 32.

10. Burn your letter, asking the seraphim to deliver it to your Father-Mother God in the etheric octaves.

11. Give the short "Tube of Light" decree[25] 1–3 times:

Beloved I AM Presence bright,
Round me seal your tube of light
From ascended master flame
Called forth now in God's own name.
Let it keep my temple free
From all discord sent to me.

I AM calling forth violet fire
To blaze and transmute all desire,
Keeping on in freedom's name
Till I AM one with the violet flame.

12. Give this call to Archangel Michael to seal your meditation:

In the name of Archangel Michael,
I call for this ritual to be sealed in blue-flame protection!
I AM the guard in Archangel Michael's name! (3–9 times) **Amen.**

Alchemy and Transmutation

In ancient times the physical science of alchemy was practiced to transform lead into gold. But mystics know alchemy as a spiritual science that involves transmuting the base elements of the lower self into the divine nature of the Higher Self. Saint Germain, Master Alchemist, explained, "the key to alchemy that must precede the acquisition of all other keys is the mastery of yourself, to a greater or lesser degree."[26] This includes mastery of our four lower bodies.

God-mastery can be accomplished through various spiritual practices and especially by invoking the violet flame, the "cosmic eraser" that can create refreshing transformation in our lives. Saint Germain explained that the violet flame brings about alchemy within the personality. It goes after the schisms causing psychological problems dating back to early childhood and previous incarnations that have been difficult for the soul to shake, recurring lifetime after lifetime. As these divisions are gradually dissolved, we find the dense "lead" of our human creation being purified and changed into the "gold" of the Christ consciousness through the transmutative action of the seventh ray.

Have mercy upon me, O God, according to thy lovingkindness: according unto the multitude of thy tender mercies blot out my transgressions.
—PSALM 51:1

Mrs. Prophet said that the moment we call for transgressions to go into the flame of transmutation, they are no longer real. The Holy Spirit releases through us the action of the seventh ray, the violet flame of freedom. As the violet flame begins

25 This decree is printed in *Prayers, Meditations and Dynamic Decrees,* p. 34, no. 1.30.
26 Mark L. Prophet and Elizabeth Clare Prophet, *Saint Germain on Alchemy: Formulas for Self-Transformation,* (Gardiner, Mont: Summit Publications, Inc., 1993), p. 17.

to pulsate, the energies of sin, sickness, death and negativity are drawn into the vortex of the flame. Those energies that were once crystal clear but have been imposed upon by our incorrect use of freewill are then stripped of imperfection and the burdens of the carnal mind. When the atoms and molecules are freed, they are truly liberated—and we are free because we are one with the divine energy within us. When people disobey the laws of God, they suffer in their four lower bodies. Therefore, healing can result from the transmutation of error.

Causal Body

The science of alchemy also involves the use of other decrees and mantras to help us become the Christ and access the gifts of our causal body.[27] Saint Germain said we do not need to know what these gifts are. We just need to use the science of the spoken Word to command in the name of the Lord—which man as a co-creator with God has the right to do—an alchemical precipitation of the gifts and graces of the Spirit that will endow us with the qualities of the Christ. These will make us more capable as spiritual alchemists and more integrated with the universal plan.

Amplifying the Violet Ray

Amethyst crystal

As with all of the rays, you can enhance the violet ray by wearing that color and using it in your surroundings. Displaying amethyst or lilac colors and images in your home or office can brighten your day. Violet-colored clothing is especially beneficial when worn on Saturday, as the seventh ray is released to the earth most abundantly on that day of the week. Saint Germain also recommended "keeping a chalice, preferably of amethyst or amethyst color, wherever you have your altar or wherever you work, on or near your desk, and consecrating that chalice to the violet flame."[28] The gemstones amethyst, aquamarine, and diamond can also be used effectively as uncut crystals or jewelry to magnify the uplifting qualities of the violet ray.

The Seat-of-the-Soul Chakra

The seat-of-the-soul chakra, located midway between the navel and the base of the spine, contains the energy of the seventh ray within six violet-colored petals. Its Sanskrit name is *svadhishthana,* meaning "sweetness" or "abode of the self." The reproductive organs of man and woman are located in the same area as the seat of the soul. Just as this chakra houses the soul within the four lower bodies, the organs of procreation give rise to the birth of the body another soul will inhabit.

The light of the seat-of-the-soul chakra is used constructively to express freedom, mercy, forgiveness, justice, transcendence, alchemy, transmutation, diplomacy, intuition, prophecy and revelation. It is also possible to misapply its light. Some misuses of the seventh ray are intolerance, disregard for others, and cruelty as well as lack of forgiveness, tact, justice or mercy.

---

27 See *Prayers, Meditations and Dynamic Decrees* for a complete selection of decrees, mantras and fiats on each of the seven rays.

28 *Pearls of Wisdom,* vol. 37, no. 25.

Seat of the Soul

This chakra is where we experience soul freedom—the freedom to become all we are meant to be and to fulfill our divine potential. Soul freedom then provides access to special faculties of the soul that are a function of the etheric plane. Even though the etheric realm is the highest vibrating plane in the dimension of matter, it is concrete and even more real than the physical plane. But instead of being experienced through the five senses, it is experienced through the senses of the soul in a dimension and awareness beyond the physical.

We have five soul faculties, which are the perceptions of the etheric octave and inner planes relating to inner sight, inner smell, inner sensitivity and everything we need to apprehend God in the seven chakras. These faculties are telepathy, premonition, clairvoyance, psychometry and telekinesis. Soul senses can also manifest as flashes of intuition and insight. For instance, we may take a soul reading of others upon first meeting them or get a gut feeling about whether or not to do something. We may just "know" something, but not know how or where the impression originated. In fact, these instances of knowing arise from the seat-of-the-soul chakra and are guided by the soul.

The violet flame can clear the seat-of-the-soul chakra as well as the other chakras so that the soul can be free from the density she has created in her many embodiments. Archangel Zadkiel and Holy Amethyst explained that "karma is a fine soot... and it crystallizes as it falls, deadening the soul faculties and dulling the brain."[29] As this dullness is cleared, the soul is able to access the soul faculties and fulfill her reason for being.

Assessing Your Seat-of-the-Soul Chakra Mastery

Strengthening your self-mastery of the seat-of-the-soul chakra involves several key points:

1. Feeling free to be who you really are
2. Realizing you play a unique part in God's plan for the earth
3. Seeing the need to free yourself from negative patterns imposed upon you by others
4. Forgiving yourself and others

The following exercise can help you assess how well you are using the violet ray in these ways.

29 *Pearls of Wisdom*, vol. 36, no. 14.

SELF-ASSESSMENT: YOUR SEAT-OF-THE-SOUL CHAKRA

1. On a scale of 1 to 5, where 1 is "never true of me" and 5 is "always true of me," please rate the following statements based on your current perceptions.

1	Never true of me
2	Rarely true of me
3	Sometimes true of me
4	Often true of me
5	Always true of me

a) **I feel free to be who I really am.**	1	2	3	4	5
1. I feel I can express myself freely.					
2. I can channel my energies into areas contributing to my life's goals.					
3. I realize that my gut feelings are part of my internal guidance system and I follow them when they prompt me.					
4. I do not allow others to distract me from accomplishing the important goals in my life.					

b) **I realize I play a unique part in God's plan for the earth.**	1	2	3	4	5
1. I recognize I have a special role to play on earth and because of this, I am valuable.					
2. I try to discover my own unique mission so I can fulfill it successfully.					
3. I perceive myself as one important part of the diversity making up all of creation.					

c) **I recognize the need to free myself from negative thought and behavior patterns.**	1	2	3	4	5
1. I realize I am sometimes hindered by patterns of thought and feeling that do not contribute to my well-being.					
2. I engage in practices such as therapy or self-help to nurture and heal the wounded parts of myself.					
3. I work on developing spiritual practices, habits and thought patterns that support and sustain my spiritual growth.					

d) **I forgive myself and others.**	1	2	3	4	5
1. I am able to forgive others for real or imagined wrongs.					
2. I believe it is important to forgive myself and others for things that may have happened in the past.					
3. When I know I have done wrong, I am able to ask the wronged person(s) for forgiveness.					
4. When I know I have done wrong, I am able to forgive myself and not hold on to unnecessary feelings of guilt.					

2. After completing the assessment, add up your score in each one of the four sections and divide it by the number of statements in that section to get an average.

3. Use the following action plan to formulate a personal strategy that will enhance your performance in every area where your average score was "3" or below.

Seat-of-the-Soul Chakra Action Plan

a) I feel free to be who I really am.
I resolve to improve in this area by doing the following: ____________________

b) I realize I play a unique part in God's plan for the earth.
I resolve to improve in this area by doing the following: ____________________

c) I recognize the need to free myself from negative thought and behavior patterns.
I resolve to improve in this area by doing the following: ____________________

d) I forgive myself and others.
I resolve to improve in this area by doing the following: ____________________

4. Put your action plan into practice for three months. Then take the assessment again and note the positive changes in your journal.

Saint Germain, Chohan of the Seventh Ray

Saint Germain is the chohan of the seventh ray. So great is his mastery of the violet ray that Elizabeth Prophet referred to him as "the very spirit of freedom in the heart of America."[30] In truth, he has striven for ages not only to win his own victory, but to spread the flame of freedom over the face of the entire planet. This becomes clear when we consider the lifetimes leading to his ascension, which repeatedly show his daring courage and deep desire to lead the world into a higher consciousness. Saint Germain was so dedicated to helping mankind achieve freedom that he even embodied

30 Elizabeth Clare Prophet, *Inner Perspectives* (Corwin Springs, Mont.: Summit University Press, 2003), p. 168.

on earth after he ascended—a rare event! And when the final chapter of his earthly incarnations closed, he worked with those on earth directly from heaven to sponsor a number of vital endeavors of the Great White Brotherhood.

Golden Age Ruler

Over fifty thousand years ago, Saint Germain was the ruler of a golden-age civilization in a fertile, semitropical country that is now the Sahara Desert. He was a master of ancient wisdom and of the knowledge of the matter realm, ruling every area of life by light so that heavenly patterns were manifested in the earth. His empire reached unsurpassed heights of beauty, symmetry and perfection.

The people loved him deeply and desired to emulate him, looking to him as the standard for their own emerging Christhood. He had charted their cosmic history on a great mural in the capital, the "City of the Sun," serving as a reminder of the Source from whence they had come and of their reason for being—to be extensions of the One. But over a period of time, many of the people became more interested in the pleasures of the senses than in fulfilling the larger creative plan of the great God Self. So a cosmic council instructed the ruler that he and his family should withdraw in order to let the people's karma be their teacher. The people's free will would determine what, if any, of his legacy of light they would retain.

The king then held a great banquet for 576 of his councilors and public servants. Everyone in attendance received a crystal goblet filled with "pure electronic essence," the light essence of the ruler. This elixir was his gift of soul protection so they would never completely forget the divine spark of the inner God Self. It would be sustained throughout the centuries until they found themselves in a civilization where they would again be given the full knowledge to pursue union with the I AM THAT I AM.

During the banquet a cosmic master who identified himself only by the word "Victory" upon his brow addressed those assembled, and his words were broadcast over the entire realm. He rebuked the people for their ingratitude and neglect of their God Source and warned them of the coming crisis they had brought upon themselves, prophesying that they would be ruled by a prince who sought to marry the king's daughter. Seven days later the king and his family withdrew to the etheric city counterpart of the civilization, and the next day the prince arrived and took over the realm without any opposition. This heralded a period of decline and the ultimate destruction of this once-great civilization.

High Priest on Atlantis

Thirteen thousand years ago Saint Germain served as high priest of the Violet Flame Temple on Atlantis. By the power of invocation and the light of his causal body he sustained a pillar of fire, a veritable fountain of violet singing flame, drawing people from near and far who desired to be set free from all binding conditions of body, mind and soul. Each person achieved this through self-effort in the offering of invocations and practicing seventh-ray rituals to the sacred fire. The fire was visible to some as a physical violet flame, to some as an ultraviolet light and to others not at all, though the powerful healing vibrations were undeniable. The flame was enshrined within a circular white marble railing inside the temple. The temple itself was three stories high and built of marble ranging in color from white with violet and purple veins to deep shades of the seventh-ray spectrum.

The priests and priestesses who ministered to this flame and officiated at the altar were schooled in the universal priesthood of the Order of Melchizedek at Archangel Zadkiel's retreat, the Temple of Purification, which is in the etheric realm over the island of Cuba. This priesthood combines the perfect religion and the perfect science. It was at Zadkiel's retreat where Saint Germain received the anointing from Zadkiel himself, "Thou art a priest forever after the order of Melchizedek."[31]

Before Atlantis sank and during the time Noah was building his ark and warning people of the coming flood, the Great Divine Director summoned Saint Germain and a few faithful priests to carry the flame of freedom from the Temple of Purification to a place of safety in the Carpathian foothills in Transylvania. Here they continued the sacred ritual of expanding the fires of freedom as returning karma descended on mankind. Then in succeeding embodiments, Saint Germain and his followers, acting under the Great Divine Director's guidance, rediscovered the flame and continued to guard its shrine. Sometime later Saint Germain assisted the Great Divine Director in establishing a retreat at the site of the flame and founding the House of Rakoczy, the royal house of Hungary.

The Prophet Samuel

Saint Germain returned as Samuel (c. 1056–1004 B.C.), who was a priest, judge and prophet—the last judge and the first prophet of the twelve tribes of Israel. He was trained by the high priest Eli, who accepted Samuel as a prophet when he was still a child.

Samuel anointing David

In those days the judges were charismatic leaders believed to have direct access to God who could rally the tribes against oppressors. Samuel was the messenger of God's liberation of Abraham's seed from bondage to the corrupt priests, the sons of Eli, and from the Philistines who had slaughtered the Israelites in battle. He is often named alongside Moses as a great intercessor. He courageously led the Israelites in a spiritual revival, exhorting them to "return unto the Lord with all your hearts" and to "put away strange gods."[32] The people repented and beseeched Samuel to continue asking God to save them from the Philistines. As Samuel prayed, a violent thunderstorm was unleashed, allowing the Israelites to overtake the enemy, who never rose again during Samuel's reign.

31 Psalm 110:6.

32 I Samuel 7:3.

Samuel spent the rest of his life administering justice in the land, and when he grew old he appointed his sons to be judges over Israel. But his sons were corrupt and the people demanded that Samuel give them a king to be their judge, as was done in other nations. He was deeply grieved and prayed for divine direction. God told him to do as the people wanted, explaining that they were not rejecting Samuel but were actually rejecting God. Although Samuel warned the Israelites of the dangers that would befall them through their rulers, they still clamored for a king. So he anointed Saul as their leader and charged him and the people to always obey God's voice. When Saul proved to be an unfaithful servant, Samuel pronounced the Lord's judgment upon him and secretly anointed David as king. When the prophet died, he was buried at Ramah and all of Israel mourned his passing.

Saint Joseph

Ten centuries later Saint Germain was embodied as Joseph, father of Jesus and husband of Mary. Joseph's lineage is traced back to the same King David whom he anointed in his lifetime as Samuel. Together, the three members of the Holy Family comprised the threefold flame that was not only the basis for family unity but also for the entire Christian dispensation.

The Bible recounts how an angel of the Lord warned Joseph in a dream that Herod planned to kill the young child, Jesus. Joseph heeded the warning and fled with Jesus and Mary into Egypt, returning only after Herod's death. It is believed Joseph died before Jesus began his public ministry.

Saint Germain as Joseph was overshadowed by his twin flame, the Ascended Lady Master Portia, who was not embodied then. In that lifetime, Joseph, who was a carpenter by trade, gave his most tender love, skill and care to Jesus. In a 1987 dictation, Jesus said of Saint Germain: "This beloved brother who was with me as my father Joseph (for so I called him, beloved) has been an adept of the seventh ray and of the use of the violet flame for tens of thousands of years and beyond. This has been his calling in God. This is his gift from the Father and his gift to the Father's children."[33]

In the twentieth century, Saint Germain extended his spiritual fatherhood to the children of earth from the ascended state, releasing their physical care into the hands of those in embodiment. He explained:

> In my July 4, 1995 address at the Royal Teton Ranch in Montana, I related to you that in the past month I had held every single child on planet Earth on my lap and that I had placed a portion of myself in their hearts. I promised that I would care for each child as I had cared for my Son Jesus.
>
> This I did, beloved, to nurture and to father the children and to bring them closer to my heart that I might let them know that someone loves them

33 *Pearls of Wisdom*, vol. 30, no. 27.

and someone will feed them spiritual teachings. Yes, this I did, but only you can give them their daily bread and sustenance."[34]

The Catholic Church considers Saint Joseph to be the Patron of the Universal Church and celebrates his feast day on March 19. Saint Joseph has performed many miracles on earth. For example, in the late 1800s, the Italian stonemasons who constructed the Chapel of Loretto for the Sisters of Loretto in Santa Fe, New Mexico, had neglected to build a staircase to the choir loft. When the sisters discovered the oversight, they prayed a novena to Saint Joseph for intercession. Shortly after, a carpenter arrived who miraculously completed a beautiful polished-wood spiral staircase—apparently without saw or hammer, nails or screws—and then disappeared without being paid. The miraculous staircase, which lacks a center pole, makes two complete 360-degree turns![35]

Saint Alban

Saint Alban, who embodied in the late third century, was the next known appearance of the soul of Saint Germain. Alban lived in England during the persecution of Christians under the Roman emperor Diocletian. He was a pagan who had been in the Roman army and later settled in the British town of Verulamium, subsequently named St. Albans.

Alban hid a fugitive Christian priest and was converted by him. He was then sentenced to death for disguising himself as the priest and allowing him to escape. Legend says such a great multitude gathered to witness Alban's execution that they could not pass over the narrow bridge that had to be crossed. Alban prayed and the river parted to give passage to the crowd. His executioner was converted on the spot and begged to die in his place, but his request was denied and he was beheaded with Alban the same day.

Merlin

In the fifth century, Saint Germain embodied as Merlin the Magician. Merlin was not just a mythical magician but a true alchemist, prophet and counselor in King Arthur's court. During the time when the land was splintered by warring chieftains and besieged by Saxon invaders, Merlin led Arthur through twelve battles—which were coincidentally twelve spiritual initiations—to unite the kingdom of Britain and establish a period of peace. It was Merlin's desire to have Britain be a place where Christ-achievement and devotion to the One could prosper. This was the dream behind the establishment of the sacred fellowship of the Round Table at Camelot, which was a mystery school where the knights and ladies could pursue the path of personal Christhood.

34 *Pearls of Wisdom*, vol. 39, no. 16.
35 *Pearls of Wisdom*, vol. 27, no. 29.

Merlin is described in some traditions as a godly sage who studied the stars and whose prophecies were recorded by seventy secretaries. *The Prophecies of Merlin* was popular in the Middle Ages but was later put on a list of forbidden readings. Merlin foresaw all the troubles to come upon Camelot, including his own dénouement, with the piercing anguish accompanying the knowledge of the playing out of karmic retribution.

Legend and myth have clouded the truth of what occurred in Camelot. It was witchcraft, intrigue and treachery that caused its demise—not the love of Guinevere and Launcelot as depicted by Thomas Malory, and widely accepted by civilizations steeped in a desire for forbidden romance. But the promise of Camelot and the return of the cast of characters are part of the establishment of the golden age of Aquarius that Saint Germain is sponsoring in the world today.

Roger Bacon

Saint Germain's next major appearance was as Roger Bacon (1220–1292), philosopher, Franciscan monk, educational reformer and experimental scientist who is now viewed as the forerunner of modern science. In an era in which either theology or logic or both dictated the parameters of science, he promoted the experimental method, declared his belief that the world was round, and castigated the scholars and scientists of his day for their narrow-mindedness. He predicted spectacles, a flying machine, the hot-air balloon, telescope, microscope, elevator and mechanically propelled ships and carriages, writing of them as if he had actually seen them—and he had. He was seeing the past and the future, for these things had been present on Atlantis and would come again in our time.

Bacon eventually left his position as a lecturer at Oxford and the University of Paris and entered the Franciscan Order of Friars Minor, determined to seek and find his science in his religion. But his scientific and philosophical world view, his bold attacks on the theologians of his day and his study of alchemy, astrology and magic led to charges of "heresies and novelties" for which he was imprisoned in solitary confinement for fourteen years by his fellow Franciscans. He was released just shortly before his death.

Once again in that life he was a proponent of the one Source. According to two of his biographers, he believed that knowledge "is a highly personal experience—a light communicated only to the innermost privacy of the individual through the impartial channels of all knowledge and of all thought." To those who followed after him, Bacon was "doctor mirabilis"—"wonderful teacher"—an epithet by which he has been known down the centuries. He gave the following prophecy to his students, which reflects his indomitable spirit of freedom:

I believe that humanity shall accept as an axiom for its conduct the principle for which I have laid down my life—the right to investigate. It is the credo of free men—this opportunity to try, this privilege to err, this courage to experiment anew. We scientists of the human spirit shall experiment, experiment, ever experiment. Through centuries of trial and error, through agonies of research... let us experiment with laws and customs, with money systems and governments, until we chart the one true course—until we find the majesty of our proper orbit as the planets above have found theirs.... And then at last we shall move all together in the harmony of our spheres under the impulse of a single creation—one unity, one system, one design.[36]

Christopher Columbus

Saint Germain came again as Christopher Columbus (1451–1506), discoverer of America. Roger Bacon himself had set the stage for Columbus' voyage to the new world when he stated in his *Opus Majus,* "the sea between the end of Spain on the west and the beginning of India on the east is navigable in a very few days if the wind is favorable."[37] Although the statement was incorrect as the land to the west of Spain was not India, it was instrumental in Columbus' discovery. Columbus quoted the passage in a letter to King Ferdinand and Queen Isabella in 1498, saying his 1492 voyage had been inspired in part by Bacon's visionary statement.

Christopher Columbus was certain he had been divinely selected for his mission and that God had made him to be "the messenger of the new heaven and the new earth of which He spake in the Apocalypse of St. John, after having spoken of it by the mouth of Isaiah."[38] He believed he was the instrument whereby God would, as Isaiah recorded around 732 B.C., "recover the remnant of his people... and shall assemble the outcasts of Israel, and gather together the dispersed of Judah from the four corners of the earth."[39] He not only believed this, but wrote about it in a book entitled *Las Proficias,* or *The Prophecies*—in its complete form, *The Book of Prophecies Concerning the Discovery of the Indies and the Recovery of Jerusalem.* Even though the point is rarely stressed, it is a fact so rooted in history that even the *Encyclopaedia Britannica* says unequivocally, "Columbus discovered America by prophecy rather than by astronomy."[40] This and his other embodiments so far clearly show how the soul of Saint Germain was continually striving lifetime after lifetime to return full circle to a golden age with the worship of the God Presence at its core.

---

36 Henry Thomas and Dana Lee Thomas, *Living Biographies of Great Scientists* (Garden City, NY: Nelson Doubleday, 1941), p. 15.

37 David Wallechinsky, Amy Wallace and Irving Wallace, *The Book of Predictions* (New York: William Morrow and Co., 1980), p. 346.

38 Clements R. Markham, *Life of Christopher Columbus* (London: George Philip and Son, 1892), pp. 207–8.

39 Isaiah 11:10–12.

40 *Encyclopaedia Britannica,* 15th ed., s.v. "Columbus, Christopher."

Francis Bacon

Francis Bacon (1561–1626) was also an incarnation of Saint Germain, and in that life he carried to conclusion the work he had begun as Roger Bacon. Often referred to as the greatest mind the West has ever produced, he is known as the father of inductive reasoning and the scientific method, which are responsible to a large degree for the age of technology in which we now live. He foreknew that only applied science could free the masses from misery and the toil of sheer survival in order that they might seek a higher spirituality they once knew. Indeed, his achievements in every field catapulted the world into readiness for the age of Aquarius.

Bacon was a philosopher, statesman, essayist and literary master. As a boy of just twelve or thirteen he conceived of a formula to change "the whole wide world," and in 1607 he crystallized it into a book called *The Great Instauration*. This vision of universal enlightenment launched the English Renaissance, with the help of Francis' tender care, for over the years he gathered round himself a group of enlightened writers who were responsible for almost all the Elizabethan literature. Some of them were part of a secret society, The Knights of the Helmet, formed when he and his brother Anthony were law students. Their goal was the advancement of learning through the expansion of the English language and the creation of new literature not written in Latin but in words Englishmen could understand. Determined that the common people should have the benefit of reading God's word for themselves, Francis later organized the translation of the King James Version of the Bible.

Two separate ciphers discovered in the 1890s—a word-cipher and a bi-literal cipher embedded in the words of the original printings of the Shakespearean Folios and in many other well-known works of Elizabethan literature—reveal that Francis Bacon was the real author of the Shakespeare plays and the aforementioned works, as well as being the firstborn son of Queen Elizabeth and Lord Leicester. Francis Bacon was therefore the rightful heir to the throne of England. Unfortunately, his mother was fearful of an untimely loss of power, refused to acknowledge him as her heir and forbade him ever to tell the truth about his parentage, on peril of his life. Although he knew he could be the best of leaders, he resigned himself to striving to bring about universal enlightenment through the other avenues available to him.

Francis Bacon is said to have died in 1626, but some have claimed he lived secretly in Europe for a time after that. On May 1, 1684, his soul passed through the ritual of the ascension from the Rakoczy Mansion, the retreat of his guru, the Great Divine Director, and he became the Ascended Master Saint Germain. His ascended name comes from the Latin *Sanctus Germanus* and simply means "Holy Brother."

Le Comte de Saint Germain

Saint Germain's desire to liberate God's people was so intense that after his ascension he sought and was granted an extremely rare dispensation from the Karmic Board to return to earth in a physical body. He appeared from 1710–1822 as "le Comte de Saint Germain," a miraculous gentleman who dazzled the courts of eighteenth- and nineteenth-century Europe, where they called him "The Wonderman."

The count was an alchemist, scholar, linguist, poet, musician, artist, raconteur and diplomat admired throughout the courts of Europe for his adeptship. He was known for such feats as removing the flaws in diamonds and other precious stones and simultaneously composing a letter with one hand and poetry with the other. He could bilocate and dissolve his physical body at will. In fact, Voltaire described him as the "man who never dies and who knows everything." He is mentioned in the letters of Frederick the Great, Voltaire, Horace Walpole and Casanova as well as in the newspapers of the day. Many of his demonstrations of mastery are described in the diaries of Mme. d'Adhémar, who knew him for at least half a century. She records his visits to herself and to the courts of Louis XV and Louis XVI, noting in his glowing face the unchanging appearance of a man in his early forties throughout that period.

He worked behind the scenes to prevent the French Revolution and to effect a smooth transition from the monarchy to a representative government. But, although they were quite willing to be entertained by him, the royalty and their ministers ignored his counsel and the revolution ensued. In a final attempt to unite Europe, he backed Napoleon, who misused the master's power to his own demise, and Saint Germain was forced to withdraw from this karmic situation.

Abandoning his sponsorship of Europe, Saint Germain turned his attention to the New World. He became the sponsoring master of the United States of America and of her first president George Washington, inspiring the Declaration of Independence and the Constitution. He also inspired many of the laborsaving devices of the twentieth century to further his goal of freeing people from the drudgery of life so they might have more time to pursue their God-realization.

Working on Earth from Heaven

As an ascended master, Saint Germain worked with the Ascended Master Serapis Bey and unascended adepts K.H. (Kuthumi), D.K. (Djwal Kul) and Master M. (El Morya) to establish the Theosophical Society in the late 1800s through the writings of their amanuensis,[41] Mme. H. P. Blavatsky. This was an important effort on the part of the Brotherhood to acquaint mankind with the workings of the Law and cosmic hierarchy.

In the twentieth century, Saint Germain stepped forward once again to sponsor

41 According to *Merriam-Webster's Collegiate Dictionary,* 11th ed., an amanuensis is "one employed to write from dictation or to copy manuscript."

an outer activity of the Great White Brotherhood. In the early 1930s he contacted his "general in the field," the reembodied George Washington, whom he trained as a messenger for the Great White Brotherhood and who, under the pen name of Godfré Ray King, released the foundation of Saint Germain's instruction for the New Age in the books *Unveiled Mysteries, The Magic Presence* and *The "I AM" Discourses.* Since the late 1930s, many cosmic beings and ascended masters have come forth to assist Saint Germain in his work of bringing the teachings of the sacred fire to mankind and ushering in the golden age.

Then, in 1961 Saint Germain contacted the messenger Mark L. Prophet and established the Keepers of the Flame Fraternity. His purpose was to quicken all who had originally come to earth with the Ancient of Days, Sanat Kumara, to keep the flame of life on earth. The fraternity was intended to restore the memory of their ancient vow and reason for being on earth today—to serve as world teachers and ministering servants in their families, communities and nations at this crucial time. Through this fraternity Saint Germain is calling to the original keepers of the flame to reconsecrate their lives to the rekindling of the flame of life—the threefold flame in the heart—and the sacred fires of freedom in the souls of God's people.

Saint Germain's Offices in Cosmic Hierarchy

Presently, Saint Germain holds a number of spiritual offices in cosmic hierarchy, which include:

- Knight Commander of the Keepers of the Flame Fraternity;
- Chohan of the Seventh Ray, an office received in the latter part of the eighteenth century from the Ascended Lady Master Kuan Yin, who was the previous seventh-ray chohan;
- The seventh angel spoken of in the Book of Revelation who is helping to disclose the mysteries of God to earth's people;
- Hierarch of the Age of Aquarius. On May 1, 1954, Saint Germain and his twin flame, the Ascended Lady Master Portia, received the scepter of power from Sanat Kumara and the crown of authority from Jesus to direct the consciousness of mankind for the next 2,000-year period.

As the New Age dawned, the Lords of Karma also granted Saint Germain the opportunity to release the knowledge of the violet flame outside of the mystery schools and retreats of the Great White Brotherhood. This dispensation allows humanity to invoke the violet transmuting flame, thereby purifying the divine energy mankind has misqualified for tens of thousands of years and cutting the human race free from fear, lack, sin, sickness and death to walk as God-free beings.

During this age, Saint Germain especially extends his heart to humanity, offering to help each of us toward our soul's victory and the ascension. In a 1975 dictation he offered himself as our teacher:

> You are mortal. I am immortal. The only difference between us is that I have chosen to be free, and you have yet to make the choice. We have the same potential, the same resources, the same connection to the One. I have taken mine to forge a God-identity. For long ago, the still small voice within spoke the fiat of Alpha and the living God: "Children of the One, forge your God-identity." And in the stillness of the night, I heard the call and I answered, "I will!" And when I said, "I will," all of cosmos echoed, "I will!" The will to be summons the vastness of the potential of being. . . .
>
> I am Saint Germain, and I have come to claim your soul and the fires of your heart for the victory of the Aquarian age. I have set the pattern for your soul's initiation. . . . I am on the path of freedom. Take that path, and you will find me there. I am your teacher if you will have me.[42]

Saint Germain's Retreat

Grand Teton

Saint Germain uses several etheric retreats. He teaches classes at his own retreat, the Cave of Symbols, as well as at the Royal Teton Retreat. He also maintains a focus in the golden etheric city over the Sahara Desert and works out of the Great Divine Director's focuses—the Cave of Light in India and the Rakoczy Mansion in the Carpathian Mountains of Transylvania, Romania—where he presides as hierarch. More recently he established a base in South America at the retreat of the God and Goddess Meru. Let's take a closer look at his main retreat, the Cave of Symbols.

The Cave of Symbols

The Cave of Symbols is a physical-etheric retreat located in the North American Rockies in Table Mountain in Wyoming. Upon entering it, we see a cavern lined with pink and white crystal, leading into a vaulted chamber two hundred feet wide covered with rainbow-hued stalactites in the formation of occult symbols. The cave derives its name from these symbols, which serve as focuses of the rainbow rays of divinity and geometric keys to the release of fohat or sacred fire. The light-energy blazing through the symbols extends throughout the United States and has a significant influence upon her people, keying into their consciousness the matrix of the golden age and the remembrance of their lost spiritual inheritance.

The east wall of the crystal chamber contains a unique Cosmic Mirror. When a disciple has reached a certain degree of attainment, the master takes him before the Cosmic Mirror, which reflects the original blueprint of the divine plan that was placed upon his etheric body when his soul was born in the Great Central Sun. The Cosmic Mirror also keys into his etheric body and reflects all his past lives, including the cause

42 *Pearls of Wisdom,* vol. 18, no. 30.

and effect of his every thought, feeling, word and deed. In viewing these embodiments, the disciple may learn what portion of his divine plan he has fulfilled. He may also see what conditions in his world must be corrected and what good momentums he has developed that he can now use to overcome the difficulties of the past and present and thus fulfill his divine plan in the near future.

On the far side of the chamber are three arches spaced twenty feet apart—the first a deep rose, the second a penetrating white and the third a cobalt blue. These arches are focuses of great cosmic beings for the victory of the Christ consciousness in America. Moving through an entrance in the center archway, one walks several hundred feet through a tunnel and then comes to a door on which there are more ancient symbols. Through the doorway is a twelve-sided, domed room sixty feet in diameter. Four of the twelve sides are a brilliant white (focusing the purity of the Christ consciousness in the four elements and the four lower bodies of the planet), and the other sides are the pastel hues of the rays.

The room houses a fantastic radio by which one can communicate with other planets in this solar system, with the center of the earth or with any point on its surface. There are chemical and electrical laboratories where scientists are perfecting formulas and inventions they have been permitted to take from the hermetically sealed cities at the bottom of the Atlantic Ocean that have been protected since the sinking of Atlantis. These discoveries will be brought forth for mankind's use, along with a wealth of information that has been guarded in their retreats for ages, to be released when mankind will have learned to harness greed, selfishness and the desire to control others through war and dishonest financial policies. Unascended scientists and students come here in their finer bodies while asleep or between embodiments. Saint Germain is training a large cadre of souls devoted to the Christ and to the science of the Christ who at the proper time will have lowered into their outer consciousness all that they have learned in this and other retreats of the Brotherhood.

In this room also sits a magnificent golden chair called an "atomic accelerator" or "ascension chair." Initiates who have proven their merit by service and devotion to the light and who have already balanced a considerable amount of their karma are allowed to sit in this chair for a length of time prescribed by Saint Germain and the Karmic Board. The chair passes electronic currents through the four lower bodies that quicken the vibratory pattern of their atoms and electrons. This acceleration of the light frequency in the four lower bodies balances a measure of their karma, as a portion of the misqualified substance is thrown off by the centrifugal action produced by the revolving electrons and transmuted by the sacred fire. In this way, a person's four lower bodies can be accelerated in ascension currents and the soul raised into the ascension. Under the sponsorship of Saint Germain, many souls have ascended from this very room.[43]

43 For more information on Saint Germain's retreats, see Prophet and Prophet, *The Masters and Their Retreats,* p. 239.

There is an elevator here as well, which descends a hundred feet into the heart of the mountain. At that level lies a circular room twenty feet in diameter with a door leading into a huge hall equipped with furnaces and machines for the production of materials used in the experimental work carried on in the chemical and electrical laboratories in the upper level of the retreat.

Keys for Working with Saint Germain

Saint Germain is always willing to assist us to achieve soul freedom. Here are some helpful ways to draw nearer to him as we go about our daily tasks.

1. **Listen to music that ties into Saint Germain's consciousness.**
    - Strauss waltzes are especially good since they carry the vibration of the violet flame.
    - "Tales from the Vienna Woods" by Johann Strauss II is the keynote of Saint Germain's retreat at the Rakoczy Mansion.
    - The "Rakoczy March" by Franz Liszt carries the flame of the master's heart and the formula of the violet flame.

2. **Meditate upon or wear the Maltese cross, Saint Germain's electronic pattern.**
3. **Wear essential oils with the smell of violets, Saint Germain's scent.**
4. **Give violet-flame mantras and decrees.** Here are some special suggestions.
    - As an experiment, repeat Saint Germain's mantra for the Aquarian age for 5–10 minutes daily for six weeks. Write the resulting positive changes in your life and relationships in your journal.

I AM a being of violet fire
I AM the purity God desires!

www.SummitLighthouse.org/SA3-22

- Chant the bija mantra for the seat of the soul chakra:

GLOUM
[pronounced *Glaum*]

- Give violet-flame decrees and call to violet-ray angels to be with you as you go about your daily tasks, and take note of how much easier it seems to accomplish your work. It is especially fun to decree while you are doing everyday things like washing dishes, vacuuming, showering and skateboarding. You can also sing and dance to the violet flame. Watch how it starts to sing in your mind even when you aren't thinking about it.

5. **Attend Saint Germain's classes at the Universities of the Spirit.** They are two weeks long and are held every sixteen weeks at the Royal Teton Retreat. Ask Archangel Michael to escort you there during sleep according to the schedule set by the seven chohans of the rays.[44]

6. **Visit the Cave of Symbols, Saint Germain's retreat.** Before you retire at night, ask Archangel Michael and Saint Germain to take you there to stand before the Cosmic Mirror. This is a very real and enlivening experience, but you need to be ready to look through your own illusions, fantasies and synthetic self and be willing to own up to the deceits that the ego continually practices against itself.

7. **Reflect on your decisions.** Take a few minutes each night to look back over the day and reflect on the right decisions you made and those that were wrong. Saint Germain said it took two million right decisions for him to gain his mastery and make his ascension. He didn't say how many wrong decisions he made in the process but we know everyone makes mistakes, and it helps to recognize what they are so we do not repeat them.

> *Thus, beloved, the call does compel the answer: When you invoke the light of our violet-flame legions, know that millions of angels of the seventh ray—who serve Saint Germain and his twin flame, Portia, the Goddess of Justice, and God at the Elohimic level personified as Arcturus and Victoria in the seventh ray—do answer your call with us, for we are one.*[45]
>
> —ARCHANGEL ZADKIEL

44 You can find the Fourteen-Day Cycles at the Universities of the Spirit chart and more information at http://www.ascendedmastersspiritualretreats.org/spiritual-retreat-information/universities-of-the-spirit.html.

45 *Pearls of Wisdom,* vol. 30, no. 58.

Lady Master Portia

Portia is the twin flame and divine complement of Saint Germain. She spent thousands of years serving on the seventh ray of justice, freedom, mercy, forgiveness, alchemy and sacred ritual. Her attainment expanded until she became the embodiment of the flame and divine consciousness of justice as cosmic opportunity. She is therefore known as both the Goddess of Justice and the Goddess of Opportunity.[46] Portia serves as the member of the Karmic Board who represents the sixth ray of service and ministration. In this capacity she keeps the flame of justice and opportunity on behalf of earth's evolutions.

Portia

Justice reigned supreme during earth's past ages of beauty, perfection and abundance, and Portia made her ascension in that era before discord began to erupt upon the planet. Mankind's sense of justice later became warped and caused an imbalance in all Portia tried to accomplish. Since the ascended masters never interfere in the lives of humanity unless they are invoked, Portia folded her mantle about her and remained in the Great Silence in higher realms of consciousness.

On May 1, 1954, Saint Germain and Portia were officially crowned at inner levels as the hierarchs or directors of the Aquarian age. A new and permanent golden age was ordained to be established for earth during this seventh-ray dispensation. In the early twentieth century, the cycles of life demanded that the scales of justice be balanced in preparation for the golden age. Since some among mankind had begun to request that divine justice be reestablished, on April 9, 1939, Portia came forth from the Great Silence and spoke in a dictation for the first time since her ascension. Her words given in dictations anchor her divine attribute of perfect balance, symbolized by the scales, in the auras of all who will receive it. Portia especially emphasizes the balance of justice and mercy, two primary qualities of the seventh ray.

It is worth noting that in his embodiment as Francis Bacon, the true author of the Shakespearean plays, Saint Germain wrote the character Portia into *The Merchant of Venice*. She played a significant role, speaking eloquently about the qualities of mercy.

46 The title "Goddess" signifies that the one who bears it has internalized the light or the God consciousness of a certain materialization and spiritualization of a ray.

The quality of mercy is not strained;
It droppeth as the gentle rain from heaven
Upon the place beneath. It is twice blest;
It blesseth him that gives and him that takes;
'Tis mightiest in the mightiest: it becomes
The thronèd monarch better than his crown.
His scepter shows the force of temporal power,
The attribute to awe and majesty,
Wherein doth sit the dread and fear of kings;
But mercy is above this scept'red sway;
It is enthronèd in the hearts of kings,
It is an attribute to God Himself,
And earthly power doth then show likest God's
When mercy seasons justice.[47]

—SHAKESPEARE, *The Merchant of Venice*

Freedom and Justice Arch

Portia focuses the flame of God's justice in her retreat over Ghana in Africa. South of Ghana in Luanda, Angola, is the violet-flame retreat of the Elohim Arcturus and Victoria, which anchors the flame of freedom. Notably in Accra, the capital of Ghana, there is a monument called the Freedom and Justice Arch—the very flames that are focused in these two retreats. This arch serves as an outer physical arc for Portia's inner etheric retreat. Portia has said the music of the "Rakoczy March" by Franz Liszt will magnetize her presence.

Let this world be a place of the violet flame, and may you be exonerated by your service. Beloved Portia is gratified that you understand the urgency of her need to bring divine justice to every household upon earth. That divine justice, beloved, will bring all the souls of the world (save those who move against my beloved Portia) to that place of opportunity whereby they might move forward.[48] —SAINT GERMAIN

47 Shakespeare, *The Merchant of Venice,* act 4, sc. 1, lines 184–97.

48 *Pearls of Wisdom,* vol. 41, no. 31.

Dispensations of Cosmic Light

Over the course of time, the ascended masters have given many grants of energy, or dispensations of spiritual light, for the benefit of their students and all mankind. These releases came through dictations and direct instruction to the messengers to help humanity evolve toward the ascension. Quite a few relate to the violet flame; others apply to different decrees and situations. All represent unprecedented opportunities for our spiritual growth, protection and perfection in the light.

The Action of Dispensations

How does a dispensation work and what are its characteristics? Elizabeth Clare Prophet explained: "A dispensation consists of a grant of energy that often comes all the way from Alpha and Omega to the cosmic councils, from the cosmic councils to our own Karmic Board, from the Karmic Board to Lord Gautama, Lord Maitreya, and so forth."[49] The grants of energy can apply to the earth body, to those who have the highest attainment on earth or to all of humanity. A dispensation can also be time-sensitive; it may last only for a specific period or it may remain in effect indefinitely.

Mrs. Prophet said dispensations do not come without accountability. They are like going to the bank and asking for a loan. The bank will lend someone money only if it believes the person will use the funds wisely and pay back the loan. The same thing is true when grants are given by God—we have to use them wisely. We cannot assume the dispensations will always be available, so it is important to make good use of them when they are offered.

Omri-Tas' Violet-Flame Multiplier

A number of dispensations for the violet flame have been given to increase its potential and impact. Since the violet flame is capable of incredible transmutation, it is one of the most powerful tools for the salvation of the planet. In 1991, Omri-Tas, Ruler of the Violet Planet, gave a tremendous grant of energy for the multiplication of 15 minutes of violet flame by the power of ten, resulting in 150 minutes of violet flame for every 15 minutes of pure violet flame invoked.

Omri-Tas gave this dispensation because he knows what the violet flame can do.

49 *Pearls of Wisdom*, vol. 43, no. 14.

The evolutions of the Violet Planet once approached a crisis similar to the one now faced by the people of Earth. In response to the rallying call of the representative of the Divine Mother, the servants of God were galvanized and turned the tide by the violet flame. Omri-Tas explained, "They heard the call to give their invocations at altars around that planet. There was a saturation of the planetary body with the violet flame. That saturation therefore did flush out the fallen angels, who then could be bound by the legions of light and removed. . . . We went on into a golden age because of the few who responded, and today that planet is sustained in that golden age because the people have not lost the memory of that which was almost a planetary holocaust."[50]

The evolutions of the Violet Planet have served the violet flame for aeons and use its radiant energy to tend to all the needs of daily life—cleaning their homes, caring for and purifying the planet, and even washing and bathing. Menial chores are performed by violet-flame angels and elementals, which allows the inhabitants time to pursue the path of adeptship and to serve other planetary homes. Across the Violet Planet, 144,000 priests of the sacred fire tend the violet flame day and night and perform seventh-ray ceremonies and rituals at thousands of altars. Earth can have the same future if we but take advantage of Omri-Tas' dispensation. He explains exactly what it involves:

> If in all reverence, with inner attunement, a sense of yourself in your Christ Self as priest or priestess of the sacred fire, if with all your heart and deep within your heart you will take, then, fifteen minutes each day to give *profound* and loving invocations to the violet flame in my name (and please remember to use my name, for I am the one from whose causal body this dispensation comes), then we will take that offering, measure for measure as it is devoted, as it is profound and sincere, the very weight of its power and light. Therefore, by the quality of it, quality for quality, it shall be multiplied in your life ten times![51]

Mrs. Prophet explained precisely how to use this dispensation. She said that the fifteen-minute period counts only for the actual violet-flame decrees given. It does not include preambles to the violet-flame decrees, personal calls or the closing. This is because the energy is being multiplied by the momentum we each have on the violet flame, and by the extent to which we magnetize the violet flame from the causal body of Omri-Tas. This magnetization occurs through every person's heart, love, momentum and the flow of the sacred Word.

50 *Pearls of Wisdom,* vol. 34, no. 26.
51 *Pearls of Wisdom,* vol. 27, no. 50A.

SPOKEN WORD PRACTICE: USING THE DISPENSATION OF OMRI-TAS

The high-frequency energy of the violet flame has the power to transmute negative energy manifesting at physical, mental, emotional and spiritual levels. Such energy may take the form of illness, stress, anxiety, fear or unwanted habits. It can also be simultaneously directed into any unwanted condition on the planet such as drugs or pollution. It truly is a cosmic eraser and a precious gift we cannot afford to ignore because, like any dispensation, it may not always be available. As Saint Germain said, "Beloved, I tell you this: the time will come when I will not have these dispensations. May you count the hours precious wherein you can pursue through the violet flame the bonding to your Holy Christ Self, wherein you can pursue that pillar of fire in the midst of your being. Such offerings, beloved, almost go begging on the earth today."[52]

The following exercise activates the 15-minute dispensation of Omri-Tas. Be sure to name all the negative conditions you would like to see transmuted because after giving the decree to Saint Germain below, it will count for 150 minutes of violet flame as long as the conditions are met. Please set aside approximately 20 minutes for this spoken Word practice. You will need a clock or a watch to time your violet-flame decree.

1. Sit upright with your feet flat on the floor; your hands and legs uncrossed.
2. Breathe deeply until you are calm and centered.
3. Focus your attention in your heart, connecting with your threefold flame. Pour out your adoration to God in reverence for the life beating within.
4. Give the following preamble and insert your personal calls in the blank.

O SAINT GERMAIN, SEND VIOLET FLAME

Beloved mighty victorious Presence of God, I AM in me, thou immortal unfed flame of Christ-love within my heart, Holy Christ Selves of all mankind, beloved Ascended Master Saint Germain, beloved Mother Mary and beloved Jesus the Christ, the beloved Maha Chohan, Archangel Zadkiel, Prince Oromasis, all great beings, powers, and activities of light serving the violet transmuting flame, beloved Guru Ma and Lanello, the entire Spirit of the Great White Brotherhood and the World Mother, elemental life—fire, air, water, and earth!

In the name and by the power of the Presence of God which I AM and by the magnetic power of the sacred fire vested in me, I invoke the mighty presence and power of your full-gathered momentum of service to the light of God that never fails, and I command that it be directed throughout my entire consciousness, being, and world, through my affairs, the activities of The Summit Lighthouse, and all ascended master activities, worlds without end.

Threefold Flame

52 *Pearls of Wisdom*, vol. 34, no. 26.

In thy name, O God, I decree for the violet-flame transmutation of [*name any negative conditions you would like to change*]**. *I call to beloved Omri-Tas to multiply these violet-flame decrees ten times!* According to God's will, let it be done.**

5. Start timing your decrees for at least 15 full minutes as you give the following decree. Repeat the body of the decree as many times as needed to fill the time period, giving the refrain after each verse and concluding with the coda.

www.SummitLighthouse.org/
SA3-23

1. **O Saint Germain, send violet flame,**
Sweep it through my very core;
Bless'd Zadkiel, Oromasis,
Expand and intensify more and more.

Refrain: **Right now blaze through and saturate,**
Right now expand and penetrate;
Right now set free, God's mind to be,
Right now and for eternity.

2. **I AM in the flame and there I stand,**
I AM in the center of God's hand;
I AM filled and thrilled by violet hue,
I AM wholly flooded through and through.

3. **I AM God's flame within my soul,**
I AM God's flashing beacon goal;
I AM, I AM the sacred fire,
I feel the flow of joy inspire.

4. **The consciousness of God in me**
Does raise me to the Christ I see.
Descending now in violet flame,
I see him come fore'er to reign.

5. **O Jesus, send thy violet flame,**
Sanctify my very core;
Blessed Mary, in God's name,
Expand and intensify more and more.

6. **O mighty I AM, send violet flame,**
Purify my very core;
Maha Chohan, thou holy one,
Expand, expand God's lovely sun.

Coda: **He takes me by the hand to say,**
I love thy soul each blessed day;
O rise with me into the air
Where blossoms freedom from all care;
As violet flame keeps blazing through,
I know that I'll ascend with you.

6. At the end of 15 or more minutes, seal the decree with the following closing.

 And in full faith I consciously accept this manifest, manifest, manifest! (3x) **right here and now with full power, eternally sustained, all-powerfully active, ever expanding, and world enfolding until all are wholly ascended in the light and free!**

 Beloved I AM! Beloved I AM! Beloved I AM![53]

7. Following this same matrix, you can give any other violet-flame decrees any time you choose.

Omri-Tas' and Saint Germain's Day

On November 16, 1991, the messenger announced a dispensation from Omri-Tas in which he said he would be present on earth on the third of each month to render service by his great causal body. Omri-Tas carries such an intensity of violet flame and the seventh ray in his aura that it extends far beyond the actual size of the planet. Mrs. Prophet said, "What this does for Omri-Tas and for the evolutions of earth is that it puts up a wall of violet flame that will transmute everything that touches it, which means Omri-Tas has given us the means through his causal body to put the brakes on planetary war, planetary momentums of evil—and this is exciting."[54]

As it is the third of the month in at least one time zone somewhere on the planet for a span of forty-eight hours, the monthly Omri-Tas' Day violet-flame vigil begins on the second day of the month and ends on the fourth.[55] Saint Germain also announced that he is present with Omri-Tas during this time: "We gather both on Earth and on the Violet Planet in celebration of Omri-Tas and Saint Germain's Day. And for forty-eight hours, my beloved Keepers of the Flame sustain a perpetual prayer vigil to the violet flame."[56]

Saint Germain spoke with profound gratitude for our service of giving violet flame on Omri-Tas' Day: "For I, Saint Germain, make you this promise: that those who stand and still stand with me and Omri-Tas in these hours, giving tirelessly the calls to the violet flame and all other calls that you give, shall have a reward personally from me from my causal body that shall be great indeed. And it shall be great indeed because my gratitude to you shall be great indeed forever and forever!"[57]

---

53 This decree is printed in *Prayers, Meditations and Dynamic Decrees*, p. 463, no. 70.15.

54 *Pearls of Wisdom*, vol. 46, no. 26.

55 For more information and for an explanation of how to calculate the beginning and ending times of the Omri-Tas' Violet Flame Day vigil in your time zone, see "Omri-Tas' Day: A 48-Hour Opportunity," 1993 *Pearls of Wisdom*, "I AM the Witness," pp. 72–76 and accompanying time zone map. See also 1993 *Pearls of Wisdom*, vol. 36, no. 31, pp. 453, 458; and 1994 *Pearls of Wisdom*, vol. 37, no. 1, p. 7.

56 *Pearls of Wisdom*, vol. 39, no. 22.

57 *Pearls of Wisdom*, vol. 35, no. 3.

CHAPTER 8

Your Path of Personal Christhood

Follow Your Ray to Christ-Mastery

As the Sacred Adventure series draws to an end, there are two big topics left to discuss: the path of personal Christhood and actively working with the ascended masters.

These two topics may seem unrelated but in reality, they are deeply intertwined. One is not possible without the other. In this chapter we will put the pieces together into a meaningful whole that will reveal to you the next steps on the spiritual path.

What Is Christhood?

Throughout the three books in the Sacred Adventure series, the word "Christhood" was used to point to a specific level of consciousness just above the human. In the West, the greatest exemplar of this level of consciousness was Jesus Christ—so Christhood in essence points to the type of advanced awareness and abilities that Jesus demonstrated for us.

In the East, this same level of consciousness has also been recognized and made a focus of spiritual striving. Hinduism recognizes Krishna, for instance, as a similar exemplar of this higher state of consciousness. Taoism speaks of the "Perfect Man"—the ideal human being who is one with the great Tao and has fully perfected himself.

> The Tao Te Ching *says:*
>
> *If you are one with the Tao, to the end of your days you will suffer no harm.*
>
> *The Perfect Man could ascend the loftiest heights without fear, could enter the water and not get wet, could enter the fire and not get burned.*

Spiritual traditions such as Theosophy have used the word "adept" to point to this more-than-human level of self-mastery. Developing one's "higher mental body" has also been a popular way of referring to it. Modern-day psychological schools have identified the concept of the transpersonal self to refer to this same spiritualized, exalted state of being.

Chart of Your Divine Self

In short, we are talking about a universally recognized higher state of consciousness and are simply using the Western word "Christhood" to make it easily discussable.

You've learned in these books that attaining Christhood is not the ultimate goal. There is an even higher state of consciousness that could be called our divine consciousness. The Chart of Your Divine Self depicts these different stages.

Above the human or soul level (shown as a person invoking the violet flame), there is the image of the Holy Christ Self. This Higher Self is the midway point in our quest to reach the highest state of consciousness available to us while still unascended. Buddhists call this ultimate state of being "enlightenment."

The Chart is therefore not a static image; it depicts a journey of spiritual growth and self-mastery. The first station in the journey is to fully bond with our Holy Christ Self and live permanently in the Christ consciousness, as Jesus demonstrated.

From that point of oneness with our Christ Self, our consciousness evolves to the next station: bonding and blending with our Divine Self or I AM Presence, which leads to the state of oneness with the divine consciousness and to our ascension—our liberation from the wheel of birth and rebirth and our permanent entry into the realms of Spirit as an immortal being.

The Importance of Christhood

The ascended masters place supreme importance on attaining our Christhood. The great Lord Sanat Kumara once said in a dictation, "The hour of Christhood in you is more important than any other event taking place upon this planet."[1]

Why is this so?

The first reason is personal: once we are fully bonded with our Holy Christ Self, there is not much left that can deter us from making our ascension. And making our ascension is our very reason for being in embodiment in the first place, as you've seen in Book 1.

The second reason is planetary. The higher our state of consciousness, the more spiritual light we are able to contain and retain and the more we can do for this world. Someone who is in the process of bonding with their Christ Self, whom we call a Christed one, can hold a tremendous balance for other people, communities and nations.

This is illustrated by the example of the Ascended Master Igor. Igor was a simple Russian peasant boy who lived at the time of the Russian Revolution. Igor had a deep devotion to Mother Mary and Archangel Gabriel. The archangel often visited him and

1 *Pearls of Wisdom*, vol. 31, no. 44.

showed him visions of the things that could come upon the nation. During and after the revolution Igor engaged in hours and hours of prayer to help his countrymen who were suffering under the yoke of communism. He rendered them invaluable service by this simple life of prayer and devotion and made his ascension at the conclusion of that embodiment.

So, striving for your Christhood is very important. It can revolutionize how you set priorities and live your life. It can inspire and enfire you to be up and doing whatever it takes to attain that oneness. It can also lay the foundation for a sense of spiritual co-measurement that spurs you on as you are engaged in the seemingly mundane activities of daily existence. The pursuit of your personal Christhood leads to the realization that those activities and how you do them are integral stepping stones to attaining your spiritual victory.

> *Take note that you are becoming your Holy Christ Self as you merge with him, not just once in a while but hour by hour and every twenty-four hours as you walk and talk with this very special teacher.*
>
> *Beloved ones, there is no such thing as a carbon copy of the Holy Christ Self. Each one's Holy Christ Self is totally and utterly unique. . . . Your individual Holy Christ Self has a very special personality. That personality has been developed over aeons of being the Christ in action.*
>
> *Thus, beloved, you have unique talents. Those talents come from your Holy Christ Self and from your labors in the fields of this civilization and others on the planetary home.*[2]
>
> —LANELLO

Seven Paths to Christhood

How do we go about attaining our Christhood?

It's important to remember that to become a Christed one does not happen overnight. It's a gradual process of overcoming, of leaving behind the undesirable aspects of our lower or everyday self and identifying more and more with the light of God that dwells within.

The ascended masters teach that there are seven unique paths, not just one, to the victory of personal Christhood, each related to one of the seven rays.

The Elohim of Purity explained why this is the case: "Out of the white-fire core of the Holy Spirit come forth the seven rays of the Christic light. These denote the evolution of mankind's consciousness on the path of Christhood. And thus there are seven paths whereby mankind might evolve to the fullness of the stature of Christ."[3]

An exciting part of your spiritual journey is discovering which of these seven rays your soul has chosen to pursue—and then following it all the way to your ascension in the light.

2 *Pearls of Wisdom*, vol. 40, no. 42.
3 *Pearls of Wisdom*, vol. 21, no. 8.

Let's briefly review the origin of this spiritual pursuit.[4] Going back to our soul's creation can help explain why we serve on a specific ray.

In the beginning, each I AM Presence was made in the image and likeness of God, endowed with the potential to manifest individuality and creativity. While the divine essence of everyone's I AM Presence is the same, the Father-Mother God imprinted upon the fiery white core of each Presence a unique divine blueprint that we share only with our twin flame.

This spiritual blueprint holds the keys to our unique destiny in life. It contains our divine plan, the purpose of being for which we were created.

Long before we came into physical embodiment, we journeyed through the energy spheres of God's consciousness. As we magnetized and gathered skeins of light around our I AM Presence, these began to form the rings of colored light in our causal body. It's at that very early point in our spiritual existence that we began to develop a preference for one or two of the seven rays.

After the causal body was formed, our twin flames separated into two identical spheres as Alpha and Omega polarities—the plus and minus, positive and negative energies—for the purpose of descending from Spirit into matter. And that started our long journey into physical existence, with the purpose of mastering ourselves and becoming conscious co-creators with God.

Our souls have been evolving for as long as they have been sojourning in the material universe. When we first came into physical form, we were still very much aware of the Presence of God with us. During our thousands of years of evolution, we adapted more and more to the denser vibrations of the earth plane, which resulted in a loss of memory of our origin and of the true nature of ourselves as spiritual beings.

Following Your Ray to Self-Mastery

In his book *The Chela and the Path,* the ascended master El Morya explained how the seven rays and the path of personal Christhood are related. In his usual terse way he also introduced the concept of working with the specific chohan, or lord, of the ray who governs our own native ray. He said:

> All mankind are born to serve and to master the self on one of the seven rays. Their first guru,[5] then, after the Christ Self, who is the true teacher of each man and woman, is the chohan of the ray on which they serve. Therefore, those who would be chelas,[6] those who would pursue the path of soul liberation, will be happy to know that there are seven distinct paths of Christhood, that one of these paths is best fitted to your soul personality and inner calling, and that a

4 For more information, see chapter 1 of *The Spiritual Quest.*

5 *Guru* is a Sanskrit word for a spiritual teacher; it means "dispeller of darkness."

6 *Chela* is a Sanskrit word that connotes a disciple of a guru. The ancient root of this term is the word *ceta,* which means a slave.

El Morya

second will complement the first. And so you might say that on the seven rays you have a major and a minor concentration of study and application in the law of becoming the Christ.

Now it is your supreme privilege to define in your world and in your life the path that you will pursue on the homeward way. As you learn more of the ascended masters and their teachings, as you play their recorded dictations given at quarterly conferences, as you read and meditate upon their words, you will begin to identify the positioning of your soul on one of the paths of the seven rays.

Realize, too, that it is the requirement of the ascension that you garner a sufficiency of the white light in your four lower bodies; for the white light is the source of all of the color rays. It is the fiery core of the flame out of which is spun the wedding garment. Your momentum of the white light is the means whereby you magnetize the flame of the ascension in the hour of your victory.

In order to achieve the mastery of the white light, you must have a certain mastery on all of the seven rays; for as you master the rays, they lead you back to the center of the white light, back to the prism of the Christ consciousness whence they came. Moreover, it is impossible to gain mastery on one of the seven rays without this mastery carrying over through the oneness of the white-fire core to other aspects of the Christ consciousness. Nevertheless, your high calling as a son or daughter of God which we term the sacred labor—which involves the perfecting of the talents that God has placed within your soul—will be achieved on the ray of your major with the support of your minor. All else will be an adornment of that central fiery purpose.

Every soul by free will elects the path of his own ascension. Your soul has already chosen and developed a considerable momentum on the ray of its destiny. This occurred while the soul was yet cycling within the spheres of the causal body prior to incarnation in the planes of Matter. The causal body of every son and daughter of God reflects this larger momentum of concentration on the chosen ray.[7]

There are five key points in this excerpt that form the backbone of the soul's spiritual path under the ascended masters:

1. Your Holy Christ Self is your true teacher or guru.
2. There are seven distinct paths to Christhood related to the seven rays.
3. Your soul has elected one path towards Christhood—your major ray.
4. A second path complements the first—your minor ray.
5. Your first guru (after your Holy Christ Self) is the chohan of the ray on which you serve.

The word *guru* has special significance in Morya's comments. It indicates that one is moving from a teacher-student relationship to a deeper tie—that of guru-disciple (or

7 El Morya, *The Chela and the Path,* pp. 53–55.

guru-chela). This conveys a more serious commitment to the path of personal Christhood. Anyone can read books and study on his own. A student with a teacher has the added benefit of the teacher's experience and perspective. But the fastest way to pursue our own Christhood, our own higher consciousness, is to apprentice ourselves to one of the seven chohans whose lives we have studied in detail in these pages and in Book 2 of the Sacred Adventure series.

In some ways, striving to become a living Christ is similar to becoming a concert pianist or an Olympic athlete. Each requires attentive learning, the application of solid principles and hard work. Studying with an expert in your chosen field of endeavor is an added boon of priceless benefit because he knows how to help you achieve your highest potential. When it comes to spiritual evolution, the seven chohans are unequalled teachers on the seven rays, and studying under them provides tremendous assistance in gaining self-mastery.

As we have seen, the path of self-mastery doesn't end with attaining our Christhood. There are steps beyond it that lead to our full divinity, our Godhood. The seven chohans are simply the appointed teachers who have the task to take us to that point of personal Christhood. Once we arrive there, other ascended master teachers stand ready to receive us and lead us to the next stage in our spiritual development.

A Review of the Rainbow Rays

El Morya's teaching shows the importance of establishing a relationship with the chohan of our major ray. Yet it may not always be clear which ray and chohan we are most strongly connected with. A brief review of the rays and chohans is therefore included here as a refresher.

Each of the seven rays can be seen as a refraction of the white light of the Holy Spirit. And each of these rays is a unique path leading back to the center of the white light, back to the prism of the Christ consciousness from whence they came.

Let's review some basic facts about the seven rainbow rays.

The Chohans of the Rays

- Every ray has unique qualities that are expressions of the divine consciousness.
- The seven rays are anchored in our seven main chakras, which gives us a mechanism to get to know them and put them into action.[8]
- The chohan of a specific ray has excelled in developing and embodying the qualities of that ray; he or she is therefore especially qualified to teach us how to master that ray.
- Each of the seven rays is released most abundantly on one of the seven days of the week.
- Different gemstones amplify particular rays.

8 For more information, see chapter 4 of *The Spiritual Quest.*

The following chart can help with the process of discovering—or more accurately, *remembering*—the ray on which you chose long ago to give your gifts. It displays a concise summary of the rays, including the related chakras, positive and negative qualities, and gemstones. It also lists the chohans and archangels of the rays and their retreats. As you look it over, notice which characteristics naturally draw your attention. Take note of them mentally or write them in your journal; you may want to come back to this chart later as an aid in developing your Christhood.

THE SEVEN RAYS

RAY COLOR DAY	CHOHAN	CHAKRA PETALS	POSITIVE QUALITIES	NEGATIVE QUALITIES	CHOHAN'S RETREAT LOCATION	ARCHANGEL'S RETREAT LOCATION	GEMSTONES
First Ray Blue Tuesday	**El Morya**	**Throat** 16	Power Divine will Faith Goodwill Leadership Obedience Protection Perfection	Abuse of power Human will Doubt Lack of interest Fear or cowardice Disobedience Not protecting self/others Imperfection/ mediocrity	Darjeeling, India	**Michael and Faith** Banff and Lake Louise, Canada	Diamond Lapis lazuli Sapphire
Second Ray Yellow Sunday	**Lord Lanto**	**Crown** 972	Wisdom Illumination Discrimination Intelligence Insight	Ignorance Pride/arrogance/vanity Lack of discernment Mental density Narrow-mindedness	Grand Teton, Teton Range, Wyoming, USA	**Jophiel and Christine** South of the Great Wall Near Lanchow, North Central China	Yellow diamond Yellow sapphire Topaz Citrine quartz
Third Ray Pink Monday	**Paul the Venetian**	**Heart** 12	Love Compassion Creativity Caring Beauty	Hatred/anger Human sympathy Negligence Selfishness Sensuality	Southern France	**Chamuel and Charity** St. Louis, Missouri, USA	Diamond Garnet Rose quartz Pink beryl Ruby
Fourth Ray White Friday	**Serapis Bey**	**Base of the Spine** 4	Harmony Purity Discipline Joy Hope Law and order Excellence	Inharmony Impurity/lust/ sensuality Lack of self-control Depression/lack of joy Discouragement Lawlessness/chaos Mediocrity	Luxor, Egypt	**Gabriel and Hope** Between Sacramento and Mount Shasta, California, USA	Diamond Pearl Zircon Quartz crystal
Fifth Ray Green Wednesday	**Hilarion**	**Third Eye** 96	Wholeness/Healing Science Vision Truth Abundance/ Precipitation Music	Disease Degeneration Superstition Error/lying/ omission of facts Lack/insufficiency Dissonance/ discordant sound	Crete, Greece	**Raphael and Mother Mary** Fátima, Portugal	Emerald Diamond Jade Quartz crystal

(Continued)

RAY COLOR DAY	CHOHAN	CHAKRA PETALS	POSITIVE QUALITIES	NEGATIVE QUALITIES	CHOHAN'S RETREAT LOCATION	ARCHANGEL'S RETREAT LOCATION	GEMSTONES
Sixth Ray Purple & gold with ruby flecks Thursday	**Nada**	**Solar Plexus** 10	Service/Ministration Brotherhood Judgment Resurrection Desirelessness Peace	Ego-centeredness/ harmfulness War Criticism/ condemnation Degeneration/ disintegration Desirefulness Emotional turbulence	Saudi Arabia	**Uriel and Aurora** Tatra Mountains, South of Cracow, Poland	Pink/yellow topaz Ruby Alexandrite Diamond with pearl
Seventh Ray Violet Saturday	**Saint Germain**	**Seat of the Soul** 6	Freedom Justice Mercy/Forgiveness Alchemy/ Transmutation Tact/Diplomacy Tolerance	Servitude/bondage Injustice Hardness of heart Dogmatism Lack of savoir faire Intolerance	Transylvania, Romania; Table Mountain, Rocky Mountains, USA	**Zadkiel and Holy Amethyst** Cuba	Amethyst Aquamarine Diamond

Tips for Discovering Your Major Ray

Your divine blueprint has been with you since your inception in Divinity. If you are not immediately able to recognize your major ray, don't become worried or give up. A lot of time may have passed, but your destiny is still intact! Here are some helpful suggestions for finding clues to the ray on which you serve.

1. Think back to the chapters and topics of Books 2 and 3 in the Sacred Adventure series—especially the ones that discussed the seven chohans. Which of these chohans and topics appealed to you most? Were there any chohans that stood out to you as familiar or whose lives and rays you felt particularly drawn to?

2. Reflect on your childhood and try to remember what was your favorite color when you were young.

3. Consider how your occupation, avocation or favorite types of work could indicate the ray on which you serve.[9]

4. Recollect any memorable experiences in your life that may point to your affinity on a certain ray. For example, one individual made an inner vow to uphold the truth when she was a teenager; she now sees herself as serving on the fifth ray, which most expresses this quality.

5. Give decrees and/or fiats on each of the seven rays. Your favorites may reveal the ray or rays to which you're most naturally attracted. Some sample fiats are provided below.

9 You may want to review the chapters on the rays in *The Spiritual Quest* and *Meeting the Masters* to help you recognize your major ray.

FIATS ON THE SEVEN RAYS		
RAY	CHOHAN	FIAT
Blue	El Morya	Thy will, O God, is good!
Yellow	Lord Lanto	I AM the golden flame of illumination!
Pink	Paul the Venetian	I AM perfect love casting out all fear!
White	Serapis Bey	LORD, I AM worthy of thy purity!
Green	Hilarion	In the name of Jesus Christ, be thou made whole!
Purple and gold	Nada	I AM my brother's keeper!
Violet	Saint Germain	I AM the light of the heart!

6. While your consciousness is a symphony of attainment in the rainbow rays, your favorite musical instruments and colors may also reflect the rays and chakras to which you most relate. The following chart shows the seven rays along with their corresponding chakras, colors and musical instruments. Which instruments please you the most?

CHAKRAS AND MUSICAL INSTRUMENTS ON THE SEVEN RAYS		
RAY/COLOR	CHAKRA	INSTRUMENT
First/Blue	Throat	Brass
Second/Yellow	Crown	Strings
Third/Pink	Heart	Harp
Fourth/White	Base of the Spine	Drums
Fifth/Green	Third Eye	Piano
Sixth/Purple and gold with ruby	Solar Plexus	Organ
Seventh/Violet	Seat of the Soul	Woodwinds, especially flute

EXERCISE: ASSESSING YOUR PREFERENCES ON THE RAYS

The following pages contain an informational tool developed by Summit University that is designed to help you tune in to your major and minor rays. Please note that this exercise is not definitive; it simply helps indicate your preferences. People often shift their concentration on particular rays at various periods during their lives, so a strong preference may indicate the ray(s) on which you are currently working rather than your soul's ultimate major and minor rays. Regardless, the exercise can help point you to rays you may want to look at as possibly being your major and/or minor ray.

Preparation

The exercise takes roughly 20–30 minutes. Take the following steps to get the best results:

1. Play some soft meditative music to help you attune to the promptings of your Holy Christ Self.
2. Close your eyes and center in your heart.
3. Take a few deep breaths.
4. Spend a few minutes tensing and relaxing your muscles from your toes to your head.
5. Open your eyes, then read the instructions below and complete the exercise.

Instructions

The exercise consists of three pages of choices related to the seven rays. Simply follow the instructions at the top of each page on how to select your preferences. The instructions differ per page so please read them carefully. Please note: You'll get the most out of this exercise if you go by intuition rather than think too much about your choices.

MAJOR AND MINOR RAYS PREFERENCES EXERCISE

PART 1 – VIRTUES

Instruction: In each horizontal row, there are seven words or phrases. Rate each of the words or phrases on a scale of 1 to 7, where 7 stands for "This appeals to me most" and 1 stands for "This appeals to me least." Use each number in the series 1 - 2 - 3 - 4 - 5 - 6 - 7 only once in each row. When you're done with all the rows, add up your scores for each column. Then go to Part 2 of the exercise.

MAJOR AND MINOR RAYS PREFERENCES EXERCISE PART 1 – VIRTUES

A		B		C		D		E		F		G	
Comfort		Rejuvenation		Mercy		Humility		Joy		Obedience		Altruism	
Selflessness		Abundance		Justice		Wisdom		Self-discipline		Will		Fairness	
Beauty		Science		Tolerance		Reason		Morality		Protection		Service	
Communion		Generosity		Transmutation		Enlightenment		Blueprint		Power		Brotherhood	
Grace		Gratitude		Forgiveness		Understanding		Hope		Direction		Balance	
Harmony		Healing		Liberty		Intelligence		Totality		Faith		Desirelessness	
Creativity		Wholeness		Ritual		Consciousness		Symmetry		Construction		Harmlessness	
Compassion		Constancy		Transcendence		Resourcefulness		Geometry		Love of God's law		Righteousness	
Unity		Regeneration		Poise		Open-mindedness		Lawfulness		Communication		Calm	
Charity		Precipitation		Tact		Clarity		Order		Dominion		Assistance	
Love		Truth		Freedom		Illumination		Purity		Perfection		Peace	
Desire to be God in action through the love of the Holy Spirit		Desire to precipitate the abundance of God through the immaculate concept of the Holy Virgin		Desire to make all things new through the application of the laws of alchemy		Desire to know God through the mind of the Son		Desire to know God through purity of body, mind and soul through the consciousness of the Divine Mother		Desire to do the will of God through the power of the Father		Desire to be in the service of God and man through the mastery of the Christ	
SCORE A:		**SCORE B:**		**SCORE C:**		**SCORE D:**		**SCORE E:**		**SCORE F:**		**SCORE G:**	

MAJOR AND MINOR RAYS PREFERENCES EXERCISE PART 2 – HUMAN QUALITIES

H		J		K		L		M		N		O	
Lack of self-control		Destructiveness		Sloth		Warring in one's members		Selfishness		Hardness of heart		Superstition	
Discouragement		Doubt		Vanity		Self-centeredness		Negligence		Stagnation		Degeneration	
Amorality		Defiance		Stupidity		Instability		Human sympathy		Intolerance		Carelessness	
Separateness		Lawlessness		Lethargy		Emotional turbulence		Decay		Dogma		Error	
Anarchy		Cowardice		Intellectualism		Harmfulness		Ugliness		Rote behavior		Greed	
Chaos		Rebellion		Pride		Cliques and gangs		Discord		Cruelty		Envy	
Incompleteness		Imperfection		Density		Worry		Sensuality		Injustice		Possessiveness	
Lust		Vacillation		Ignorance		Free love		Discomfort		Bondage		Lack	
Negative spirals		Controlling others		Narrow-mindedness		Antisocial behavior		Disintegration		Depravity		Disease	
SCORE H:		**SCORE J:**		**SCORE K:**		**SCORE L:**		**SCORE M:**		**SCORE N:**		**SCORE O:**	

MAJOR AND MINOR RAYS PREFERENCES EXERCISE
PART 2 – HUMAN QUALITIES

Instruction: Rate each of the phrases in each row on a scale of 1 to 7, where 7 stands for "I dislike this the most" and 1 stands for "I dislike this the least." Use each number in the series 1 – 2 – 3 – 4 – 5 – 6 – 7 only once in each row. When you're done with all of the rows, add up your scores for each column. Then go to Part 3 of the exercise.

MAJOR AND MINOR RAYS PREFERENCES EXERCISE
PART 3 – MISCELLANEOUS ASPECTS

Instruction: Rate each of the words in each row on a scale of 1 to 7, where 7 stands for "This attracts me the most" and 1 stands for "This attracts me the least." Use each number in the series 1 – 2 – 3 – 4 – 5 – 6 – 7 only once in each row. When you're done with all the rows, add up your scores for each column. Then go to Part 4 of the exercise.

MAJOR AND MINOR RAYS PREFERENCES EXERCISE PART 3 – MISCELLANEOUS ASPECTS

P		Q		R		S		T		U		V	
Flute		Organ		Trumpet		Piano		Drums		Harp		Violin	
Purple Fiery Heart		Righteous Heart		Diamond Heart		Immaculate Heart		Pure Heart		Magnanimous Heart		Wise Heart	
Saint Germain		Jesus		Lanello		Hilarion		Serapis Bey		Paul the Venetian		Kuthumi	
Amethyst		Pearl		Lapis lazuli		Emerald		Rock crystal		Garnet		Yellow Topaz	
Alchemist		Attorney		Leader		Scientist		Architect		Artist		Educator	
Goddess of Liberty		Magda		Amazonia		Pallas Athena		Goddess of Purity		Rose of Light		Theosophia	
Violet		Purple and gold		Blue		Green		White		Pink		Yellow	
Taoism		Mystical Islam / Sufism		Judaism / Kabbalah		Confucianism		Hinduism		Mystical Path of Christianity		Buddhism	
Priest / Minister		Judge		Statesman / Politician		Healer		Builder		Designer		Philosopher	
SCORE P:		**SCORE Q:**		**SCORE R:**		**SCORE S:**		**SCORE T:**		**SCORE U:**		**SCORE V:**	

MAJOR AND MINOR RAYS PREFERENCES EXERCISE
PART 4 – TABULATION OF RESULTS

Fill in your scores from Parts 1–3 in the following table and add them up horizontally:

COLUMN / SCORE		COLUMN / SCORE		COLUMN / SCORE		TOTAL SCORE	RAY
F		J		R			First Ray
D		K		V			Second Ray
A		M		U			Third Ray
E		H		T			Fourth Ray
B		O		S			Fifth Ray
G		L		Q			Sixth Ray
C		N		P			Seventh Ray

Fill in your two highest scores below:

My highest score is ______________	______________ **Ray**
My second-highest score is ______________	______________ **Ray**

Reflect on your scores and write down your realizations in your notebook.

Disclaimer: This exercise is a tool to help you reflect on strong and weak preferences in relationship to the seven rays. It does not necessarily indicate your major and minor rays, though it may be helpful in trying to identify your major and minor rays.

Connecting with the Master of Your Ray

Hopefully you have gained some clarity in terms of tuning in to what could be your native major and minor rays. Now what?

Knowing your ray is only the beginning. The more important step is to connect with your ascended master teacher on your ray: one of the seven chohans!

It may be an intimidating thought to be working directly with an ascended master. But consider this: Your outer mind may not be aware of it, but if you have been striving as an aspirant on the spiritual path, your soul has already been tutored for a long time by the masters at inner levels in preparation for the time when you would have the conscious recognition of their presence in your life.

Who Is Your Chohan?

Discovering which of the seven chohans is your master is a wonderful way to help pinpoint your major ray and your spiritual mission in this life. Below are some recommended ways to intuit who this special master is.

1. Read about the past lives of the chohans.[10] There may be an individual or historical period that you relate to especially well or that brings back memories of a shared path in the past.
2. Study dictations released by the chohans or the books they wrote while embodied to get a better feel for who is the master teacher on your ray.[11]
3. Sing the songs of the seven chohans and let your heart tell you which of these seven masters is the guiding light in your life. You'll find these songs in the online resource collection.

www.SummitLighthouse.org/SA3-31

- "More," to El Morya www.SummitLighthouse.org/SA3-24
- "Lanto, Beloved Lanto" www.SummitLighthouse.org/SA3-25
- "Paul the Venetian" www.SummitLighthouse.org/SA3-26
- "All Hail, Mighty Serapis Bey" www.SummitLighthouse.org/SA3-27
- "Master Dear, Hilarion" www.SummitLighthouse.org/SA3-28
- "Beloved Nada, Our Chohan Divine" www.SummitLighthouse.org/SA3-29
- "I Love You Waltz to Saint Germain" www.SummitLighthouse.org/SA3-30

Once you have a sense of who your chohan is, you can ask him or her to accept you as a chela and tutor your soul in Christ-mastery. You can do this by simply speaking to the chohan or by writing a letter to him or her and burning it.

Another way to establish a bond with them is by doing the meditation below.[12] This is a beautiful way to formally request the acceptance and blessing of chelaship under your favorite chohan.

If at this moment you are still unclear about your major ray and not sure which chohan you should try to build a relationship with, there are two recommended courses of action:

1. You can simply pick a chohan that you like and ask him or her to be your teacher until such time as you discover with greater certainty who your actual chohan is.
2. You can ask El Morya, the chohan of the first ray, to work with you at inner levels and prepare you for the connection with the chohan of your ray when you are ready.

10 The previous lifetimes of each chohan are reviewed in detail in the book *Lords of the Seven Rays*, by Mark L. Prophet and Elizabeth Clare Prophet.

11 *Lords of the Seven Rays* contains several dictations by each of the seven chohans.

12 This meditation is adapted from Kuthumi and Djwal Kul, *The Human Aura*, pp. 162–63.

www.SummitLighthouse.org/ SA3-32

MEDITATION: THE ISLAND OF THE SEVEN RAYS

1. Be seated in an upright position in a place where you will not be disturbed. Play soft meditation music in the background if you like.

2. Draw an outline in your mind of an island located in the midst of a glistening nectar sea. The island is composed of jewel-like crystals—emeralds, diamonds and rubies.

3. Imagine yourself approaching this island. Now see yourself walking from the shore of the sea through the tropical trees and vegetation to the center and highest promontory of the island. Visualize tropical birds and flowers of delicate and brilliant colors. You hear the songs of the birds as they sing the song celestial and key your soul to the frequencies of the etheric place.

4. As you stand in the center of the island, bathed in the sunlight, visualize a platform and on it see seven ornate thrones that are consecrated to the image and the sacred presence of the seven chohans. These thrones are exquisite—richly carved, gold-leafed and inlaid with precious and semiprecious stones. On each throne there is a cushion in the color of one of the seven rays.

5. Now visualize the seven chohans in all their regal splendor.

   - On the blue throne sits El Morya, Chohan of the First Ray, in all of his radiant power, majestic and stern but with a twinkle in his eyes.
   - On the yellow throne is seated Lord Lanto, Chohan of the Second Ray, deep in meditation. The soft golden glow of his threefold flame can be seen shining through his chest.
   - On the pink throne sits beloved Paul the Venetian, Chohan of the Third Ray. He is smiling, beaming vast oceans of love from his heart.
   - On the white throne in the center you see Serapis Bey, Chohan of the Fourth Ray, emanating the disciplined essence of purity's fire.
   - On the green throne sits Hilarion, Chohan of the Fifth Ray, radiating the healing vibrations of wholeness and truth.

- On the purple and gold throne sits Lady Master Nada, Chohan of the Sixth Ray, smiling graciously with a welcoming aura of peace.
- On the last throne, the violet, sits Saint Germain, Chohan of the Seventh Ray. His aura blazes with brilliant violet fire that conveys his desire for your soul's victory.

6. Approach the chohan of the ray whom you feel most attracted to. Kneel before him or her.
7. In the silence of your heart, ask the chohan to accept you as a chela on his or her ray and to tutor your soul in attaining personal Christhood.
8. After you have communed with the chohan in this profound and intimate way, thank him or her. Rise, slowly turn around and walk back down the hill to the shore, carrying the light of this encounter with your guru in your heart.
9. With your inner sight, gaze out across the ocean, which seems as vast as God's consciousness, until you feel like opening your eyes. Move your arms and legs and slowly bring your consciousness back into your body.
10. Give the following prayer:

Teach me, O chohan of my life,
How to be thyself,
How to walk the earth
As heart and head and hand
Responding to thy will at thy command.
Teach me, O chohan of my love,
How to feel the flow,
How to give thy succor
To all hearts below.
Teach me now, O chohan of the law,
To fulfill the promise of the seven rays
And to be forevermore
Prism'd awareness of thy grace.

11. Record your realizations in your journal.

Developing a Relationship with Your Chohan

Once you have requested the sponsorship and guidance of a chohan, it is important to develop a guru-chela relationship with that master. El Morya's definition of a disciple, or chela, is "the one striving to become the Christ, [which is] your Real Self."[13] Our chohan's main task is to help us do that very thing—becoming the Christ—and he will spare no effort to guide us to that goal.

There is a significant difference between this sacred relationship with the chohan

13 *Pearls of Wisdom*, vol. 28, no. 11.

or guru of our ray and any other person on earth. We cannot count on those in embodiment to always uphold their side of a relationship. But in the guru-chela relationship, we can always count on the chohans of the rays. The question is whether or not we will uphold *our* side of the bond.

If we strive earnestly to be a dedicated chela to the best of our abilities, the chohans stand ever ready to offer their assistance as we pursue our Christhood. They will provide unerring guidance. They will also point out our faults and make us aware of those things that stand in the way of our Christhood and need to be surrendered on the altar of transmutation.

Here are some ways to discover the deeper meaning of this special relationship and strengthen your tie to the master:

1. Regularly ask to go to the chohan's retreat to be tutored there in the next steps of your soul's development.

2. Meditate on a picture of the chohan and/or his retreat. Pictures allow the master to radiate grace and blessings to you through his image that you gaze upon.[14]

3. Ask the chohan to superimpose his heart chakra over your heart chakra to amplify the exchange of energy between you. Visualize this interchange taking place as a figure-eight flow between your heart and the heart of the chohan.

4. Continually ask the master for guidance in all things great and small—and cultivate a listening ear and discerning heart that will teach you how to identify the unique vibration of your master.

Five Stages of Discipleship

Chelaship is a process and a relationship that evolves over time. The ascended masters recognize a step-by-step path of spiritual development that consists of five stages, culminating in full-fledged Christhood. It's helpful to review these stages to see where we fit as aspiring chelas on the path: where we came from, what our current tasks are, and what lies ahead of us.

1) Student

Under this phase the individual studies, becomes a student of the writings and the teachings of the master. He is free to come and go and has declared no particular responsibility to the person of the master. He has taken no vows, made no commitment, but may be studying to "show himself approved"[15] in order to be accepted as a servant (otherwise known as "chela") of the master.

14 Pictures of the seven chohans are available from The Summit Lighthouse online bookstore (SummitLighthouse.org/store).

15 II Timothy 2:15.

2) Servant or Chela, a Disciple

The individual desires to enter into a bond with the master—to be taught directly by the master rather than through his published writings alone. The individual receives initiations in the course of his service to the master. His heart, mind, and soul have begun to unfold a greater love as appreciation and gratitude for the teachings received in the previous level of student. This love is translated into action as self-sacrifice, selflessness, service, and surrender to the Christ; when this step has been accelerated to the level of the "acceptable offering," and the chela is engaged in balancing his threefold flame and his karma, he may be considered for the next step.

3) Friend

Those counted as friend of the master—"Henceforth I call you no more servants but friends"[16]—enter by invitation into a relationship as companion and co-worker on the path of world salvation. The friend bears the cross as well as the burden of light of the master. He demonstrates the qualities of friendship as in the life of Abraham and other chelas who have risen to a level of understanding the very heart and the experience of the master—providing comfort, consolation, advice, and support out of loyalty to both the purposes and the person of the master.

4) Brother

The degree of brother is the level where the oneness of the guru-chela, Alpha-Omega relationship is complete through the horizontal figure-eight exchange heart-to-heart. The guru has actually made his disciple a part of his own flesh and blood and has offered to him the full momentum of his attainment and portions of his mantle and authority in preparation for the master's ascension and the disciple's assuming of a part or the whole of the master's office. This is the love relationship exemplified between Jesus and his disciple John the Beloved, and perhaps his own flesh-and-blood brother (or cousin) James.

5) Christ

The full incarnation of the Word.

Working with the Masters

The seven chohans are among a subgroup of ascended masters who occupy a special place on earth. Contrary to many beings who made their ascension and then moved on to other places of cosmic service, they have pledged to stay with our planet to help earth's evolutions attain their own soul liberation. This puts them squarely in the category of enlightened beings whom we speak of as *bodhisattvas*,[17] albeit bodhisattvas in the ascended state.

16 See John 15:15.

17 A *bodhisattva* is an advanced student of the Buddha who forsakes entering nirvana in order to help all sentient beings find liberation.

It's obvious that the seven chohans and other ascended beings who work with humankind have a lot of work to do. These masters come together in their councils to determine how to best assist us in the midst of all of the preoccupations and distractions of daily life that keep spiritual seekers from realizing their full potential.

As we have seen in the Sacred Adventure series, there are strict rules that govern the interactions between ascended and unascended beings. Each of these groups exist in their own realm or slice of the spiritual-material world. Due to the gift of free will that has been extended to mankind, the ascended masters may not intervene or intercede in the human realm unless they are invited by some among mankind to do so.

Our prayers and decrees are tools that give the masters access into our world. A second way in which the chela renders assistance to the master is by calling upon the master's ability to radiate energy and light into the world via the chela's aura and chakras.

The masters also direct their chelas to assist with specific work for planetary advancement that takes place on the master's ray. For instance, those working with El Morya on the first ray may be directed to encourage and inspire others or to take up critical leadership positions in their city or nation that will help advance the cause of light. Those working with Lord Lanto on the second ray tend to find themselves in positions where they are expected to convey spiritualized understanding and illumination. Each of the chohans is thus connected to a group of embodied chelas who assist him in his tasks by these various means. Some chelas are more conscious of it than others, but all who align themselves with a chohan and strive to do right become invaluable players in heaven's great opus.

It is this dedicated partnership between the ascended master and the chela that allows the master to instruct and correct the chela, which affords the chela maximum opportunity to transcend his old self and become more like his master. El Morya explained this process as follows:

> In the Eastern tradition, the chela is the slave of his master for a good reason—not for the loss of his true identity, but for the replacement of the pseudoimage with the Real Image of selfhood. The chela, by submission, day by day is weaving into consciousness the threads of the garment of his master. The master's garment (as the much sought-after robe of the Christ) is synonymous with the master's consciousness.[18]

Charles W. Leadbeater, an author from the early days of Theosophy, sums up the work done by the chelas or "pupils" in this quote:

> I have already mentioned that the pupils of the Masters are also apprentices, that at their lower level they serve as transmitters of force, and also do a great variety of work in every branch of civilization and human culture, all of which is part of the Adept's work in the world. A vast amount of this is done

18 El Morya, *The Chela and the Path*, p. 20.

> by others who have received inspiration or suggestion from these pupils, or through the various societies and agencies that they have set going or influenced. Without these influences humanity would be poor indeed, though for the most part it knows little of the source of its true wealth. The Adepts themselves cannot turn aside from their exalted work to do these lower and easier tasks, because if they did the whole machinery of evolution would suffer.
>
> Men sometimes ask why these Great Ones have not written books, for example. They forget that the Adepts are carrying on the evolution of the world; they can hardly drop that in order to give people information with regard to some part of it. It is true that if one of the Great Ones had the time to write a book, if his energy could not be better employed, that book would be far superior to any that we have. But if it were the plan of things that all work should be done by those who can already do it perfectly there would be no field for the exercise of our faculties, and it would be difficult to see any utility in our existence in this world.[19]

Testing and Initiation

Our exploration of chelaship under the seven chohans is not complete without a reflection on how the ascended masters help their chelas expand in self-awareness. They use a tried and true process that evolved in the East over many centuries: testing and initiation.

In essence, initiation is a precious gift of light from the master to the chela. It is a conditional gift: the chela must be ready for the gift; he must have gained enough self-control to be able to retain the gift and not squander the light. In El Morya's words:

> In return for illumined obedience and self-sacrificing love, the chela receives increments of the master's attainment—of the master's own realization of his Real Self. Through the acceptance of the word of the master as inviolate, the chela has imparted to him the Christ consciousness of his master, which in turn is the means whereby the base elements of the chela's subconscious and the momentums of his untransmuted karma are melted by the fervent heat of the sacred fire which comprises the master's consciousness.
>
> Thus, by freely and willingly setting aside the momentums of his human consciousness, the chela discovers that these are soon replaced by his teacher's mastery, which, when he makes it his own, serves as the magnet to magnetize his own higher consciousness and attainment.[20]

Morya's words make it very clear: our path to personal Christhood under the ascended masters requires committed and dedicated chelaship and love. This is where testing comes in. A chohan will test his chelas regularly to see if they have conformed enough to his expectations to allow him to convey to them the next initiation. Likewise, after an initiation the master will test his chela to see if he is able to retain the

---

19 C. W. Leadbeater, *The Masters and the Path* (various editions), chapter 11.

20 El Morya, *The Chela and the Path,* p. 20.

newly conferred "increments of the master's attainment" in harmony, peace and love.

Testing is not always easy. It may involve a steady confrontation with an element in the chela's not-self that stubbornly refuses to go away. At times like that, the chela may feel like he will never be able to live up to the master's requirements and expectations. But when a victory is gained and the initiation is conferred, the chela is flooded with an indescribable love and knows for certain that there is no higher bond and no more exciting and rewarding path than chelaship under the ascended masters!

The great yogi Milarepa endured many hardships on the path, including the unlearning of the false teachings of the dark ones who imparted to him a knowledge of the manipulation of energy. Thus he had to overcome the practice of black magic and to balance the karma of his misdeeds whereby he had wreaked vengeance upon his neighbors who had deprived him of his patrimony, first causing the death of many and then a hailstorm which destroyed their fields of barley ripe for the harvest. When he finally earned the right to be the chela of a true master, his pride had been broken and in humility he walked the way of attainment.[21]

Putting on Your Christhood

And so, the path of Christhood on your ray is ready for you to explore and embrace. The ascended masters don't project the day of our Christhood into a distant future. They spur us on and tell us that the time is now!

In a dictation given on November 1, 1987, the Ascended Master Jesus Christ said: "The hour has come for you to understand, beloved, that nothing less than becoming the Christ will suffice as fulfillment or requirement of the Law. . . . This is the day that the path of thy Christhood must begin in earnest."[22]

What does achieving our Christhood mean in a down-to-earth, practical sense? Elizabeth Clare Prophet gave a wonderful explanation of this process in 1993, which is summarized below:

> In becoming the Christ, we gradually put on the garments of the Christ. El Morya said that before becoming the Christ, the disciple often or occasionally becomes the vessel of his Christ Self. So first we are the vessel. In the process of being the vessel of the love of Christ, the truth of Christ, the qualities of the Christ, we are putting on that oil of truth, the oil of love. We are becoming saturated with it and we are beginning to take on its characteristics and beginning to think as Jesus thinks. And when we say, "What would Jesus do?" we know exactly what he would do and therefore what we should do. So it is a very gradual process. It doesn't happen overnight and that is why we

21 Ibid., pp. 19–20.

22 *Pearls of Wisdom,* vol. 30, no. 74.

have to be attentive day by day, weaving the cycles, weaving the garment of our Christhood.

How can you tell when you are the vessel of your Christ Self? Beloved Archangel Jophiel and Archeia Hope tell us: "When you hear yourself saying things that you know your Holy Christ Self would not say, then you know that that Holy Christ Self has ascended far above you and cannot enter in. When you say things with a tone of voice of condescension, with criticism, with burden or depression, sarcasm or the vibration of gossip, then you will know your Holy Christ Self cannot enter; for it is the law of God.

"Therefore pursue the path of the imitation of Christ."[23] And so it is important to have that book by Thomas à Kempis, *The Imitation of Christ,* reading pages of it daily, reminding yourself what it is to walk in Christ's footprints. "Speak as you know or believe Christ would speak, with love but firmness, sternness where required, mercy when it is due, soft-spoken when needed, in the intensity of the sacred fire when you would awake a soul who will not be awakened.

"Speak as Christ would speak and Christ will speak through you. Think as Christ would think and Christ will think through you and the mind of God will become congruent with the physical vessel. When you think thoughts impure, unkind, critical, intolerant, the mind of Christ is not in you"[24] in that moment. And when you catch yourself, you make your calls to the violet flame, you apologize to someone, you make things right and you get right back into that communion with God with ever more alertness to see to it that you are in control of thought, feeling and spoken word.

"When you have feelings that are not feelings of the compassionate Christ, then you know Christ is not in you."[25] At that point you ask yourself, "Well, why do I have those feelings?" And you start getting out your books on psychology and you read about the inner child and you get to the bottom of why you have those feelings so that you will not repeat them. Some feelings, some expressions of emotions are repetitive throughout a person's lifetime. When you get to the bottom of why you do things and you solve that problem by love, by decrees, even by therapy with a professional, then you will find that you will not repeat those negative patterns anymore. And you will have your victory through and through because you have seen your psychology for what it is and you are getting past it and beyond it, and gaining control of it. And this is the path of mastery.

So "practice sweet thoughts, sweet feelings, sweet words and soon they will come naturally. Demonstrate them to your children, to one another, and others will speak as you speak, for all humans are imitators."[26] Implicit in this teaching is that someone is going to imitate you whatever you are doing and not necessarily because they are around you, but because there is a subconscious

23 *Pearls of Wisdom,* vol. 32, no. 36.
24 Ibid.
25 Ibid.
26 Ibid.

communication through the level of the soul throughout the world. And so whether you are alone or whether you are with people, you are setting an example and other people are imitating you.

"Finally, beloved, perform deeds that you know Christ would perform and shun those which Christ would not engage in."[27]

Avoiding Pitfalls on the Path

Christhood is indeed a treasure worth having! But no treasure hunt comes without pitfalls along the way and certain obstacles to overcome. No matter what our major ray is, there are common barriers to the pursuit of self-mastery that span all seven rays. Perhaps we have already lessened them or removed some of them from our consciousness altogether, but there may still be remnants blocking the way to full Christ-awareness. Many of these stumbling blocks are familiar to people on the spiritual path and this knowledge gives us hope. Since all of the ascended masters have overcome these challenges, we can too; it's simply a matter of applying ourselves and not giving up.

Some of the most common pitfalls are:

- Fear of becoming the Christ
- Lack of belief that we can become the Christ
- Low self-esteem
- Procrastination
- Laziness
- Anger and irritation
- Pride and ego
- Self-centeredness

Each of these pitfalls aims at usurping the exalted place of our Holy Christ Self as our innate teacher—so each must be carefully examined and cast out.

It takes time to manifest Christ-mastery, so it's very helpful to take some time each day to devote to this pursuit. Take a few moments with the following exercise to contemplate your challenges to becoming the Christ.

EXERCISE:
ELIMINATING BARRIERS TO YOUR CHRISTHOOD

1. Reflect on how you have lived your life thus far to discover any personal hindrances to Christhood that may be lingering in you from the past or the present. They may be listed above or they may relate specifically to your major ray. The chart, "The Seven Rays," on page 237, includes the negative qualities on the rays, so you may want to use it for reference. The reading material and self-assessment exercises in Books 2 and 3 of the Sacred Adventure series can also be very useful to review your strong and weak points on the seven rays.

27 Ibid.

2. Write down your insights in your journal and take note of how much or how little progress you have made regarding these challenges over the course of time.

3. Develop a plan for clearing these negative patterns and replacing them with positive qualities. Write this plan down in your journal. To help with formulating this plan, you may want to:

    - Ask your chohan to assist you in overcoming particular traits or negative habits on your major and minor rays. This is a great way to experience the difference that the grace and light of the chohan can make in your life.

    - Every day use decrees and mantras to help you eliminate the pitfalls you are aware of in your life. In so doing you will gradually but continuously put on a little more of the mantle of your Christ Self. Then finally, one day, you will realize that you have indeed grown into more of your treasured Christhood.

4. After three months of doing this, review your plan and assess your progress. Revise your plan as needed and continue your progress toward Christ-mastery one day at a time.

The Violet Flame: Key to Victory on Every Ray

A critical key on the path of personal Christhood is giving decrees to the violet flame. Elizabeth Clare Prophet explained that by definition, Christhood means that we must bear our own burden of karma. Sometimes devotees feel that because they give mantras or perform good deeds, their karma should not descend on them. However, each of us is ultimately fully responsible for the misuse of God's energy in our present and past embodiments.

No matter which of the seven rays is your major or minor, the violet flame is an unequaled tool for excelling on that ray. Lady Master Leto said that the violet flame facilitates fusion with our Holy Christ Self. The violet flame is also the hallmark of the Aquarian age, the key to soul freedom that unlocks the energy within you that is trapped in negative energy patterns. It is even able to penetrate your physical form in order to remold your inner being and body in the fullness of the Christ image. You can create entirely new momentums and habits by invoking light to fill in the gaps in your consciousness and remake yourself in the image of your Christ Self.

In his book *The Chela and the Path,* El Morya takes two entire chapters to extol the virtues of the violet flame and explain how it can free the soul. He describes how this cosmic energy works to clear the karma of negative interactions with other individuals along with the causes, cores, effects, records and memories that are associated with them. We invoke this powerful spiritual flame to blaze forth the action of transmutation, changing darkness into light. El Morya explains:

Coils of fire are formed like the curly shavings that fall from planed wood. These coils rise and fall, rise and fall, intensifying the action of transmutation. And now they burst into a wide circle of energy and then return to the center. All of this is the action-formation of the fires of transmutation, flaming fire moving up and down and in and out; and then, following the circle of the cycles of individual karma in the electronic belt—a scrubbing action, a boiling action, a bubbling and a buoyant energy. . . . Scene by scene, step by step, the angels of the violet flame remove the record from the etheric body, the concepts from the mental body, the emotions from the feeling body, and the scars upon the physical matrix.[28]

SPOKEN WORD PRACTICE: INVOKING THE VIOLET FIRE OF FREEDOM

1. Let your mind's eye drink in the image of the violet flame in all of its beautiful nuances.
2. Give the following call by El Morya to invoke the cleansing action of the violet flame:

In the name of the Christ Self and in the name of the living God, I call forth the energies of the sacred fire from the altar within my heart. In the name of the I AM THAT I AM, I invoke the violet flame to blaze forth from the center of the threefold flame, from the white-fire core of my own I AM Presence, multiplied by the momentum of the blessed Ascended Master Saint Germain. I call forth that light to penetrate my soul and to activate my soul memory of freedom and the original blueprint of my soul's destiny.

I call forth the violet transmuting flame to pass through my four lower bodies and through my soul consciousness to transmute the cause and core of all that is less than my Christ-perfection, all that is not in keeping with the will of God for my lifestream.

So let it be done by the cloven tongues of the fire of the Holy Spirit in fulfillment of the action of that sacred fire as Above, so below. And I accept it done this hour in the full power of the living God who even now declares within my soul, "I AM WHO I AM."[29]

3. Give this violet-flame mantra for at least five minutes:

I AM a being of violet fire
I AM the purity God desires!

4. Visualize violet fire coursing through your veins, penetrating the layers of your physical body—your bloodstream, nervous system and brain. See it pressing through your chakras, swirling through your etheric body and passing over the pages of the written

28 El Morya, *The Chela and the Path*, pp. 41–42.
29 Ibid., pp. 46–47.

record of your incarnations on earth. Directed by the mind of God, see this intelligent, luminous flame setting free the energies, electron by electron, of all your past misuses of the sacred fire.

5. Give the mantra again to increase the cleansing action.
6. Seal your exercise by chanting the *Aum*.

In Conclusion

Following the path of your major ray and studying under the chohan of that ray is the sure road to attaining Christ-mastery. Nothing could be more precious than this spiritual pursuit and to use the gift of your Christhood to bless all of life. In the words of Elohim Cyclopea:

> One individual who knows his Christhood is more valuable in the earth in this hour than any other individual of any other capacity. You must place supreme value upon your emergent Christhood. Treat it as a diamond that must be cut and polished and treasured, beloved.[30]

As you embrace your sacred adventure on the path of personal Christhood, may you follow your ray all the way home to God's heart!

30 *Pearls of Wisdom*, vol. 29, no. 66.

For those who would keep
the flame of life
on earth
KEEPERS
of the FLAME®
FRATERNITY

Keepers of the Flame® Fraternity

In this book we've talked extensively about the seven chohans of the rays and the world service they render to humanity. Chances are, you were inspired to want to work with them and assist in this great effort.

One of the best ways to combine forces with the seven chohans is to join the Keepers of the Flame Fraternity. Keepers of the Flame are students of the ascended masters who have pledged to uphold and tend the flame of life—the divine spark in the heart—for themselves as well as for the millions of souls of light on planet Earth.

The Keepers of the Flame Fraternity was founded in 1961 by the Ascended Master Saint Germain through the messenger Mark L. Prophet. Those who join the fraternity receive monthly lessons with teachings by the ascended masters dictated specifically for these lessons.

Keepers of the Flame come together at many centers around the world for weekly decree services (or participate online), since they recognize that the science of the spoken Word is the spiritual technique to make a major difference in world affairs.

Perhaps most importantly, Keepers of the Flame receive direct, personal sponsorship from Saint Germain, the Knight Commander of the fraternity. This is an invaluable assistance to each one's spiritual path!

To find out more and to join this unique fraternity, visit:

https://www.summitlighthouse.org/keepers-of-the-flame

You may also write or call for a brochure:

The Summit Lighthouse
63 Summit Way
Gardiner, MT 59030-9314

Email: TSLinfo@TSL.org
Tel: 1-800-245-5445 / 406-848-9500

NOTES

Akasha. Primary substance, the subtlest, ethereal energy vibrating at a certain frequency so as to absorb, or record, all the impressions of life. This substance fills the whole of space. Akashic records can be read by adepts or those whose soul faculties are well developed.

Alpha. The masculine polarity of the Father-Mother God in the Great Central Sun of cosmos. His twin flame is Omega. Together Alpha and Omega express the divine wholeness of the Father-Mother God.

Angelic evolution. The third kingdom, or realm, of cosmic hierarchy. This kingdom represents the Holy Spirit, which penetrates and nurtures all of creation. It manifests the love of God, reflected in the color pink. The Angelic evolution includes archangels, angel devas and angels. They express God's love through compassion, care, guidance, protection and assistance.

Aquarian age. The 2,150-year cycle following the age of Pisces. The age of Pisces gave us the understanding of God as the Son, exemplified by the sponsor of that age, Jesus Christ. The age of Aquarius brings us the awareness of God as the Holy Spirit and as the Divine Mother. It is sponsored by the Ascended Master Saint Germain and his divine complement, the Ascended Lady Master Portia. During this cycle, the opportunity will be given to mankind to apply the laws of freedom and justice, the science of precipitation and transmutation, and rituals of invocation to God that can bring in an age of enlightenment and peace such as the world has never known.

Archangels. The highest rank in the orders of angels. One specific archangel, along with his divine complement, or archeia, presides over each of the seven rays. These seven archangels embody the God consciousness of the ray on which they serve and direct legions of angels who specialize on that ray. The archangels, their archeiai and the colors of their rays are as follows: Archangel Michael and Faith, first ray, blue; Archangel Jophiel and Christine, second ray, yellow; Archangel Chamuel and Charity, third ray, pink; Archangel Gabriel and Hope, fourth ray, white; Archangel Raphael and Mother Mary, fifth ray, green; Archangel Uriel and Aurora, sixth ray, purple and gold with ruby; Archangel Zadkiel and Holy Amethyst, seventh ray, violet.

Archeia. [plural, archeiai] The divine complement and twin flame (feminine polarity) of an archangel.

Ascension. A spiritual acceleration of consciousness that takes place at the natural conclusion of one's final lifetime on earth whereby the soul reunites with God and is free from the rounds of karma and rebirth.

Astral plane. The frequency of time and space immediately above physical matter. The astral plane is the repository of mankind's thoughts and feelings, conscious and unconscious. Though it was originally intended to reflect pure thoughts and emotions, the astral plane has been polluted by mental and emotional negativity, multiplied many times over by cycles of repetition.

Bija mantras. *Bija* is a Sanskrit word meaning "seed." Bija mantras are seed syllables, specific combinations of vowels and consonants that represent the essence of a cosmic being, chakra or principle. The seed syllables of the chakras correspond to the wavelength, or vibration, of the chakra's inner core. When a chakra's seed syllable is intoned, it activates that chakra's petals. This causes the life force to rise up the spine. These seed syllables come out of the Aum, the original seed syllable of creation.

Bodhisattva. A Sanskrit term, meaning literally a being of *bodhi,* or enlightenment. A bodhisattva is one who is destined to become a Buddha but has forgone the bliss of nirvana with a vow to save every being on earth. Two of the primary virtues of a bodhisattva are kindness and fearless compassion—the courage to be compassionate and to give love without fear.

Builders of Creation. The first kingdom of cosmic hierarchy. Associated with the Father aspect of God, this kingdom expresses the divine attribute of power, reflected in the color blue. Powerful beings called Elohim occupy the top position in this realm. The Elohim preside over the creation of all physical life and they are assisted in this ongoing task by nature spirits, or elementals. Together these Builders of Creation construct and sustain the material world.

Call. A direct means of communication between man and God. The call is a quick summons to God and other members of the cosmic hierarchy for assistance in accomplishing a particular result. It is especially helpful when the situation requires immediate action or when there is not enough time to give a more lengthy prayer or decree. Calls can also be given after decree preambles to invoke specific action for personal or planetary change.

Causal body. Interpenetrating spheres of light surrounding each one's I AM Presence at spiritual levels. The spheres of the causal body contain the records of the virtuous acts we have performed to the glory of God and the blessing of man through our many incarnations on earth.

Chakra. (Sanskrit, meaning "wheel," "disc" or "circle") A term used to denote the centers of light anchored in the etheric body that govern the flow of energy to the four lower bodies of man.

Chela. A disciple of a religious teacher or guru. *Chela* generally refers to a student of the ascended masters and their teachings. Specifically, it is a student of more than ordinary self-discipline and devotion who is initiated by an ascended master and who serves the cause of the Great White Brotherhood.

Chohans. *Chohan* is a term that is used to mean "lord" or "master." A specific chohan presides over each of the seven rays. These seven chohans, or lords, of the rays have specialized in the application of their ray throughout their many incarnations on earth, and they can instruct us in self-mastery on that ray. The names of the chohans and their rays are as follows: El Morya, first ray; Lanto, second ray; Paul the Venetian, third ray; Serapis Bey, fourth ray; Hilarion, fifth ray; Nada, sixth ray; Saint Germain, seventh ray.

Christ consciousness. The consciousness or awareness of the self in and as the Christ; the attainment of a level of consciousness commensurate with that which was realized by Jesus, the Christ. The Christ consciousness is the realization within the soul of that mind which was in Christ Jesus.

Cosmic beings. Highly evolved spiritual beings who have vast attainment. Their consciousness can ensoul an entire universe and they command immense fields of energy. Cosmic beings, along with the Elohim, carry the greatest concentration and highest vibration of light that we can comprehend.

Cosmic Christ. An office in hierarchy held by the one who keeps the focus of the universal Christ on behalf of all mankind. The Cosmic Christ is the embodiment of the combined momentum of the Christ consciousness of every individual soul evolving in the matter cosmos. The Ascended Master Lord Maitreya currently holds this office and demonstrates the cosmic consciousness of the Christ to earth's evolutions and throughout cosmos.

Cosmic hierarchy. A universal ordered system in which the members are ranked according to their levels of spiritual attainment and divine awareness. It consists of beings throughout cosmos who identify with God's consciousness and embody a certain aspect of that awareness. Cosmic hierarchy is based on pure standards of spiritual attainment and evolution in consciousness. It is the ideal upon which the earthly standards of hierarchy were originally founded.

Cyclopea. Elohim of the Fifth Ray, the emerald-green ray, of science, truth, healing, vision and abundance. Also known as the Great Silent Watcher, Cyclopea uses the power of the All-Seeing Eye of God to hold the immaculate concept for every individual on this planet and for the entire spiritual-material creation. With his divine counterpart, Virginia, Cyclopea helps mankind and the elementals bring the abundance of God into physical form.

Decree. A dynamic form of spoken prayer used by students of the ascended masters to direct God's spiritual energy into individual and world conditions to produce constructive change.

Divine Mother. Also known as the universal Mother and Cosmic Virgin. The Divine Mother is the feminine polarity of the Godhead, the manifestation of God as Mother. Matter is the feminine polarity of Spirit, and the term *matter* is used interchangeably with *mater,* a Latin term meaning "mother." In this context, the entire material world becomes the womb of creation into which Spirit projects the energies of life as Mother.

Djwal Kul. A great master of the Far East; foremost disciple of Kuthumi in the nineteenth century, known at that time as "D.K." and "the Tibetan." Djwal Kul assisted El Morya and Kuthumi in their work with the Theosophical Society. At the time of Jesus' birth, he was one of the three wise men, Caspar, along with El Morya and Kuthumi, who were Melchior and Balthazar. Now ascended masters, these three represent the plumes of the threefold flame. Djwal Kul represents the pink plume of love. He assists souls in practicing and expanding love and in balancing their threefold flame.

El Morya. Chohan of the First Ray, the blue ray, of divine power. He tutors souls in gaining self-mastery in the throat chakra and in developing faith, goodwill, leadership, protection, perfection and surrender to the divine will. Some of his embodiments that exemplify these virtues are Abraham, King Arthur, Thomas Becket, Sir Thomas More and Akbar the Great. El Morya counsels many types of people, including those who serve in the governments of the nations, teachers, scientists, economists, the avant-garde and servants of the will of God. He is the teacher and sponsor of Mark and Elizabeth Clare Prophet and founder of The Summit Lighthouse.

Electronic Presence. Also called the I AM Presence or the I AM THAT I AM. The Electronic Presence is the individualized Presence of God focused for each soul. It is each one's God-identity.

Elementals. Nature spirits who are the servants of God and man; also known as the beings of fire, air, water and earth. As part of the first kingdom of cosmic hierarchy (the Builders of Creation), the elementals establish and maintain the physical platform for earth's evolutions. Their job is to care for various aspects of nature in the four planes of the physical world, which are characterized by the elements of fire, air, water and earth. The elementals who serve the fire element are called salamanders; those who serve the air element, sylphs; those who serve the water element, undines; and those who serve the earth element, gnomes.

Elohim. Powerful beings in the highest level of the realm of the Builders of Creation. The Elohim, with the elementals and their hierarchs, represent the power of the Father as Creator. Elohim preside over the creation of star systems, planets and all physical life evolving anywhere in the universe. Along with cosmic beings, they carry the greatest concentration and highest vibration of light that we can comprehend.

Etheric plane. The highest plane or octave in the dimensions of matter; a plane that is as concrete and real as the physical plane, but that is experienced through the senses of the soul in a dimension and a consciousness beyond physical awareness.

Etheric retreats. Places of enormous spiritual light located in the etheric plane, or heaven-world, the highest vibrating plane in matter. The retreats consist of entire etheric cities, temples of light and structures with various rooms dedicated to specific purposes. Each retreat has unique characteristics and maintains a reserve of light-energy, which is used to help humanity on its evolutionary path. During sleep and between embodiments, the soul can travel to the retreats in her etheric body to receive in-depth instruction from members of the cosmic hierarchy.

Fiat. A short exclamatory statement to invoke God's light, given with fervor, power and great determination. Fiats are fiery, quick and intense. When uttered by the power and authority of the individual Christ Self and God Presence, the fiat can effect profound change.

Fifth ray. The emerald-green ray of divine wholeness. Qualities of the fifth ray include healing, vision and science. The energy of the fifth ray is focused in the third-eye chakra.

First ray. The blue ray of divine light-energy from God. Qualities of the first ray include faith, divine will, power, perfection and protection. The energy of the first ray is focused in the throat chakra, the power center of one's spiritual being.

Fohat. The electrical power of cosmic consciousness. It is the creative light-energy that can be released from the chakras in response to the spoken Word. When called into action by divine fiat, fohat is the impelling vital force that can move a single human being or entire evolutions from the beginning to the completion of a mission. It comes from the white fire of the Divine Mother within all of the chakras, from the base-of-the-spine chakra to the crown. The ascended masters have said that students on the path will have fohat when they allow this sacred fire to rise within them.

Four lower bodies. The four sheaths surrounding the soul; the vehicles the soul uses in her journey on earth: the etheric, or memory, body; the mental body; the desire, or emotional, body; the physical body.

Fourth ray. The white ray of divine purity. Qualities of the fourth ray include harmony, order and discipline. The energy of the fourth ray is focused in the base-of-the-spine chakra.

Golden age. An age of enlightenment, peace and harmony, characterized by the bonding of souls to their Holy Christ Self. Before the fall of Adam and Eve, there were three golden ages, which existed in the etheric plane. Other golden ages have been sustained on Atlantis and Lemuria, continents in the Atlantic and Pacific Oceans that were destroyed, some authorities estimate, around twelve thousand years ago. The writers of the Bible and others have prophesied an upcoming golden age of Aquarius.

Great Central Sun. The Great Central Sun, also called the Great Hub, is the center of cosmos; the point of integration of the Spirit-Matter cosmos and the point of origin of all physical-spiritual creation. The focus of the Great Central Sun in our sector of the galaxy is the God Star, Sirius.

Great Divine Director. A cosmic being who represents divine direction for earth's evolutions. The Great Divine Director helps people in hearing the inner voice of divine guidance and in fulfilling their divine plan. He also works to establish the inner blueprint of God-government for the nations. Known as the Master R and also as a Guru of gurus, he is the teacher of the Ascended Masters Saint Germain and El Morya. He exemplifies the Father aspect of God and is a master of the first ray, the blue ray, of God's power, protection and divine will. (For more information, see the ascended master profile in chapter 2.)

Guru. A personal religious teacher and spiritual guide. The word *guru* comes from a Sanskrit word meaning "dispeller of ignorance or darkness." The guru comes to remove darkness, ignorance and all that is not the Divine Self. The guru teaches the seeker about the spiritual path and is also an example of how to walk that path. The true guru is overshadowed by a mantle, or authority, from God to lead the soul back to God.

Higher Self. The I AM Presence and Holy Christ Self; one's innate higher consciousness.

Hilarion. Chohan of the Fifth Ray, or green ray, of wholeness, vision and science. He was previously embodied as the apostle Paul.

Holy Christ Self. Our inner teacher, guardian and friend; the advocate and mediator between our soul and God; the universal Christ individualized for each of us.

I AM Presence. The Presence of God, the I AM THAT I AM, individualized for each of us.

I AM THAT I AM. The individualized Presence of God focused for each soul; the I AM Presence.

Immaculate concept. The highest and most perfect possible vision of an individual's divine nature. The immaculate concept is the pure concept or image of the soul that is held in the mind of God. It is also any pure thought held by one part of life for and on behalf of another. The ability to hold the immaculate concept is a science that has been taught to students of the ascended masters by Mother Mary.

Initiation. The testing of the soul that occurs as a logical, natural process in orderly stages. Every day each soul receives an allotment of energy. What a person does with that energy determines whether or not he passes his spiritual initiations, or tests. Each test failed delays the hour of ultimate spiritual freedom, but it is also part of the learning process. Each test passed represents a milestone of spiritual achievement and progress. When the soul passes a test, she receives an increase of light, graces and keys to self-mastery. These are transferred to the soul from her Higher Self and the spiritual hierarchy.

Karma. (Sanskrit, meaning "act," "deed," "work") Karma, both positive and negative, is the effect of causes we have set in motion in the past, whether ten minutes ago or ten embodiments ago. The law of karma necessitates the soul's reincarnation until all negative karma is balanced.

Karmic Board. A group of eight ascended masters and cosmic beings, also called the Lords of Karma. The ascended masters and lady masters comprising this board are: the Great Divine Director; the Goddess of Liberty; the Ascended Lady Master Nada; the Elohim Cyclopea; Pallas Athena, Goddess of Truth; Portia, Goddess of Justice; and Kuan Yin, Goddess of Mercy. Vairochana, a Buddha of great attainment who has never embodied on earth, became the eighth member of the Karmic Board in 1993. The Lords of Karma dispense justice to this system of worlds, adjudicating karma, mercy and judgment on behalf of every soul. See also Lords of Karma.

Keepers of the Flame Fraternity. An organization sponsored by the ascended masters for students who vow to keep the flame of life on earth and support the activities of the Great White Brotherhood. Keepers of the Flame receive graded lessons in cosmic law dictated by the ascended masters to their messengers Mark L. Prophet and Elizabeth Clare Prophet. The fraternity was founded in 1961 by the Ascended Master Saint Germain.

Kuan Yin. The Ascended Lady Master Kuan Yin is known as the Goddess of Mercy because she ensouls the God-qualities of mercy, compassion and forgiveness. Kuan Yin ascended thousands of years ago and has vowed to serve planet Earth until all its evolutions are free. From her etheric retreat, she ministers to the souls of humanity, teaching them to balance their karma and fulfill their divine plan through loving service to life and the application of the violet flame.

Lanello. The name of the ascended master who was embodied as Mark L. Prophet, messenger for the Great White Brotherhood. Along with other masters, the Ascended Master Lanello spiritually directs the activities of The Summit Lighthouse from the heaven-world as the "Ever-Present Guru."

Lanto. Chohan of the Second Ray, the yellow ray, of divine wisdom. He embodies the qualities of wisdom, understanding and illumination. Lord Lanto teaches the path of attainment through enlightenment and dominion in the crown chakra. He spent many of his embodiments in China, focusing the flame of illumination that helped infuse the culture of China with great wisdom. During his final incarnation, Lanto adored God's indwelling presence so fervently that the flame in his heart could be seen emanating as a soft golden glow through his chest.

Maha Chohan. The hierarch of the seven chohans of the rays. His name means "the Great Lord." He embodies the white light of the seven rays and teaches the balance and integration of these rays. The Maha Chohan is also the representative of the Holy Spirit to earth and her evolutions. Because of his pledge to all mankind to keep the flame of life until they are able, he is called the Keeper of the Flame.

Maitreya. An ascended master who holds the office of Cosmic Christ and Planetary Buddha, serving in cosmic hierarchy under Gautama Buddha. He demonstrates the cosmic consciousness of the Christ in all areas of endeavor. Lord Maitreya was the guru and initiator of Jesus Christ, and he was also the one referred to in the Bible as the LORD God in Eden. From ascended levels, he continues to initiate souls on the spiritual path. In the East, Lord Maitreya is known as the Coming Buddha.

Mantle. A spiritual cloak, or forcefield of light, worn at inner levels by someone who is sponsored by one or more members of the Great White Brotherhood. The mantle contains specific spiritual keys that are anchored in the wearer's four lower bodies. These keys are formulas or qualities of light, hieroglyphs of the Spirit. Through these keys, the Brotherhood is able to perform specific acts of service for unascended humanity. A mantle can be passed from a spiritual teacher to his student when the student has passed the necessary initiations. With the transfer of the mantle comes the transfer of responsibility as the disciple pledges to carry on the mission of the master.

Mantra. A short spoken prayer consisting of a repeated word or group of words that invokes a particular aspect or quality of God.

Mother Mary. Mother of Jesus Christ. Her name means Mother Ray (Ma-ray). Throughout her embodiments on earth, she ardently exemplified the Motherhood of God. Mother Mary is now an ascended lady master who is known as a great healer and intercessor on behalf of mankind. She teaches the science of the immaculate concept—the ability to hold the image of the perfect pattern for any part of life and thereby help to bring it into manifestation. She is the twin flame of Archangel Raphael.

Nada. Chohan of the Sixth Ray, the purple and gold ray, of peace, ministration and brotherhood. Nada was previously embodied as a lawyer and advocate of the people on Atlantis. She also serves on the great Karmic Board.

Omega. The feminine polarity of the Father-Mother God in the Great Central Sun of cosmos. Her twin flame is Alpha. Together Alpha and Omega express the divine wholeness of the Father-Mother God.

Omri-Tas. A cosmic being whose aura carries a tremendous intensity of the violet flame and is so large that it exceeds the size of Earth. Omri-Tas is known as the Ruler of the Violet Planet, a golden-age planet at the etheric level whose evolutions have invoked and served the violet flame for aeons. Once, at a time of great crisis, they saved their planet and brought in a golden age by invoking the violet flame.

Paul the Venetian. Chohan of the Third Ray, the pink ray, of divine love. He teaches the way of divine love through love in action. His last and most widely known lifetime was as the Italian Renaissance painter Paolo Veronese. Paul the Venetian is devoted to beauty as an essential element of the soul, and he is dedicated to the development of the intuitive and creative faculties of the heart chakra. Paul works with students of art, music, architecture and engineering in the creation of beauty, symmetry and design.

Portia. Known as the Goddess of Justice and the Goddess of Opportunity, she is an ascended lady master who embodies the essence of divine justice and divine opportunity on behalf of the evolutions of earth. Portia represents the sixth ray of service and ministration on the Karmic Board. She is the twin flame of Saint Germain. Together they are responsible for directing the earth's next two-thousand-year cycle for the planetary body, the seventh dispensation known as the Aquarian age.

Saint Germain. The ascended master who is Hierarch of the Aquarian Age and sponsor of the United States of America. Saint Germain also initiates souls in the ritual of transmutation through the violet flame by the power of the spoken Word, meditation and visualization.

Sanat Kumara. (From Sanskrit, meaning "always a youth") Hierarch of the planet Venus; known as the Ancient of Days spoken of in the Bible, and in the East as Karttikeya. Thousands of years ago, mankind's departure from cosmic law became so great that cosmic councils decreed the dissolution of the planet. Sanat Kumara volunteered to come from his home star, Venus, to keep the threefold flame of life on behalf of the evolutions of Earth. They had willfully ignored and forgotten the God flame within their hearts. He descended to Earth with 144,000 souls who volunteered to keep the flame with him until the children of God would respond and turn once again to serve their mighty I AM Presence.

Science of the Spoken Word. The science of invoking the light of God to produce constructive change in oneself and the world. Practitioners use the science of the spoken Word in affirmations, spoken prayers and mantras to access divine energy from the Christ Self, the I AM Presence, and the ascended masters and direct it into spiritual, mental and physical conditions.

Second ray. The yellow ray of illumination. The qualities of the second ray include wisdom, understanding and inspiration as well as discernment and discrimination. The yellow ray is focused in the crown chakra, which has the highest frequency of all the chakras.

Serapis Bey. Chohan of the Fourth Ray, the white ray, of purity; the ascended master who prepares and trains candidates for the ascension. Serapis Bey is the hierarch of the Ascension Temple, a retreat located in the etheric plane at Luxor, Egypt.

Seraphim. Intense fiery beings known as the seraphic hosts. Seraphim are members of the order of angels dedicated to focusing the flame of purity and the consciousness of purity throughout cosmos. Under the direction of Justinius, Captain of Seraphic Bands, the seraphim serve at the Ascension Temple in the fourth-ray etheric retreat at Luxor, Egypt. Periodically, they journey from far-off worlds to the Great Central Sun and back again. After they recharge at the Central Sun, they bring a portion of its light back to the earth and other planets. The seraphim have a tremendous healing quality. They can place their angelic presence over those who call to them and purify, purge and heal them of all that is not of the light.

Seven rays. The seven spiritual light rays of God; the seven rays that emerge out of the white light of the Christ consciousness. Each ray focuses a frequency, or color, and has specific qualities. First ray: blue—faith, will, power, perfection and protection; Second ray: yellow—wisdom, understanding, enlightenment and illumination; Third ray: pink—compassion, kindness, charity, love and beauty; Fourth ray: white—purity, discipline, order and joy; Fifth ray: green—truth, science, healing, music, abundance and vision; Sixth ray: purple and gold with flecks of ruby—ministration, service, peace and brotherhood; Seventh ray: violet—freedom, mercy, justice, transmutation and forgiveness.

Seventh ray. The violet ray of divine freedom. Qualities of the seventh ray include transmutation, alchemy, diplomacy and transcendence. The energy of the seventh ray is focused in the seat-of-the-soul chakra.

Sixth ray. The ray of divine peace. Its color is purple and gold flecked with ruby. Qualities of the sixth ray include service, brotherhood and ministration. The energy of the sixth ray is focused in the solar-plexus chakra.

Sons and Daughters of God. Those who are joint heirs with Christ, or Christed Ones. The realm of sons and daughters of God includes human beings, ascended masters and cosmic beings, and is the second kingdom of cosmic hierarchy. This kingdom expresses the divine attribute of wisdom, reflected in the color yellow. The inner meaning of the word *wisdom* is "wise dominion." When individuals mature into responsible sons and daughters of God, they possess the wise dominion of the Christ.

Soul. The soul is the living potential of God, projected from the I AM Presence into physical evolution. The soul is not immortal but can attain immortality through fusion with the Holy Christ Self and the I AM Presence in the ritual of the ascension. Since the soul is the feminine counterpart of Spirit (the masculine polarity), we refer to the soul as "she," regardless of whether it is the soul of a man or a woman.

Soul travel. A method by which the soul can journey to the etheric plane to receive instruction at the retreats of the Great White Brotherhood. By using the etheric body, the highest vibrating of the four lower bodies, the soul can travel at inner levels while the body sleeps. During these out-of-the-body sojourns, the soul is able to visit the etheric retreats, where she can receive tutoring and guidance from members of the spiritual hierarchy.

Spirit. The masculine polarity of the Godhead, in relationship to the feminine coordinate of matter. God as Father, of necessity, includes within the polarity of himself God as Mother and is therefore known as the Father-Mother God. The plane of the I AM Presence; the dwelling place of the ascended masters in the kingdom of God.

Third ray. The pink ray of divine love. The colors of the third ray range from pink to rose to ruby. Beauty, creativity, compassion and love are the qualities of this ray, whose mastery comes through the heart chakra.

Tube of light. The white light that descends from the heart of the I AM Presence in answer to the individual's call. About nine feet in diameter, it is a cylinder that originates in the I AM Presence and extends three feet below the person's feet. The tube of light acts as a shield of protection from negative energies and is sustained twenty-four hours a day as long as one maintains harmony in his thoughts, feelings, words and deeds.

Universities of the Spirit. Spiritual classes in the etheric retreats where souls receive instruction and guidance from members of cosmic hierarchy. At the universities of the Spirit, students can visit each one of the seven chohans of the rays for fourteen consecutive days and then go on to study with the Maha Chohan. In this way, they receive step-by-step instruction on the rays, which enables them to increase their self-mastery. While studying at the retreats, souls also prepare to more efficiently balance their personal karma in daily life.

Violet flame. The seventh-ray aspect of the Holy Spirit. The sacred fire that transmutes the cause, effect, record and memory of sin, or negative karma. Also called the flame of transmutation, freedom and forgiveness. When the violet flame is invoked through the science of the spoken Word, it brings about powerful, constructive change.

World Mother. An office in hierarchy that represents the flame of the Divine Mother. Traditionally, this office was held by a different ascended lady master each year. On January 1, 1974, the honor of holding the office of the World Mother was given to the messenger Elizabeth Clare Prophet by the Goddess of Liberty. In 1988 Mrs. Prophet confirmed that she continued to hold this office.

FURTHER STUDY

Books by Summit University Press®

These books can be ordered from The Summit Lighthouse, 63 Summit Way, Gardiner, MT 59030.
To purchase books, audios, videos, CDs and DVDs, or to request a catalog:
Go to www.SummitLighthouse.org • E-mail TSLinfo@TSL.org
Call 1-800-245-5445 or 406-848-9500 • Fax 1-800-221-8307 or 406-848-9555

ACCESS THE POWER OF YOUR HIGHER SELF
by Elizabeth Clare Prophet
Your Higher Self is your Real Self. The Self that you identify with today is just a tiny fraction of the mighty being that you are. Learn how to connect with the Higher Self, how to access its unlimited energy, and how to protect and sustain this contact throughout the day.
POCKET GUIDE 110 PP. #4423

ALCHEMY OF THE HEART
How to Give and Receive More Love
by Elizabeth Clare Prophet and Patricia R. Spadaro
This book of sensitive and profound insights shows us that, while love can be compassionate and nurturing, it can also be powerful, dynamic and practical—a catalyst for spiritual growth.
POCKET GUIDE 204 PP. #4492

ANGELS
Decree booklet
by Elizabeth Clare Prophet
Words to decrees, mantras, songs and bhajans celebrating the seven archangels and the seven rays. The pages are color coded according to the seven rays.
BOOKLET 18 PP. #3600

THE ANSWER YOU'RE LOOKING FOR IS INSIDE OF YOU
A Commonsense Guide to Spiritual Growth
by Mark L. Prophet
Weaves anecdotes from everyday life with universal truths to create a profound yet thoroughly enjoyable guide to spiritual growth. Mark Prophet, one of the great spiritual teachers of our time, believed that our quest for meaning in life, though challenging, should be fun.
SOFTBOUND 118 PP. #4378

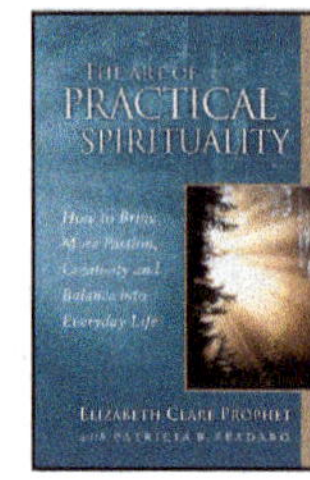

THE ART OF PRACTICAL SPIRITUALITY
How to Bring More Passion, Creativity and Balance into Everyday Life
by Elizabeth Clare Prophet and Patricia R. Spadaro
This commonsense guide offers practical steps for staying in tune with Spirit midst the hustle and bustle of everyday life. For listening to the still small voice within—for living in the here and now.
POCKET GUIDE 154 PP. #4484

ASHRAM NOTES
by El Morya, compiled and edited by Elizabeth Clare Prophet
In these profound reflections on mysticism and spirituality, the Himalayan Master El Morya offers spiritual advice, meditations and techniques to achieve gnosis—self-knowledge.
HARDBOUND 215 PP. #2675

THE CHELA AND THE PATH
Keys to Soul Mastery in the Aquarian Age
by El Morya
Contains personal instruction from El Morya for all spiritual seekers and chelas (students of a spiritual teacher). It is foundational for those who would not only know their true potential, but fulfill it.
SOFTBOUND 164 PP. #420

CORONA CLASS LESSONS
. . . for those who would teach men the Way
by Jesus and Kuthumi
Learn how to break habits of all kinds—keys that will help you fully experience the joys and navigate the challenges of the spiritual quest.
SOFTBOUND 466 PP. #1654

COSMIC CONSCIOUSNESS
One Man's Search for God
by Mark L. Prophet
as recorded by Elizabeth Clare Prophet
Mark illustrated truth as a day-to-day experience of God that can come to all. Includes a guided meditation for nourishing the heart and the soul.
SOFTBOUND 298 PP. #424

THE CREATIVE POWER OF SOUND
Affirmations to Create, Heal and Transform
by Elizabeth Clare Prophet
For centuries, mystics of East and West have believed that sound creates matter. Seven fundamental principles for using prayers, affirmations, decrees and mantras to generate spiritual energy.
POCKET GUIDE 108 PP. #4447

DREAMS
Exploring the Secrets of Your Soul
by Marilyn Barrick, Ph.D.
Not only are our dreams meaningful and connected with events in our lives, but they also hold valuable keys to our spiritual and emotional development.
SOFTBOUND 248 PP. #4497

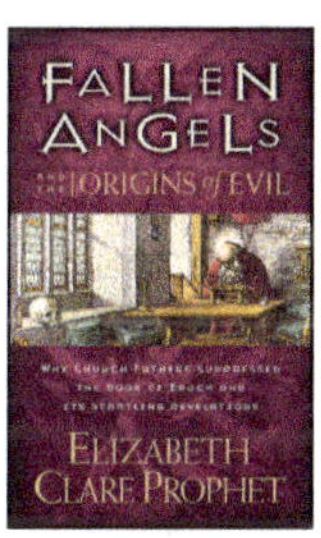

FALLEN ANGELS AND THE ORIGINS OF EVIL
Why Church Fathers Suppressed the Book of Enoch and Its Startling Revelations
by Elizabeth Clare Prophet
Takes you back to the primordial drama of good and evil, when the first hint of corruption entered a pristine world—earth.
POCKETBOOK 524 PP. #4483

THE MASTERS AND THEIR RETREATS
by Mark L. Prophet and Elizabeth Clare Prophet
compiled and edited by Annice Booth
An encyclopedia for the serious student! Includes stories of the ascended masters' lives on earth, locations of their retreats, instruction for soul travel at night and how to get the most out of your retreat experience.
SOFTBOUND 557 PP. #7100

HEART, HEAD AND HAND DECREES
A convenient pocket-size booklet of meditations, affirmations, mantras, prayers and decrees for contacting and increasing the divine qualities of power, wisdom and love within you.
BOOKLET 48 PP. #4444

HOW TO WORK WITH ANGELS
by Elizabeth Clare Prophet
Learn ten steps to make angels a part of your life. "Whether for love, healing, protection, guidance or illumination, angels stand ready to help you in many practical and personal ways."
POCKET GUIDE 118 PP. #4445

THE HUMAN AURA
How to Activate and Energize Your Aura and Chakras
by Kuthumi and Djwal Kul
In this book, Kuthumi unveils the mysteries of the human aura, from the meaning of its colors to how you can strengthen, purify, expand and protect it. Djwal Kul reveals the science of the chakras and their relationship to the aura.
POCKETBOOK 442 PP. #1483

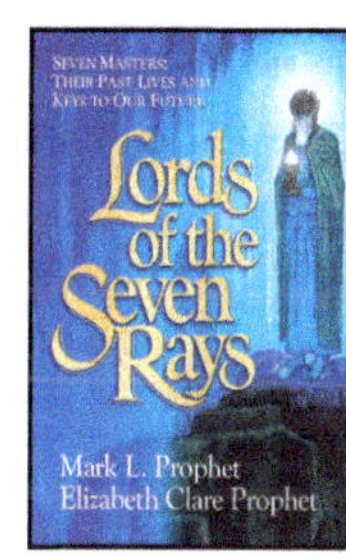

LORDS OF THE SEVEN RAYS
Seven Masters: Their Past Lives and Keys to Our Future
by Mark L. Prophet and Elizabeth Clare Prophet
Tells the stories of seven mystics who reached for and accomplished the goal of self-transcendence on each of the seven initiatic paths or "rays" of spiritual growth.
SOFTBOUND 428 PP. #2079

THE STORY OF YOUR SOUL
Recovering the Pearl of Your True Identity
by Elizabeth Clare Prophet
The soul has been likened to a pearl cast into the sea of the material universe. The goal of our life is to go after that pearl and recover our true identity. This book champions your profound worth and nobility, which only you can make a reality.
POCKET GUIDE 128 PP. #7276

THE LOST TEACHINGS OF JESUS SERIES
by Mark L. Prophet and Elizabeth Clare Prophet
The authors show that many of Jesus' original teachings were lost, removed from the Gospels, suppressed or kept secret.

The Lost Teachings of Jesus: Missing Texts • Karma and Reincarnation
SOFTBOUND #6479

Lost Teachings of Your Higher Self
POCKETBOOK #6330

Lost Teachings on Keys to Spiritual Progress
POCKETBOOK #6350

Lost Teachings on Finding God Within
POCKETBOOK #6365

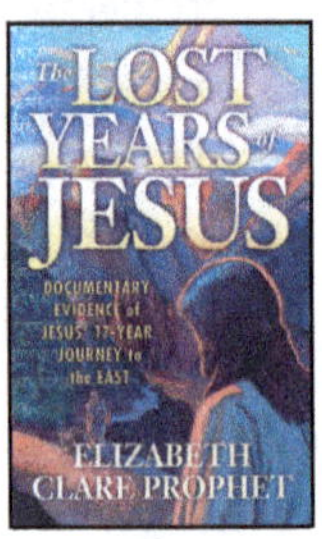

THE LOST YEARS OF JESUS
Documentary Evidence of Jesus' 17-Year Journey to the East
by Elizabeth Clare Prophet
The Gospels record Jesus at age 12 in the temple, then age 30 at the river Jordan. Where was he in the interim? Ancient Buddhist manuscripts say that Jesus traveled to India, Nepal, Ladakh and Tibet. Prophet brings together the testimony of four eye-witnesses of these remarkable manuscripts plus three different translations of the texts.
POCKETBOOK 468 PP. #2156

MEMORIES OF MARK:
My Life with Mark Prophet
by Annice Booth
The author shares the magic and mystery of her friendship and student-teacher relationship with this twentieth-century prophet.
SOFTBOUND 198 PP. #4477

MESSAGES FROM HEAVEN:
Amazing Insights on Life After Death, Life's Purpose and Earth's Future
by Patricia Kirmond
SOFTBOUND 254 PP. #4474

PRAYER AND MEDITATION
by Mark L. Prophet and Elizabeth Clare Prophet
An inspiring combination of Christian mysticism and Eastern meditation that teaches the art of unceasing communion with God and the way of higher meditation to open the heart. An illuminating guide for achieving spiritual renewal and overcoming adversity.
SOFTBOUND 314 PP. #569

PRAYERS, MEDITATIONS AND DYNAMIC DECREES
for Personal and World Transformation
Your complete handbook of decrees for personal and world action. Color coded on loose-leaf pages. #1778

QUIETLY COMES THE BUDDHA
by Elizabeth Clare Prophet
"There are some who are born to be the Christ and there are some who are born to be the Buddha..." If you would pursue the eternal quest and behold God face to face, the Compassionate One comes quietly to tell you how you can realize the Christ, the Buddha where you are. SOFTBOUND 158 PP. #4495

SACRED PSYCHOLOGY OF CHANGE
Life as a Voyage of Transformation
by Marilyn Barrick, Ph.D.
Catch the vision of your role in the 21st century. This engaging book shows how to welcome chaos and cycles of change as transformational opportunities. It is jam-packed with helpful information, from cutting-edge change theories to psychology and spirituality.
SOFTBOUND 240 PP. #4486

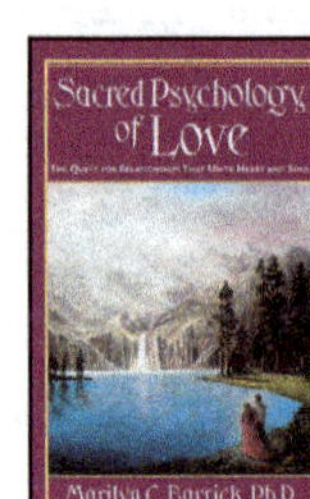

SACRED PSYCHOLOGY OF LOVE
The Quest for Relationships That Unite Heart and Soul
by Marilyn Barrick, Ph.D.
This first book in the series reveals the hidden spiritual and psychological dramas inherent in friendship, love relationships and marriage. It tells the story of each one's inner mystic and offers tender ways to spark divine love in human relationships.
SOFTBOUND 256 PP. #4469

SAINT GERMAIN ON ALCHEMY
Formulas for Self-Transformation
by Saint Germain
In this greatest of all self-help books, Saint Germain describes the principles of alchemy and how they can be used to effect spiritual, mental, emotional and physical transformation.
POCKETBOOK 540 PP. #1835

THE SCIENCE OF THE SPOKEN WORD
by Mark L. Prophet and Elizabeth Clare Prophet
The authors present the most powerful and profound message on techniques of spoken prayer in print today. This important work explains how to use worded formulas to access the full spectrum of spiritual light for personal and world transformation.
SOFTBOUND 246 PP. #104

SOUL MATES AND TWIN FLAMES
The Spiritual Dimension of Love and Relationships
by Elizabeth Clare Prophet
"Extremely powerful in revealing the inner mysteries of the soul and the true essence of love through its insightful analysis of real-life experiences and classical love stories."
POCKET GUIDE 166 PP. #4465

UNDERSTANDING YOURSELF
A Spiritual Approach to Self-Discovery and Soul-Awareness
by Mark L. Prophet and Elizabeth Clare Prophet
This insightful work offers unique perspectives into how to master the components of being—the ego, karma, and the Self beyond the self.
SOFTBOUND 222 PP. #4472

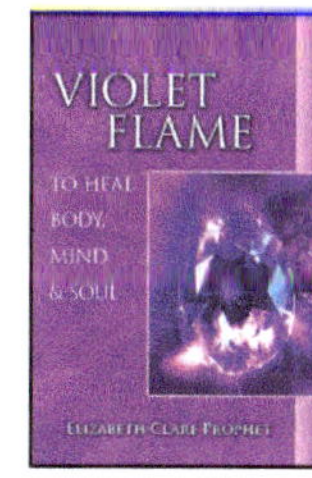

VIOLET FLAME TO HEAL BODY, MIND AND SOUL
by Elizabeth Clare Prophet
Describes how to use violet flame—unique high-frequency spiritual energy to increase vitality and spirituality, overcome blocks to healing and transmute the burden of traumatic experiences.
POCKET GUIDE 108 PP. #4424

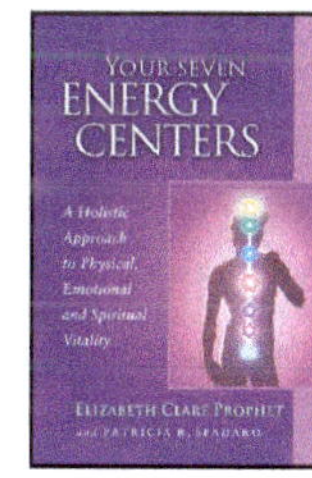

YOUR SEVEN ENERGY CENTERS
A Holistic Approach to Physical, Emotional and Spiritual Vitality
by Elizabeth Clare Prophet and Patricia R. Spadaro
Contains powerful insights and tools for wholeness based on the science of the body's subtle energy system. "Your 21st century guide to integrating and healing body, mind and soul."
POCKET GUIDE 234 PP. #4485

OTHER BOOKS

THE CHAKRAS, *by C. W. Leadbeater,* rev. ed. (Wheaton, Ill.: The Theosophical Publishing House, 1994)

HEART, *by Helena Roerich* (New York: Agni Yoga Society, 1975)

THE LITTLE FLOWERS OF ST. FRANCIS, *trans. by Raphael Brown* (New York: Doubleday, 1958)

THE MAGIC PRESENCE, *by Godfré Ray King* (Chicago: Saint Germain Press, 1982)

ST. JOHN OF THE CROSS: ***Alchemist of the Soul,*** *trans. Antonio T. de Nicolás* (York Beach, Maine: Samuel Weiser, 1989)

UNVEILED MYSTERIES, *by Godfré Ray King* (Chicago: Saint Germain Press, 1982)

THE WAY OF LAO TZU ***(Tao-te ching),*** *trans. by Wing-Tsit Chan* (New York: Macmillan Publishing Company, 1963)

HOME STUDY COURSES

For those who prefer reading as opposed to studying online, Summit University offers several self-guided study materials. These step-by-step guides bring you closer to your higher self and the ascended masters and provide practical tools for personal spiritual growth.

SACRED ADVENTURE 1
The Spiritual Quest
by the Staff of Summit University
This comprehensive introduction to the Teachings of the Ascended Masters® gives you the keys to get in touch with your soul's inner power. It includes seven interactive lessons with profound teachings, true stories, illustrations, exercises, meditations and accelerated spiritual techniques to help transform yourself and your world.

SACRED ADVENTURE 2
Meeting the Masters
by the Staff of Summit University
The second book in the Sacred Adventure series introduces you to the seven spiritual rays and the ascended masters who instruct us in their use. You'll come face to face with the masters of the first three rays: El Morya, Lord Lanto and Paul the Venetian. Come to know them intimately as you learn about their lives and passions. In addition to transformative spiritual exercises, this book also contains exciting chapters on soul travel, hierarchy, working with angels and expanding the divine spark in your heart.

SACRED ADVENTURE 3
Working with the Masters
by the Staff of Summit University
The third book in the Sacred Adventure series completes the overview of the seven rays. You'll be introduced to the Ascended Masters Serapis Bey, Hilarion, Nada and Saint Germain and will learn about the Divine Mother, the creative power of music and the mysterious world of the elemental builders of form. The book concludes with instructions on how to pursue your own path of personal Christhood as a student of one of the Lords of the Seven Rays.

WALKING WITH THE MASTER
Answering the Call of Jesus
by Elizabeth Clare Prophet and Staff of Summit University
Two thousand years ago Jesus called a small group of disciples to leave their nets and follow him. He gave them a teaching and a path of initiation, only fragments of which are found in the New Testament. This path is as real and as vital today as it was in Jesus' time. And now, at the turning of an age, the ascended master Jesus calls those who would be his disciples to take up that path to walk and work with him again. Twenty-eight steps on that path are presented here, with commentary and explanation by Elizabeth Clare Prophet and the staff of Summit University. The goal is to find and externalize the Christ within. The means is a practical path of initiation for the modern world.

SEMINARS

Every year, Summit University hosts many seminars in locations throughout the world. These powerful, affordable weekend events on a variety of spiritual topics including healing, psychology, and spiritual development, give you the opportunity to spend quality time with yourself and with God, and explore the next step on your spiritual path.

www.SummitUniversity.org

Mark L. Prophet (1918–1973) and Elizabeth Clare Prophet (1939–2009), were visionary pioneers of modern spirituality and internationally renowned authors. Their books are published in more than 30 languages, and millions of copies have been sold online and in bookstores worldwide.

Together, they built a worldwide spiritual organization that is helping thousands to find their way out of human problems and reconnect to their inner divinity. They walked the path of spiritual adeptship, advancing through the universal initiations common to mystics of both East and West. They taught about this path and described their own experiences for the benefit of all who desire to make spiritual progress.

Mark and Elizabeth left an extensive library of spiritual teachings from the ascended masters and a thriving, worldwide community of people who study and practice these teachings.

Summit University®
63 Summit Way
Gardiner, Montana 59030 USA
1-800-245-5445 / 406-848-9500
Se habla español.
SummitUniversity.org
TSLinfo@TSL.org
SummitLighthouse.org

Printed in the USA
CPSIA information can be obtained
at www.ICGtesting.com
JSHW051034030224
56298JS00001B/2

9 781609 882969